Overgrown

Overgrown

Practices between Landscape Architecture & Gardening

Julian Raxworthy

THE MIT PRESS
CAMBRIDGE, MASSACHUSETTS
LONDON, ENGLAND

© 2018 Massachusetts Institute of Technology

All rights reserved. No part of this book may be reproduced in any form by any electronic or mechanical means (including photocopying, recording, or information storage and retrieval) without permission in writing from the publisher.

Publication of this book was supported by a grant from the Graham Foundation for Advanced Studies in the Fine Arts.

This book was set in Garamond Premier Pro, Poetica, and Gotham by the MIT Press. Printed and bound in the United States of America.

Library of Congress Cataloging-in-Publication Data

Names: Raxworthy, Julian, author.

Title: Overgrown : practices between landscape architecture and gardening / Julian Raxworthy ; foreword by Fiona Harrisson.

Description: Cambridge, MA : The MIT Press, [2018] | Includes bibliographical references and index.

Identifiers: LCCN 2018001499 | ISBN 9780262038539 (hardcover : alk. paper) ISBN 9780262547123 (paperback)

Subjects: LCSH: Landscape architecture. | Landscape gardening.

Classification: LCC SB472 .R37 2018 | DDC 712—dc23 LC record available at https://lccn.loc.gov/2018001499

10 9 8 7 6 5 4 3

For Dorothy and Richard Raxworthy: missed parents,
my models for scholarship.

Contents

Foreword *by* Fiona Harrisson · *ix*

Acknowledgments · *xiii*

1 · Introduction · *1*

PART I
Figuring Growth

2 · The Persistence *of a* Line · *29*

3 · Architecture *with* Plants · *71*

4 · Changing Rooms · *113*

PART II
Gardening Design

5 · A Moving Work *of* Art · *167*

6 · Marginalia · *219*

7 · Wait *and* See · *271*

8 · Conclusion: A Manifesto *for the* Viridic · *323*

Notes · *335*

Index · *365*

Foreword

FIONA HARRISSON

IN ITS EFFORTS TO GAIN professional standing, the discipline of landscape architecture has chosen to sever itself from its roots in gardening; it has literally drawn itself into a corner. This book argues that the tradition of gardening is an essential element of the practice of landscape architecture so that design is understood as working with plants that change through time. The practice of thinking about and drawing landscape is put in its rightful place. Through careful reconsideration of plants as live matter, the project of this book is practical, philosophical, and political. It relinquishes the quest for power by questioning established hierarchies and valuing different kinds of knowledge. It is an invitation to landscape architects to get out of the office and get their hands dirty.

Gardening is portrayed as an intimate and extended conversation with the living world. The reader is offered a glimpse into an embodied mode of practice from an author who has worked as a gardener, secateurs in hand, making choices about which branch to cut, when and where. Design is viewed as dynamic improvisation which occurs through time. It is relational and ground-level rather than perceived from a bird's-eye view. This embodied mode of inquiry informs the research for the book; gardens across the globe are repeatedly visited. They are discovered by scrambling through hedges; the scale of a garden is revealed by arriving by bicycle. As the author's argument builds across the chapters, the readers are privy to an intimate, relational practice between living beings. As plants grow, so too does the gardener. For a reader of the book, the discipline is revealed anew.

Through revisiting the historical canon of landscape architecture, the author suggests that the bracketing of landscape architecture from gardening is in itself a conceit. Contemporary practitioners of the discipline stand on the shoulders of designers who were themselves gardeners. Le Nôtre, the famous garden designer of Versailles, was a gardener. Roberto Burle Marx from Brazil was first and foremost a plants man. Raxworthy rewrites the canon through the lens of plants, more specifically through an interrogation of the different ways in which *growth* is engaged with or denied. Through visiting projects over extended periods, and observing different forms of plant growth, he reveals a breadth of pruning techniques and identifies design strategies that engage with the world as a living entity.

A timely and delightful critique of the discipline of landscape architecture unfurls through the pages of this book. It arrives at a time when the discipline is taking stock in terms of its capacity to address the ecological challenges of our time. A lecture by Weller and Fleming[1] commemorating the 50th anniversary of the Landscape Architecture Foundation asked: "Has Landscape Architecture Failed?" The lecture provides an incisive overview of strategies within the profession since the 1960s, in response to the environmental crisis that we saw looming even then. Weller and Fleming identify three parallel approaches—landscape architect as artist (Walker), landscape architect as regional planner (McHarg), and landscape architect as urbanist (Waldheim); they argue that each strategy has fallen short of meeting the ecological challenges thus far. They suggest that the way forward requires incorporating all three approaches. They make an impotent conclusion to a spectacular provocation.

Raxworthy looks to the humble act of gardening as a way to question assumptions that are taken for granted in the discipline of landscape architecture. His exploration is delightful because of its directness and simplicity. He puts his finger on a fault line within the discipline and prizes open a chasm—its limited capacity to engage with the dynamic nature of the world, except through simulation in drawing. The term "the viridic" is coined to articulate the dynamic, living nature of the medium of landscape. This term identifies growth as the core of the disciplinary practice. Gardening offers tools of operation which work with the aliveness of the material as spatial construction through biological understanding, not *instead of* but as well as drawing. This way of thinking reflects a broader disquiet emerging in philosophy and science which looks to the vegetal as a way of rethinking relations between human beings and the other-than-human world (Marder and Irigaray,[2] Marder,[3] Holdrege,[4] Buhner[5]). These philosophers use close encounters with the vegetal world to explore relational ways of knowing that expand beyond human-centered ways of engaging with the world.

I too come to landscape architecture from a background in gardening. I have also distanced myself from my gardening roots. After 25 years, I have chosen to return to the garden as a laboratory for learning and research. "Don't be afraid of being a gardener," Julian told me when he invited me to write this foreword. This counsel speaks loudly about what has been unspoken: a fear that my gardening background may call into doubt my authority in the profession. Perhaps the "call to arms" described in the book is really a call to our senses. It invites us to inhabit our full selves in what we do. For landscape architects it may mean getting up close and dirty rather than flying above the landscape we seek to transform. It invites professionals to reflect on our implicit assumptions when we buy into the club of the profession. These assumptions may get in the way of expanding our modes of practice, of acknowledging other ways of knowing and admitting tools and methods of engagement, new and old, to meet the living, changing world we inhabit, and the challenges it presents.

Acknowledgments

I WOULD LIKE FIRST TO ACKNOWLEDGE the generous support of the Graham Foundation for Advanced Studies in the Fine Arts: both their funding, which enabled this book to be published in color, and their confidence in its topic, were very encouraging.

The "roots" of this book are in my PhD, which I started almost 15 years ago. Over that time I have been lucky enough to be supported by a number of institutions and people. I would like to thank, in the order in which I received the support: the University of Queensland for an APA scholarship, and my PhD supervisors Professor John Macarthur and Dr. Naomi Stead, as well as my student peers there, including Chris Brisbin, Andrew Wilson, Mark Hiley, James Davidson, and Susan Holden; the University of Western Australia, and particularly then head of school Patrick Beale, for a Research Fellowship, as well as colleagues there when I was visiting: Richard Weller, Rene van Meeuwin, Ian Weir, and Karl Kullman; my employer during my PhD candidacy, the Queensland University of Technology, and the Heads of School while I was there, including Professors Jill Franz, John Frazer, Paul Sanders, and Gini Lee, for supporting field research and granting me a sabbatical.

The book was initiated when I started working at the University of Cape Town in 2014, and I was constantly supported by UCT, a strong research university. In particular, I would like to thank the various directors of the School of Architecture, Planning and Geomatics, Alta Steenkamp, Iain Low, and Tóma Berlanda, for supporting a range of grant applications that helped to fund field research for this book. These were ultimately supported by the University Research Committee (URC) at UCT. I would also like to acknowledge the research funding provided to me as a rated researcher by the National Research Foundation (NRF) in South Africa; this supported research assistance during the writing of the book. My colleague, Clinton Hindes, as well as having great conversations about landscape architecture with me that informed the book, also allowed me the space in my workload to finish it while he was convener of the MLA program. I was invaluably assisted, particularly at the end, by my research assistant Michael Brown, who also produced the beautiful chapter-opening images in this book. I would also like to thank Amy Thompson for her help with drawings. I also had valuable conversations with my students Wallace Honiball, Timothy Snyders, and Frank Kleinschmidt about topics in this book as I was writing it. Thanks also to my architecture friends at UCT for conversations, notably Matteo Fraschini, Kevin Fellingham, and Nic Coetzer.

An earlier version of chapter 3 was published in *Journal of Landscape Architecture*, no. 12 (2011), and of chapter 4 in *Landscape Review* 16, no. 2 (2016).

I would like to acknowledge the following stakeholders and experts related to the case studies and readers of my draft:

For Courances: Marc Rumelhart, from the École Nationale Supérieure de Paysage de Versailles, together with multiple groups of students and colleagues, has been fastidiously documenting the maintenance of French baroque gardens and their configuration. Marc has been incredibly generous with me as a "go-to guy" about the French baroque garden in general as background to Château Courances, which Valentine de Ganay, one of the current owners of Courances, prefers to call a "French Renaissance water garden." Marc answered any question I asked, reading and commenting on drafts in detail. Any errors are my own. Thanks to Valentine de Ganay for commenting on my draft chapter; also to Patrick Deedes-Vincke for an interview. On a previous visit I was honored to meet the recent patriarch of Courances, Jean de Ganay, now sadly deceased, who gave me access to the château at inopportune times.

For the Miller Garden: I had a hunch that there must be a back story about its maintenance, and was very lucky to discover Benjamin L. Wever, manager of the property and gardener, who opened a window into the project and gave me an extensive interview. His employer, and the current owner of the Miller House and Garden, the Indianapolis Museum of Art (IMA), was also very generous, with respective directors answering my inquiries: first Bradley Brooks, then Mark Zelonis. I relied heavily on the IMA archives, and archivist Samantha Norling. Thanks to the IMA also for the use of images, and to Gary Hilderbrand for responding to the draft of the Miller Garden chapter.

For Marnas: Unfortunately, I never got to visit Sven-Ingvar Andersson's garden with him, meeting him for the first time a few months before his death; however, his daughter, Beata Engels Andersson, graciously gave me access to the garden and permission to reproduce his images. Thanks also to Steen Høyer for correspondence and photography. In Denmark generally, I have been lucky to find great colleagues with whom I shared many conversations related to gardens, notably Marlene Hauxner (RIP) and particularly frequent voyager on bicycle field trips Torben Dam, who rode there with me. Immense thanks to Anne Whiston Spirn, who commented not only on the draft of this chapter but, indeed, on the entire manuscript. Thank you to MIT for royalty-free access to the Marnas image archive that Spirn and the Danish Academy of Art have assembled, and that MIT hosts.

For the Sítio Roberto Burle Marx: Researching the plant collection trips of Roberto Burle Marx, I came upon a reference to Oscar Bressane, who accompanied him, and once I had tracked him down, he and I had a number of Skype chats about his experience, followed by a dinner in São Paulo. His generosity was representative of my experience generally in Brazil. Discovering his blog by deciding to search for the Sítio in Portuguese, and then digging a bit deeper using Google Translate, I was very lucky to find Roberio Dias, Professor of Landscape Architecture at the Universidade Federal do Rio de Janeiro. When I visited him in Rio we spent a day talking in his studio about his experiences both working with Burle Marx and also at the Sítio. I cannot thank him enough for his prompt answers to any questions I had, and for introducing me to Marlon Souza, his protégé at the Sítio Burle Marx, who also spent an afternoon walking around the Sítio with me, gently qualifying some misapprehensions I had picked up while talking to Roberio, which were all my own. While Roberio made strident responses to my draft, I hope he will see that I dealt with these in the revision. Thanks also to Sima Elivson's son for giving me reproduction rights to her images.

For Druimchardain: Perhaps the most moving contacts I had were with the family of G. F. Dutton, who sounds like an amazing man and reminded me of my own father. Kirsty Jones, his daughter, organized my visit generously, and both his son Alasdair and Dutton's widow Elizabeth gave me their time, as well as allowing me access to his slides—and permission to reproduce them—and library. The initial contacts with the family were made via Geoffrey's poetry publishers at Bloodaxe Books: thanks to Anthony Rudolf and Neil Astley for putting me in contact, and for the copy of *Harvesting the Edge*. I also had a great visit to Geoffrey's friends Mike and Sue Thornley, who had an interesting take on Dutton and an amazing garden. My companion on this trip, Sebastien Penfornis, was also great company: more travels next time, Seb.

For Hombroich: Thanks to Lisa Diedrich for introducing me to the Hombroich, and more generally as a friend, fellow landscape thinker, and travel companion. The protagonists in the chapter—Bernhard Korte, Burkhard Damm, and Klaus Fischedick—were all very generous with their time in interviews on, or near, the site. In particular, my walk with Fischedick made me remember my time as a gardener, and we had a great chat.

I owe major thanks to Roger Conover at the MIT Press, for his confidence in taking this book on. Beyond logistics, Roger's confidence, together with that of the Graham Foundation, made ideas that had seemed like some bizarre tangent of my own acquire weight. Thanks also to copy-editor Gillian Beaumont for early reading and feedback as well as the final edit, to Molly Seamans for her excellent graphic design, to Victoria Hindley for coordination with MIT, and to Matthew Abbate for guiding the book through the publication process.

Without respected referees who are willing to throw their support behind one's research, it is impossible to get it off the ground; therefore I owe a major debt to Elizabeth K. Meyer, Richard Weller, Sue-Anne Ware, Gini Lee, and Thaisa Way.

Sometimes tangential and odd moments "plant seeds" that end up "flowering": James Corner once attempted, in vain, to make me wear the mantle of "plant guy," which I resisted. In retrospect, I must acknowledge that his suggestion that I should focus on plants had considerable influence on this book, though I rejected his admonition that "theory is over" and chose to theorize nonetheless. In 2010 Elizabeth K. Meyer invited me to convene the Myles H. Thayer symposium at the University of Virginia, where I presented a lecture that consolidated my thinking on the topic of this book, and following this, when I taught at UVa, I had a group of students whom I regard as co-researchers on the topic of design with maintenance: Michael Geffel, Isaac Hametz, and Joey Hays. Talking about UVa, it's also important to acknowledge Anne T. Pettus, a UVa grad who taught me at RMIT in the 1990s and who introduced me to Dan Kiley and the Miller Garden.

Often friendships are like ongoing conversations, and many friends made significant contributions to my thinking about this topic, notably Marian Macken, Martin Kirkwood, Sacha Coles, Kirsten Bauer, Sebastian Penfornis, Thierry Kandjee, and more recently, Martí Franch. In this vein, conversations with fellow landscape architect-gardeners have also been very important: Tim Nicholas, Jason McNamee, Michael Howard, Heath Gifford, and Fiona Harrisson, whom I also need to thank for the foreword.

My PhD started when my parents, Richard and Dorothy Raxworthy, were still alive, but neither of them got to see its end or, now, this book. Their scholarship was an inspiration to me, and I am glad I can add this book to theirs on my bookshelf. My wife Magriet Raxworthy gave me so much love and support, never doubting that I would do it: thanks, "gorgus."

CHAPTER 1

Introduction

LANDSCAPE ARCHITECTS have an ambiguous relationship with gardens.

In answer to the obligatory question "What do you do for a living?," landscape architects know what will follow: "Can you do my garden?" In response they will patiently explain that, really, they work on more significant, more serious things like environmental projects, open space systems, streets, and other infrastructure. In silent fury they will say to themselves: "You can't afford me…I'm not 'just' a gardener."

Being called a "gardener" (or, worse, a "landscaper") is an insult for a landscape architect. Landscape architects regard gardeners as either amateurs or blue-collar members of the working class. While growing vegetables has piqued the public interest everywhere, landscape architects have rebranded this "productive landscape" to maintain its separation from gardening, appropriating the trend for themselves. For their part, gardeners are too caught up in their gardens to be interested in landscape architects.

Landscape architects regard their best work as art, and therefore think of their projects as artworks. Gardeners, on the other hand, treat the garden as a process, a process called "gardening." Gardeners enjoy the activity of gardening, and can see its fruits growing in front of them. The success of gardening can be seen in the health of a garden's plants. This means that gardeners' main concern is *growth*. The process of growth is a potent metaphor in the garden. It gives gardening a philosophical dimension apart from its physical labor.[1] Amateur garden literature abounds with analogies of life: the life of the plant in relation to the life of the gardener; while in China, gardening's relationship to religion made it an activity of both hand and mind, both physical and literary.[2]

The importance of growth unites gardeners and landscape architects. Both require successful plant growth to show that their efforts have been successful. However, despite the fact that landscape architects are often avid gardeners too, there are significant differences between the ways in which landscape architects and gardeners conceive of growth, and work with it. These differences are the focus of this book.

For the landscape architect, plant growth is the ongoing manifestation of an imagined future state. This state is imagined in representations, where size at maturity is taken for granted in drawings produced before a project gets built. On the other hand, for the gardener, interacting with plants in real time, growth rather than a drawing proves the success of their actions.

The gardener can act directly to ensure that growth occurs; the landscape architect, however, must entrust their vision to others during and after installation. These "others" include gardeners, who maintain the project after it is built and no longer in the hands of the landscape architect. Gardeners frustrate landscape architects because they change a project, inevitably modifying it from the landscape architect's original concept. Presented with the necessity to encourage the plants to grow, gardeners make immediate decisions on the basis of found conditions that have emerged since the drawing was done. These conditions are inevitably different to what the landscape architect desired, so "the gardeners" are a source of constant frustration for the landscape architect.

Despite separating themselves professionally from them, the historic champions of landscape architecture are gardeners. These gardeners have been appropriated by twentieth-century "landscape historians" like Geoffrey Jellicoe, stitching them into a fabricated historical narrative about landscape architecture.[3] "Landscape architect" for French baroque king Louis XIV, André Le Nôtre, while operating on a territorial scale, was first and foremost a gardener like his father, his coat of arms resplendent with grass, snails, cabbage, and a fork. Much-derided stylist of the eighteenth-century English garden Humphry Repton called himself a "Landscape *gardener*" (my emphasis) on his business card. And the doyens of landscape architecture, designers of Central Park Frederick Law Olmsted and Calvert Vaux, used the term "landscape architecture" as a convenience to conjoin their expertises: *landscape* gardening and *architecture*, respectively.[4] In the twentieth century, too, gifted (and untrained) gardeners were appropriated by landscape architecture—for example, Roberto Burle Marx, who was ostensibly a painter and a plantsman.[5]

Ideas of growth and change are now in the *Zeitgeist* of both architecture and landscape architecture in what I call "the process discourse." The process discourse refers to designers and theorists who see natural and cultural processes, described in scientific terms, as the source of dynamic design suited to a world that is different from the past because of flows of information, for example. The models of process they use generally come from nature. In architecture, morphogenesis and biomimicry seek to use parametric systems derived from nature to animate the inorganic. In landscape architecture, subfields like landscape urbanism look to ecology to develop instrumental ways of working with natural processes, such as hydrology, in the city.[6] By appropriating and valorizing processes, both architecture and landscape architecture seek to rid the architectural object of its static properties, and calibrate it to the world. Denatured and accelerated by computers with advanced modeling and simulating capabilities, the flux and indeterminacy of the world seems within reach, ready to be seized and mobilized. However, I would argue that this is a vainglorious illusion that mistakes simulation for the real. While the landscape architect is modeling the effects of time, the gardener is located at the point of Eddington's "arrow of time," directing the arrow while the landscape architect is mapping its wake.[7]

Landscape architecture and architecture are generally practiced behind a desk in an office rather than in the field, landscape architecture admittedly less so than building architecture. This means that their influence is removed from the systems they seek to catalyze. Even while their models of simulation get better and better, because they are derived from past events rather than current ones, the real agency of those models is nonexistent.[8]

Is it possible that the gardener is better at working with the processes that preoccupy the process discourse? For the gardener, cause and effect is not an abstract concept, but something they deal with all the time with only manual tools, human labor, and expertise gained from repetitive action. The "dynamic" systems with which the landscape architect engages in representation have a banal but reassuring tactility in the hands of the gardener, who can manipulate them with greater precision.[9]

Surely landscape architecture and gardening can get together? Landscape architecture offers a design foresight and judgment that can create beautiful spaces. Gardening uses techniques that allow the garden to gain qualities over time rather than lose them, where small deviations are serendipitous rather than a cause of concern. The convergence of both disciplines offers redemption to both, and a new synthetic practice of landscape gardening.

CURATING GROWTH

Reading landscape architecture in terms of deconstruction, "an interrogation that shakes structures…expos[ing] structural weaknesses," makes the discipline's fraught relationship to plants and gardening clear.[10] In a deconstructive reading foundational ideas are revealed to be shaky, with the potential to demolish the discipline. In these terms, I argue that the foundational idea for landscape architecture was change, but that it is now disconnected from it.

The idea that landscape architectures is about time and change is fundamental to the way the profession has defined itself. In an introductory textbook, Michael Laurie describes "time" as the fourth dimension of landscape architecture.[11] He quotes Brian Hackett: what is specific to landscape architecture "is the medium in which we work, the landscape, subject to change and growth, which has existed for millions of years and will doubtless continue to exist."[12] Landscape here is not simply the subject of the profession but also its medium, a material palette that defines the discipline. Laurie's claim that the landscape is "subject to growth" implies the primacy of plant material for landscape architecture, since it is the main landscape material that changes visibly over time.

But landscape architects do not literally work with plants; they specify them in drawings, generally produced on the computer. Any growth that occurs does so when the project is complete, when it is handed over to managers, or gardeners. Gardeners work with plants. Landscape architecture's claims to growth are revealed to be rhetorical. And so, "that which is structural [growth] cannot be recognized as such by the very tradition it organizes,"[13] because landscape architecture has separated itself from gardening.

However, in destruction lies redemption, or in our case reconciliation. Deconstructive readings "look for slippages in the tradition by questioning all its routine categories and strategies but not to simply overthrow them." By investigating the relationship between landscape designs produced by landscape architects and their maintenance by gardeners, as I do in this book, we see their vital interdependency. Once the relationship between gardeners and landscape architects becomes visible, it is possible to see how we can "intensify [tradition], ruthlessly respecting [its] specific rigor in order to see exactly what it is that [its] slippages organize."[14] This slippage is growth, and what it organizes is a conundrum about change. This is a contradiction between the discipline defining itself on the basis of dynamism and change, but having a static conception of time. It is static because the landscape architect knows what they want "in the end," regardless of the fact that the nature of time is unpredictable.

Plants are critical because the rhetoric of change in landscape architecture is tied to the growth of plants as a material. Since these material properties arise through growth, I argue that when we use plant material, our real material is growth itself, and to highlight it, I propose a new practice for working with plant material in landscape architecture and gardening that I call "the viridic." The viridic is a landscape-architectural version of the tectonic in architecture, its title derived from the Latin word for green, "viridis," which had an implicit connection with vegetation and growth, a connection I develop in chapter 4. The idea that growth is the medium of landscape architecture has radical implications for the discipline. Practical implications include recognition that maintenance, gardening in particular, is the only tool for engaging with growth. Theoretically, a focus on growth makes the form of landscape architecture projects plastic, changing spaces over time. The greatest implication, however, is disciplinary, because the representations used by professional landscape architects are not able to engage with growth, while the techniques used by garden tradespeople are. Reconciliation with gardening, then, involves a loss of control but also the acquisition of the real agency of time: novelty. In making good its claims to change through the practice of the viridic, or growth, a landscape architecture renewed by gardening will operate in completely new ways that blur the class divide between the professions and the trades.

In this book I build my argument over a presentation of six gardens, divided into two parts that progress through two gradients: from "formal" to "informal,"[15] and from a design to a gardening practice. This transition is from representation and figuration, often through drawing in an office offsite, where change is predicted, to the direct, nonrepresentational real-time activity of gardening that is largely based on onsite decisions. Both landscape architecture and gardening, I argue, exercise a kind of design judgment, contrary to convention, which treats the former as design and the latter as at best artisanal, though more often as kitsch craft.

Part I, "Figuring Growth," includes gardens that are celebrated for their clear use of plants in a strongly architectonic way: the sixteenth-century French Renaissance water garden at the Château Courances and its forests; Dan Kiley's garden for Eero Saarinen's Miller House in Columbus, Indiana (1957) and its famous Honey Locust Allée; and Sven-Ingvar Andersson's garden for his holiday house at Marnas, Sweden (1950–), with its garden rooms of hawthorn. Part I explores the relationship between garden structure and plant form as plants change (or don't) due to maintenance, the degree to which this is allowed for or encouraged, and the effect that such growth and maintenance have on the gardens' development over time. Since these gardens represent conventional examples of the planting design category "form," this part represents a debunking of the status quo, an opportunity for me to argue instead that such form is actually the result of gardening as much as, if not more than landscape design. In Part I, gardening technique is in the service of geometry.

While Part I focuses on landscape-architectural approaches, Part II is concerned with gardening-led approaches. The title of Part II, "Gardening Design," is a play on words because, on the one hand, the case studies in it are all examples of projects that were created using design decisions implemented through gardening practice onsite; on the other hand, the title also reflects my argument that landscape-architectural practice itself needs to be "gardened," brought back into the field. The gardens in this section include: Brazilian landscape architect Roberto Burle Marx's own nursery and garden outside Rio de Janeiro, the Sítio Roberto Burle Marx (1940s–); poet and scientist G. F. Dutton's "marginal garden" Druimchardain, Scotland (1980s); and Bernhard Korte's Museum Insel Hombroich, Germany (1983–). In Part II, geometry emerges from gardening technique.

Plants seem hardly to have the manifest forcefulness of architecture, so in a contrarian manner I conclude the book with a clear articulation of the viridic through a series of operative principles, proposing a "Manifesto for the Viridic." The viridic, then, is a call to arms to those landscape architects who are also gardeners, or to those gardeners who have design ambitions, to modify their modes of practice to suit the nature of their material.

Since, as I argued above, change cannot be simulated but only approximated, and growth is the most visible form of change in a designed landscape or garden, analyzing the difference between projections of growth and real growth demonstrates change. My varied background—first as a landscaper and gardener, then as a landscape architect—informs my readings of these gardens when I visited them. As a landscape architect I analyze the gardens formally and spatially, while as a gardener I look at plant growth as evidence of maintenance activity. Since the book is not an authoritative account of any one of the gardens, I use eclectic and differing evidence to advance my argument about the viridic that suits the particular case study and its position in the narrative of the book, but all evidence relates to time and change, since this is the nature of the medium: growth. For Courances and Marnas, this evidence is an analysis of plant forms resulting from a combination of plant location in the plan drawing and maintenance techniques, and I use conventional plan and section drawings to demonstrate this analysis. For the Miller garden and the Sítio, where I am talking about landscape change over longer periods of time, I have relied on documentary evidence from the Indiana Museum of Art's excellent online archive in the case of the former, and writing by the previous director for the latter. In both cases I have augmented this evidence with interviews with managers and staff who have seen the landscape change over time, relying on their informed observations of their workplaces. Perhaps the most unusual evidence I have used is for Druimchardain, where Dutton's poems were compared to my site experience and interviews with his family, to understand his working method of "marginal gardening." Since, by this stage in the book, my argument has moved to the relationship between the human subject and the vegetal subject in real time, this change is underlaid by a desire to value and treat seriously empirical evidence in the classical meaning of the word: evidence from the senses. With this in mind, by the time I analyze the Hombroich I am relying on conversations in different locales, entirely devoid of documentary evidence. Throughout the book, rather than ignoring the subjective nature of this evidence, I emphasize experience, and ask the reader to follow my logic as I examine what I find during my own analysis of the gardens onsite, deliberately focusing on what I noticed and the sequence in which I noticed it, as a kind of real-time process of developing an argument.

Ideas have lineages, and this book is no different, so I start each chapter with an introduction that provides a historical and theoretical landscape-architectural background as a context for my personal choices of the case studies. I came to landscape architecture at a point of theoretical transition from postmodernism, particularly critical theory, to landscape urbanism. Being a "late adopter," I was still immersed in a theoretical and design practice from the former, but thinking of ideas that shared a great deal with the latter. I was also very much influenced by my teacher and later colleague, Peter Connolly at RMIT University (Royal Melbourne University of Technology), who was theorizing landscape and site in a revolutionary way, exploring site representation and the use of site experience to give voice to "what the site does to you." While I appreciated the focus on change and ecology in landscape urbanism, I felt that because of its basis in design-generational techniques adopted from the architectural avant-garde, its methods were fundamentally disengaged from those parts of landscape that manifested such change, notably plants.

I strongly feel that at the moment of theoretical transition from post-modernism to landscape urbanism, a developing design discourse in landscape architecture was, if not silenced, then at least marginalized, notably in the work of scholars in the United States including Elizabeth K. Meyer, Marc Treib, and Dorothée Imbert, who were unpacking landscape form. At the same time, practitioners and theorists from France, often associated with the École Nationale Supérieure de Paysage (ENSP) in Versailles, were providing a basis for a landscape architecture embedded in gardening that could deal with change without regarding design and form as antithetical to it. It is from this position and these lineages that I seek to theorize. Often these ideas were bouncing around in my head on my site visits, finding synergies with what I saw. Landscape urbanism has rendered any other theory of landscape architecture somehow boring or conventional. I disagree: it's radical, as radical as arriving onsite and discovering that your design doesn't fit.

Three factors that bridge all the sections and gardens need to be discussed first, so that the reader can use them as a background for what will follow: form, biology, and practice. Together and separately, they describe growth and its effects, and affect how one conceives of landscape architecture and gardening as a practice, providing the background for the viridic.

The relationship between these three factors can be quickly summarized: Plants have form that is used by landscape architects to achieve desired spatial effects. Plant form arises through biological growth, "the process of increasing in size,"[16] the result of cell division and elongation over time. Gardening practices, mostly pruning in this book, affect growth processes and produce certain forms. Examining the relationship between these three, landscape-architectural practice and gardening practice are linked via design intentions made manifest through manipulation of biology by gardening practices.

PLAN FORM, PLANT FORM

Two rows of trees along a street form an avenue, creating a tunnel effect. For the driver passing in a car, the tree trunks produce a metronomic rhythm. For the pedestrian, the trees provide a cool refuge from the sun, a cathedral of branches from which leaves cast dappled shadows far below that the walker's feet cross on the pavement. The Parisian tree-lined boulevard, the English country lane, the track lined by eucalyptus in the Australian outback—in all these avenue formulations a recognizable space is created. A drawing of these configurations would use two parallel lines to guide the placement of tree centers opposite each other, pairs equally spaced along the lines. This diagram is simple, providing no sense of the sophisticated spatial experience that the driver or the pedestrian obtains. The space these trees form radiates from a uniform tree center, but is much more than a location.

This description uses the words "form" and space" implicitly. The idea of "space" is now so widespread that even business language refers to economic markets as spaces, like "the retail space," giving money spatiality, however the term is historically situated. Space forms part of what I refer to as the "form-space dialectic" of modernist architecture, which was adopted and modified by modernist landscape architects who applied it to plants.

Adrian Forty argues that ideas of form and space are foundational to the existence of modernism. Form and space are dialectical because form "produce[s] space,"[17] because "three-dimensionally a void is filled in part by the individual volumes of objects and in part by air."[18] Form and space are complementary and inverted. They are complementary because space is the silhouette left over from form, and inverted because form displaces space. The German word for space, *Raum*, literally means "room." This emphasizes the role of boundary demarcation, "the first impulse of architecture,"[19] in the definition of space. Modernist landscape architect Sven-Ingvar Andersson used space both as void and as *Raum* to describe how his hawthorn hedges made "11 rooms" with "in-between negative spaces" in his Marnas garden, the subject of chapter 4.[20]

Two other definitions of space used by Forty—space defined by people occupying it ("space itself, in the sense of inherent form, becomes effective form for the eye")[21] and abstract space ("space as a mathematical abstraction that can be plotted by coordinates and which has boundaries defined externally")[22]—were also used by modernist landscape architects. These two definitions are not distinct from each other, as we can see when Brazilian landscape architect Roberto Burle Marx, the subject of chapter 5, spoke of a garden being "a chromatic event where volumes connected and established relationships."[23] In a similar vein, American modernist landscape architect Garrett Eckbo said: "Design shall be three-dimensional. People live in volumes, not planes,"[24] where space is made by enclosing form: "Things must be around us and over us, as well as under us. A living area fails if it does not make one conscious of being within something, rather than on top of something."[25]

Eckbo's Harvard Graduate School of Design colleagues, modernist landscape architects Dan Kiley and James Rose, used plants as forms to shape architecturally. Gregg Bleam has analyzed Kiley's Miller Garden, subject of chapter 3, extensively in relation to modernist spatial theories, and demonstrated its debt to Mies van der Rohe's Barcelona Pavilion.[26] Kiley's description of the Miller Garden as "my first essentially modern landscape design. ... The sense of spaces unfolding and opening to join with one another inside is repeated outside linking the house with its landscape"[27] shows how he used the idea of "space" in the same way as his modernist architectural contemporaries used it. All these spaces were featured vegetation rather than architectural objects, though the implication of Bleam's analysis is that Kiley substituted trees into the tectonic of the wall, and that the rest of the compositional ideas were the same as Mies's. This model persists in contemporary planting design texts which treat architectural effect as the basic way of deploying plants in landscape design.[28] But surely plants are different to walls?

James Rose theorized landscape-specific spatial effects to make the modernist form-space dialectic specific to landscape architecture.[29] These effects arose from the unique properties of plants. Rose created a taxonomy of plant forms to show how different forms created differences in transparency, quantities and qualities formed by the gaps between branches and leaves where light would come through, like a trellis (if I must use an architectural analogy myself).[30] Used to shape space, plants gave a more subtle and nuanced spatial definition than their architectural counterparts. I will discuss Rose in more depth in chapter 3, but it is important to note here that Kiley and Rose provide a basic model for how plants can shape space in architectonic ways. All the gardens in this book are discussed from the perspective that plant form shapes space.

Space and form are often implicit in writing about landscape architecture. I draw attention to them because an interest in space has come to signify an ideological dimension, to which I do not subscribe. Perhaps since Gaston Bachelard's *Poetics of Space*,[31] discussion of space has become rarefied phenomenology. However, since I use my first-person observations of effects, some experiential component is inevitable. I have tried not to be too "spiritual" about this. I use the form-space dialectic more pragmatically as a way of describing the organization of the design, and the contribution of plant form to how garden spaces are shaped.

Plant form is really plant growth, since the form of a plant at any given time has arisen because of growth. Growth inflects the form-space dialectic of modernism. Although plants do not change their original position, their three-dimensional extent and size in plan do change as they grow and adapt to the ecology of their situation. Consequently, spaces too change over time as the plants that define them change. Furthermore, since each plant is genetically individual, the plan figure is even further disturbed. This makes it difficult to regard plants as combining to create a uniform structuring element in plan. These different growth effects converge to imply flux and imbue the plan with a certain waviness over time. Dynamic plant growth produces qualitative changes in three-dimensional form from static quantitative figures in plan. In other words, while plant location on the plan does not change much over time; the spaces do. The ineffectiveness of representation in describing such change demonstrates the need for a different practice than technical drawing to work with the emerging spatial change. This is why I advocate a gardening practice that uses the form-space dialectic in its decision-making.

Plants are growing form. This disturbs the modernist form-space dialectic by problematizing form. "Staticity," the condition of being static, has been a common critique of form since the process discourse began. R. E. Somol says: "forms can be beautiful or ugly but they are always serious [because] form is...an elaboration of geometry that seeks legitimacy in terms of the discipline of architecture,"[32] rendering form an anachronism that is empty when considered in its own terms. Instead, Somol prefers "shape" to form, because it is "crude, explicit, fast, material": shape "simply exists."[33] He gives shape a quality he denies form: performance. Unlike form, Somol argues, "shape adapts, is made fit for purpose, it is contingent." Correspondingly, "shape never appears as a definitive object itself but at most as the residual for *other* objects." Shape reflects the idea that design produces geometry in the context of undertaking something other than simply being form, or space creation. This sense of activity makes form provisional on a process's operation. D'Arcy Wentworth Thompson coined the term morphogenesis in the mid-twentieth century in his book *On Growth and Form*, where he argues that "the form of any portion of matter...may in all cases alike be described as due to the action of a force."[34]

Rather than polarizing form and process, weighting one or the other, Sanford Kwinter proposes a model that values both, which he calls "Manifest Form." This is built on a critique of the pejorative term "formalism," a "sloppy conflation of the notion of 'form' with that of 'object',"[35] where "form is ordering action, a logic deployed, while the object is merely the [form's] sectional image." Instead Kwinter talks about form and formation, where form is both the object and its catalytic qualities simultaneously. Formation is the process of patterns being distilled from "a less finely-ordered field."[36] On the surface this seems like a rebranding of form as process, particularly when he states: "form is resonance and expression of embedded forces."[37]

However, Kwinter argues that "the great formalists...have always been able to peer into the object toward its rules of formation and to see these two strata together as a mobile, open and oscillating system subject to a greater or lesser number of external pressures"[38] "Manifest Form," then, is still physical and complete, able to be "peered into," at the same time as it is an expression of the forces that have made it.

A process definition of form describes plants well, since plant form results from the growth process. However, in elevating process, form in its own right is often devalued. This has negative implications for landscape architecture, but positive implications for gardening. Organizing a design with plants, landscape architects require a stable form in order to produce the desired spatial effects, so changes in form due to growth potentially disturb such effects. However, if a gardener is working with plants as they grow, seeing form as process gives them agency in shaping spaces over time. In other words, process makes form, which makes space. But form is also catalytic in its own right, particularly in a landscape where forms influence microclimate, and therefore other plants. Therefore, form influences processes to create space.

For the purposes of this book, I need both definitions: Kwinter's definition of "Manifest Form" as both a process and an artifact offers such a model. I need to foreground forms as artifacts to get to the spatial structure of the gardens produced by plants. And I also need process to describe how the forms that produce spatial effects were created through gardening. Combined with plant growth, this spatial model becomes more dynamic and differentiated over time in an exciting way. Far from being just substituted for bricks in a wall, plants problematize the architectural model of form and space itself.

THE BIOLOGY OF PLANT LIVES

The avenue is on a congested road in a tropical city, so the landscape architects select a large fig tree, Ficus religiosa, *the tree under which the Buddha is said to have gained enlightenment. They have seen massive examples of this tree, so they choose a generous spacing: 20 meters apart. When the trees are planted they are only 3 meters high and 2 meters wide, leaving a space of 18 meters between them. This gap will close over in time, but each tree will have different shapes along the way, according to its own morphological responses to site factors and its unique DNA. While the figs will ultimately have large trunks and wide canopies, they will grow tall before they begin to spread. Since they are banyan figs, as their limbs spread sideways, aerial roots will drop down from the branches to the pavement, crack-*

> *ing it, finding water. Over time, across its lifespan, each tree will look like a dispersed network of trees rather than a single individual.*

Plants, like people, go through many different states in the process of their growth before they reach maturity. To ignore the states in between is to ignore the very quality of growth that makes plants unique as living rather than inert. If form is process when it comes to plants, then that process is morphology, a branch of biology concerned with the form of living things. When I talk about growth, this growth is the morphogenesis that Wentworth discussed. It requires a general description of plant morphology, since in all my case studies gardeners stimulate morphological processes in one way or another, but generally by pruning, to achieve the desired effects, including spatial ones. Biologists, ironically, call this "plant architecture."

The place on plants where cells most actively divide and grow is called the meristem. Growth proceeds continuously from the apical meristem, located at the top or ends of a shoot. Over time, "the accumulation of apical meristems by the plant and their subsequent activity results in the development of the structural architecture of the plant."[39] A plant grows from numerous apical meristems, also referred to as buds, from which shoots emerge. These eventually become woody branches, resulting in the plant's form. Bell notes that identification of a characteristic morphology for a plant suggests that such characteristics are static: "however, a flowering plant is not a static object. It is a dynamic organism constantly growing and becoming more elaborate" over time.[40] Three factors in the development of plant architecture are relevant to time: bud location (where the bud is located on the plant), potential (the potential of that bud to produce a shoot), and time of activity (the growth season). Any intervention that affects these things will affect plant form. This can be explained by using pruning as an example. When woody material, like a branch, is removed, the buds located on it that have the potential for growth are also removed. This has a less obvious effect, to do with a phenomenon known as "apical dominance." The apical meristem is located at the end of the shoot and produces more growth than the axillary, or side, meristem. The apical meristem's dominance is due to concentrations of an inhibiting hormone called auxin, which affects the axillary buds' growth potential.[41] When a branch is pruned, and its apical meristem is removed, the axillary meristem's growth potential increases significantly. This combines with the possibility of new buds emerging from the cambium tissue surrounding the branch. Together these result in greater side branching, so that a plant becomes "bushier" when it is pruned.[42] This process is manipulated by spacing out pruning actions in relation to growth periods and the desired resulting growth.

Highlighting the morphological mechanisms by which plants grow suggests a different way of thinking about plant form and how plants shape space. In architecture, materials are applied to forms more than the other way around. Working with plant form means taking actions on the plant that cause form to arise indirectly. This sets up a trajectory for the future via changes in form in the present that will yield results in future form. On the one hand this might mean that current form is devalued, and form again becomes process, not something in its own right. But since I argue that we must also value the current state, not simply the future, the gardener must have a view on both every time they prune: prune for now, prune for later. This process requires regular intervention to adjust and calibrate the trajectory to emerging form, a process undertaken by the horticulture trades—arborists or gardeners, for example—rather than landscape architects.

Emphasizing plant biology as part of spatial effect draws attention to the fact that plants are organic, like people. Like people, each plant is simultaneously an individual and a representative of a species. Focusing on the plant, as the gardener does, also necessitates a focus on particular plants since, as Ferrari says, "when gardening is art, its elements are the lives of plants."[43] Preferring to call them plant lives rather than plant material, Ferrari maintains the strangeness of manipulating a living thing in art, but also recognizing what is unique about it: that the artwork is made by one organism using another.

An avenue involves the performance of each of the plants individually, so that they can collectively create the desired spatial effect. To have a spatial effect, plants must prosper, so a "gardener wants his plants happy,"[44] because a happy plant is a growing plant. The idea of happiness for a plant is anthropomorphism; however, Ferrari says that gardeners have "a concern for plants that we feel just as one living being for another being."[45] He suggests that in the garden one of our other activities is to "share the company of plants."[46] This makes the garden less like a zoo for plants than a public space, where people physically share the company of plants.

Michael Marder, on the other hand, suggests that plants are different to humans, and proposes a different way of "being" for plants called "Plant-Thinking," when humans "encounter plants." "Plant-Thinking" is defined as "the non-cognitive, non-ideational, and non-imagistic mode of thinking proper to plants," or what he calls "thinking without the head."[47]

Plants have a different relationship with their environment than people. Plants, Marder says, "are capable, in their own fashion, of accessing, influencing, and being influenced by a world that does not overlap the human *Lebenswelt* but that corresponds to the vegetal modes of dwelling on and in the earth."[48] Plant-thinking is sensitivity to the environment and a complex feedback process between the plant and that environment, where one alters the other iteratively, perhaps recursively. While humans can move location to suit their living requirements, plants must adapt to, and in turn adapt, their immediate microclimate. Marder's model of plant-thinking has implications for Ferrari's idea, because "whenever human beings encounter plants, two or more worlds (and temporalities) intersect."[49] Even when the gardener is in their company, "the absolute familiarity of plants coincides with their sheer strangeness."[50] Marder suggests that "to accept this axiom is already to let plants maintain their otherness, respecting the uniqueness of their existence."[51]

Nonetheless, gardeners have an agenda when it comes to plants. Focused on selfish aims like a beautiful garden, they need plant growth for their own ends. Although Stefan Buczaki says that "the garden is an environment of interacting organisms," he still adds that "you [the gardener] are, or pretend to be, the most important [organism]."[52] The garden is a dictatorship, making gardening both "an aesthetic art [but also] the art of politics."[53] It is political, because "both the gardener and the politician organize lives. The garden is a society of plants, a society established, maintained, cared for, and ruled over by its gardener."[54]

Correspondingly, gardeners can never have an equal relationship with plants. Marder says that "when [we] instrumentalize plants, we do not yet encounter them, even though their outlines become to some extent more determinate."[55] Recalling disinterestedness in Kantian aesthetics, where qualities can be truly appreciated only if one does not have an agenda in relation to the subject, Marder suggests that "perhaps we are in a better position to encounter the plants themselves—for instance, sunflowers—when we do not know what to do with them."[56]

Talking about plant-thinking is strange, bearing in mind that we started from a drawing of an avenue. However, moving from the architecture of plant forms and their resultant spaces to an understanding of the biology of growth, and finally to the plant as growing being, demonstrates that the implications for designed form of embracing growth and gardening are enormous and radical. From being a wall that is transparent and green, a hedge, for example, now appears to be a living, breathing community of organisms with individual levels of "happiness." To engage with plants at this level will never be possible for the landscape architect unless they become a gardener. But isn't this going backward?

LANDSCAPE GARDENER

The avenue was planted beneath overhead power lines. The trees have been steadily growing toward them, their top leaves now brushing against them. The council landscape architect has been working behind the computer and hasn't noticed, but a concerned ratepayer has contacted the council. The landscape architect is concerned that the power company will demand that the council remove trees in proximity to the lines. Meeting onsite, the arborist, dressed in high-visibility work wear, and the "smart casual" landscape architect survey the scene. Before returning to the office, the landscape architect directs the tree gang to prune the trees around the power lines. Fifteen meters in the air in a cherry picker, covered in sawdust from the chainsaw, the arborist judiciously cuts some limbs and not others. As she carefully maintains shape and conceals cuts, the arborist's aim, based on her experience, is to cause the new growth to bypass the power lines. In this way, the avenue will continue to grow, with the power lines going through it, until they eventually disappear and the avenue closes over.

Gardeners and landscape architects are different, despite having much in common. The gardener is "a person who tends and cultivates a garden as a pastime or for a living," while the landscape architect is one who undertakes "the art and practice of designing the outdoor environment."[57] Their similarity is that both focus on "the outdoor environment." It is their practices, or actions, which are different, because the gardener tends or cultivates, "organiz[ing] plant lives,"[58] while the landscape architects designs. The gardener and the landscape architect work with the outdoor environment very differently: the landscape architect produces drawings of it while the gardener literally has her fingers in it, as a kind of performance.[59]

The gardener has a critical role to play in the dynamic model of form and space I am proposing. Their actions direct the production of new plant forms by optimizing emerging characteristics. I am also arguing that the gardener uses a design judgment that is not so different from the landscape architect's, but very different in practice. The practices and expertise of each are required to work with growth, and each needs the characteristics of the other: landscape architects need gardeners to realize their original propositions, while gardeners need landscape architects to realize the formal and spatial possibilities of their practices. However, the two disciplines are separated professionally, and it is now very difficult for the landscape architect to engage meaningfully with growth, because they cannot engage with gardening.[60]

I shall examine the historical roots of this problem, arguing that landscape architecture has its roots, as it were, in gardening, and that its shift toward architecture reflects two tendencies: a society-wide process of professionalization, as Baird and Szczygiel have demonstrated,[61] and a class-based perception of gardening as an unskilled trade.

The English term landscape architecture has its roots in the English landscape garden, and gardens such as Stourhead, whose creator, Henry Hoare, was, according to Edward Hyams, "the first landscape *gardener* [emphasis added], who showed in a single work, genius of the highest order."[62] While Hyams calls Hoare a landscape gardener, J. C. Loudon suggested in his book *The Landscape Gardening and Landscape Architecture of the Late Humphry Repton, Esq.*, published in 1840,[63] that the term "landscape gardener" is attributable to Repton, though Uvedale Price was critical of this self-attribution, "assuming a title with no small pretensions," since he "determined to make that pursuit his profession which had hitherto been only his amusement."[64] In the title of Loudon's book we also see the earliest use of the term "landscape architect" in English, as a qualification of "landscape gardening," though Waldheim notes an earlier usage in Gilbert Measons's *On the Landscape Architecture of the Great Painters of Italy* (1828).[65] Indigenous to England, this type of gardening had been called *English gardening*, but Loudon found this term inappropriate, since it emphasized gardening "in its more confined sense of *Horticulture*." He preferred *landscape gardening*, because "the art can only be advanced and perfected by the united powers of the *landscape painter* and the *practical gardener*," since "the former must conceive a plan which the latter may be able to execute."[66]

When the American Society of Landscape Architects (ASLA) was established in 1899, this debt to landscape painting was evident in the description of landscape architecture as "an art." Writing about the beginning of landscape architecture in the United States, Baird and Szczygiel note that it was initially a profession for both "landscape architects" and "landscape gardeners." Although the reference to gardener was dropped by 1907, Thomas Whateley's *Observations on Modern Gardening* was still included in the ASLA's "authoritative library" for the landscape-architectural profession.[67]

For Loudon, landscape painting and gardening had a dynamic relationship because, on the one hand, the gardener's knowledge was vital, since "the luxuriant imagination of the *painter* must be subjected to the *gardener's* practical knowledge in planting, digging and moving earth."[68] On the other hand, "if the knowledge of painting be insufficient without that of gardening... the mere gardener, without some skill in painting, will seldom be able to *form a just idea of the effects before they are carried out in execution*."[69] Although Repton used his famous Red Books to show how his improvements would look before and after his endeavors, these were primarily for marketing purposes, and his design practice was based on Repton directing work onsite himself.

Repton was practicing like a gardener but thinking like a landscape architect. Proposition and action were thus located in the same time interval. While Loudon decried how "Time makes unrelenting havoc with designs which, during the first ten or twenty years, may have afforded unmixed satisfaction,"[70] he nonetheless saw too that this change is entirely natural: "The facility with which any alterations may be made, aiding the love of change which is natural to most minds, in the course of years leaves no trace of that master hand which first laid the foundation of future improvement."[71] Repton's practice could be a model for the kind of landscape architecture practice I am proposing in this book. However, though the root of landscape gardening may have been the garden, the profession quickly distanced itself from garden workers on the basis of class.

Baird and Szczygiel argue that "by keeping the 'irregulars' out of competition (for example, mid-wives and homeopaths in medicine; women and amateur gardeners in landscape architecture), a controlled base of operation could be delineated and power established over not only the market, but also over production of future professionals."[72] Drawing on the sociology of professions, they call this "credentialism." Landscape architecture was distancing itself from both amateur and trade gardeners. Early on in the establishment of the ASLA, landscape architects decried "engineers [that] think of landscape architects as planting flowers."[73] Landscape architects were distancing themselves from "planting," "getting your hands dirty": either an amateur endeavor or, worse, a working-class trade.

The birth of landscape gardening had a relationship to taste, inherited from painting. The mobilization of cultivated judgment in landscape gardening was a class-based distinction. Thus for Loudon, the requisite qualification for being a landscape gardener was that "culture and education should have refined his taste," and he should have "a knowledge of the habits of polished life [which can be] acquired only by an admittance into the best society."[74] While he might have wished it otherwise, Repton complained, like the early landscape architects who founded the ASLA sixty years after him, that "it is the misfortune of every liberal art to find amongst its professors some men of uncouth manners; and since my profession has more frequently been practiced by day labourers, and persons with no education, it is the more difficult to give it that rank in the polite arts which I conceive it ought hold."[75] Correspondingly, while Loudon acknowledged the skills of gardening in implementing a landscape garden, he was careful to distinguish its practitioners from the ranks of the gardener—characterizing them as uneducated and uncouth.

The status of gardeners is still very variable across the world. More than a century later, in many First World countries gardeners are treated as lower-class, unvalued and underpaid. Sally-Ann Murray notes that in South Africa, "garden knowledge was permitted to black people only through the menial labour of 'the garden boy,'"[76] a term applied to men working in gardens despite being on average 33.86 years old,[77] and generally initiated,[78] therefore men rather than boys.[79] Gardeners are included as domestic workers in the Basic Conditions of Employment Act (BCEA) in South Africa, where "domestic work is one of the few employment opportunities open to poor and often uneducated men and women," of which gardening is the only type of domestic work available to men.[80] Du Preez et al. "contend that, when it comes to the employment relationship in the domestic workspace, the legacy of apartheid is not in racialising relationships, but in reinforcing the economic structures that facilitate and perpetuate unequal relationships."[81] This demonstrates that class distinctions continue to play out in relation to gardeners in the twenty-first century, but now through inequality and economic migration, which nonetheless consolidates the racial profile of the gardener.

The racial difference between clients and gardeners due to inequality is not confined to South Africa, but also prevails in America, where Mexican gardeners who work as contractors in an informal economy are similarly affected, though as entrepreneurs they can gain significant financial rewards from garden work over time.[82] In both these examples, from the

United States and South Africa, a lack of education and skills allows men to work as gardeners, tying gardening as a trade to inequality and a particular working-class position. In relation to an international comparison of the situation of domestic workers, Du Preez et al. find that "improved education levels [and] professionalisation of domestic work...leads to reduced income inequality."[83]

The much-photographed masterworks by landscape architects—the Miller Garden, for example—all have two stories: the story of the designer's intentions and the stories of the gardener's labor. These two stories about the same garden are often very different but very instructive about how much work it takes to make a spatial effect persist over time. I talk to the gardeners of almost all the gardens in this book, and hear their descriptions of what they do to keep the masterworks in their care in a state of peak performance. Informed by the oral history practice of my father, Richard Raxworthy, I try both to capture both what they do to maintain the spatial effects in terms of gardening, and to glean stories of their lives: to bring to life the labor and personalities of key workers whose efforts are generally either derided or ignored by landscape architects.

The history of landscape gardening demonstrates how landscape architecture and gardening have become separated, but also provides a model for how they might come together again. It shows that both have something to contribute and that growth is something which they share, and which can bring their practices together too. This reveals my political position, one for which I make no apology. Gardeners need to be trained; their expertise should be recognized and treated with respect.

GARDEN OR LANDSCAPE?

Issues of maintenance are important to all landscape architects. Since this book is directed at them, landscape architects might ask: "Why talk about gardens?," when public landscapes are also in desperate need of care. I will conclude this introduction by setting out why I believe that the garden is the ideal place to consider growth, and the relationship between landscape architecture and gardening.

The garden is the root of landscape architecture, yet a fraught site for the profession. It is the birthplace of the discipline, yet one that it seeks to suppress due to its association with the trade of gardening, or amateur gardening. Nonetheless, by the time modern ideas like outdoor living were becoming of interest to suburban homeowners in postwar America,[84] the residential garden again became a site for landscape-architectural practice, once the link to gardening and gardeners had been broken, and the profession was well established. The garden as the root of the profession is periodically invoked by designers who talk about "getting back to basics," and is synonymous with a call to renew interest in plant material.

The garden has always been a place where modernist landscape architects "test" ideas—Swiss landscape architect Dieter Kienast, for example, who famously explored topiary and wetlands in his home garden in Zurich. Both Rose and Eckbo used the garden as a testing site for ideas. In his graduation design project from Harvard, "Small Gardens in the City," Eckbo designed a series of 18 hypothetical residential gardens. Using the same site issues and design palette in different ways, he developed a project that was "purely abstract and experimental, designed to stimulate thought and provoke comment, discussion and flow of new ideas."[85] Sven-Ingvar Andersson, Roberto Burle Marx, and Geoffrey Dutton all tested ideas and ways of using plants in the gardens featured in this book.

Another reason why the garden is trivialized by landscape architects—more so than by architects—is that it lacks many of the constraints faced by public landscapes. While I hope that my discussion of the political dimension of gardening as a trade demonstrates that I am not interested in autonomy, it is true that I am focusing on the garden because it is less easily hijacked by other issues than public landscapes are. The garden allows a specific focus on plants. In so doing, though, I acknowledge that having a garden is a privilege acquired through economic advantage and is not available to everyone, a fact that does potentially undermine some of my claims about gardening as a trade.

The garden is always practical and philosophical, and these two are and always have been linked. Dixon Hunt, reading Cicero, suggests that gardens are "third nature": first nature is wilderness, second nature is mobilized for human gain, like agriculture, and third nature is the garden, essentially functionless, where nature—that is, plants—are mobilized for aesthetic purposes.[86] While the garden as third nature has different intentions to second nature, it shares with it the manipulation of plants, albeit for different ends. In the garden, this manipulation is gardening. Therefore, I argue that the garden and gardening are synonymous, and that this activity is foregrounded in the garden. Correspondingly, since gardening is one of the foci of the book, the garden is the logical place to discuss it.

Mark Francis, in *The Meaning of Gardens*, discussing the "everyday garden" of the amateur home gardener, argues that gardens are "*a place to exert creativity*, … to experiment with creative fantasy [and] to experience the joy of creating something."[87] Acknowledging the amateur roots of gardening by focusing on the garden, I hope that this book will also appeal to regular gardeners who might be interested in the relationship between gardens, as they understand them, and the profession of landscape architecture. Much of the gardening techniques and biology that I discuss will be familiar to gardeners; therefore the spatial and formal discourse of landscape architecture might allow them to see what they do in their garden from a perspective more informed by design.

Landscape has come to mean either public landscape or urban landscape, despite its English landscape garden roots. Landscape is now linked to infrastructure, to programs like schools or building types like business parks. The garden, on the other hand, is self-referential, and about plants. This alone is a reason for landscape architects to be less interested in it. Indeed, efforts by the early profession to distance itself from plants show the trivial regard for plants by landscape architects generally. Due to its association with plants, the garden is also regarded as trivial, compared to public landscapes and infrastructure. My primary reason for choosing the garden is that gardens are acknowledged to foreground growth, which is the central focus of this book.

That does not mean the book has no relevance for landscape maintenance—very much to the contrary. Maintenance means to "keep (something) at the same level or rate."[88] A narrow focus on landscape maintenance would cause the creative potential of growth to be obscured by the instrumentality of maintenance. Ideas about growth in the garden can stand separate from the banal pragmatism of landscape maintenance. It is from this perspective of creative growth that, I believe, a conjunction of landscape architecture and gardening offers a whole new realm of design practice.

PART I

FIGURING GROWTH

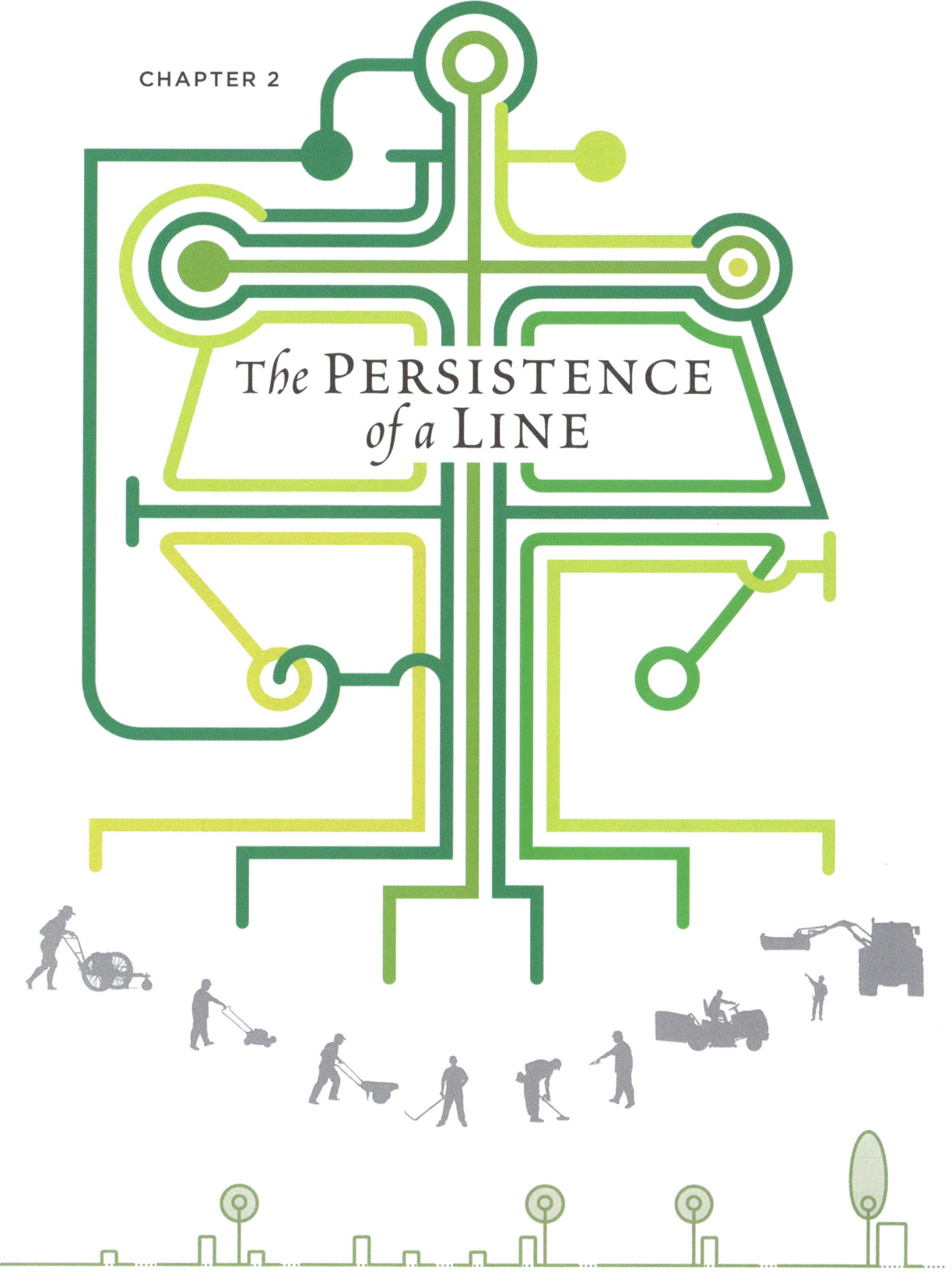

Duchamp the years of postmodernism, the garden at the Château Vaux-le-Vicomte by André Le Nôtre was celebrated as a masterpiece of French landscape design.[1] Readings of this garden tended to focus on the French garden either as animated spectacle or as proto-modernism. Allen Weiss's essay "Vaux-le-Vicomte: Anamorphosis Abscondita" discussed Vaux as a place of calculated visual distortion, expected readings of myth recast through optical effects.[2] At the same time, landscape historians revealed the admiration modern landscape architects like Dan Kiley had for Le Nôtre's work; its articulation of space at scale and clear organization.[3] The idea that a garden can structure a territory continues to be an exciting and liberating one for landscape architecture, making Vaux a logical stop on the mandatory European grand tour.[4]

Walking along the central axis at Vaux, taking photographs at the transition from one terrace to the next, even as I was awed, I was bored. Advancing toward the transverse canal, I expected the perverse visual trick described by Weiss: what appear from a distance to be sculptures turn out to be amorphous piles of shit-like cement up close. Instead, during the deviation along the canal, I saw that the characteristic "cuts" of the French garden through forest were in fact constructed. The power

FIGURE 2.2
London plane trees line the *pièce d'eau des Platanes simples* on one side of the Allée d'Honneur at the Château Courances.

FIGURE 2.3
The central axis at the Château Vaux-le-Vicomte, designed by André Le Nôtre.

FIGURE 2.4
The edge between garden and forest along *le Grand canal* at Château Vaux-le-Vicomte.

of the French garden lies in how its geometries operate on a geographic scale. Forests were organized around territorial routes, their geometry's desire-lines meeting garden diagrams, forest the space in between. Using hedges and rows of trees as an edge for regenerating forest, the transition between forest and garden is much more sophisticated than a simple "manipulation of nature." At Vaux I saw that to make the diagram of the French garden, to render geometry on this territorial scale, was to use the garden's edge as a device to negotiate the formality of the territorial diagram and the different time intervals of agriculture. The French garden was a structuring mechanism that was interchangeably ornamental and infrastructural, not urban but definitely territorial: a territory defined by trees, by growth.[5]

Leaving Versailles by l'avenue Saint-Cloud, on a circuit around Paris between Château Vaux-le-Vicomte and Château Dampierre, lies another garden often attributed, incorrectly, to Le Nôtre: Château de Courances. Courances has an intriguing description. In their guidebook *The Gardens of Europe*, Hobhouse and Taylor say: "André Le Nôtre is said to have had a hand in the design. If he did, he was certainly in an uncharacteristically intimate frame of mind."[6] Intrigued by their comment, I deviated from my planned route. My visit to Courances was serendipitous, since it turned out to be my favorite French garden, one that I visited four more times over the next ten years. It also exemplified the characteristic vegetated edge that I had seen at Vaux, negotiating between garden and territory in a much simpler way.

Hobhouse and Taylor describe a mood not normally associated with the French garden and its massive scale. They describe Courances's "grave formal beauty" made up of "a series of green rooms…[and] a stately harmony of trees, water and grass." Vincent Scully also noted the unusually romantic quality of Courances, with its "little canals [that run] beneath the trees, reflecting them and sparkling with light…indicating as it does how 'natural,' how unforced, the regular effects of the French classic garden may be made sometimes to seem."[7] At Vaux the focus of attention is clearly its detailed *parterres*, complex grade changes, and visual effects rather than its forest edges. The simplicity of Courances's language—"trees, water and grass," together with its "unforced, regular effects"—make it an ideal candidate for describing the mediation between territorial and garden-scale characteristic of the French baroque garden, a mediation that revolves around growth and time.

The relationship between territorial scale and management provides an important demonstration about how individual organisms, plants, can be aggregated to create broader organizational effects, so I start this chapter by setting out a model for defining this relationship—which I call "*parti-parterre*"—between large-scale geometry and the small spaces of management, using it to introduce Courances.[8] With Hobhouse and Taylor's description of Courances's intimacy in mind, I then focus on the changes to one particular vegetated space, the Allée d'Honneur, showing both how geometry can persist over time when it is made out of living, and dying, things, but also how it has changed qualitatively, spatially, even as it has persisted quantitatively, in extent, because it is made of living things. Building on both this quality/quantity dynamic, and the *parti-parterre* model, I then look in detail at a range of different contemporary edge conditions at Château de Courances that describe the transition of the ornamental garden space to the productive forest space, focusing on how management acts give design qualities to this transition, as well as imply different intervals of time and natural process. I conclude by arguing that a key quality of the viridic is recognition that any formal effect that one expects from landscape architecture using vegetation is always primarily a management effect.

PARTI-PARTERRE

I call this relationship between large-scale territorial and small-scale management "*parti-parterre*," bringing together terms from two different periods. The sixteenth-century term *parti pris* means "take a view," from the phase *prendre parti*, which means to take a position.[9] The usage of the term during the Beaux-Arts period referred to the idea of the project generally, but since the advent of modernism it has come to refer to the diagrammatic expression of an idea in plan. I use *parti* literally to refer to the large-scale organizing figure of the French garden, following this modernist model. For many French gardens, like Vaux-le-Vicomte and

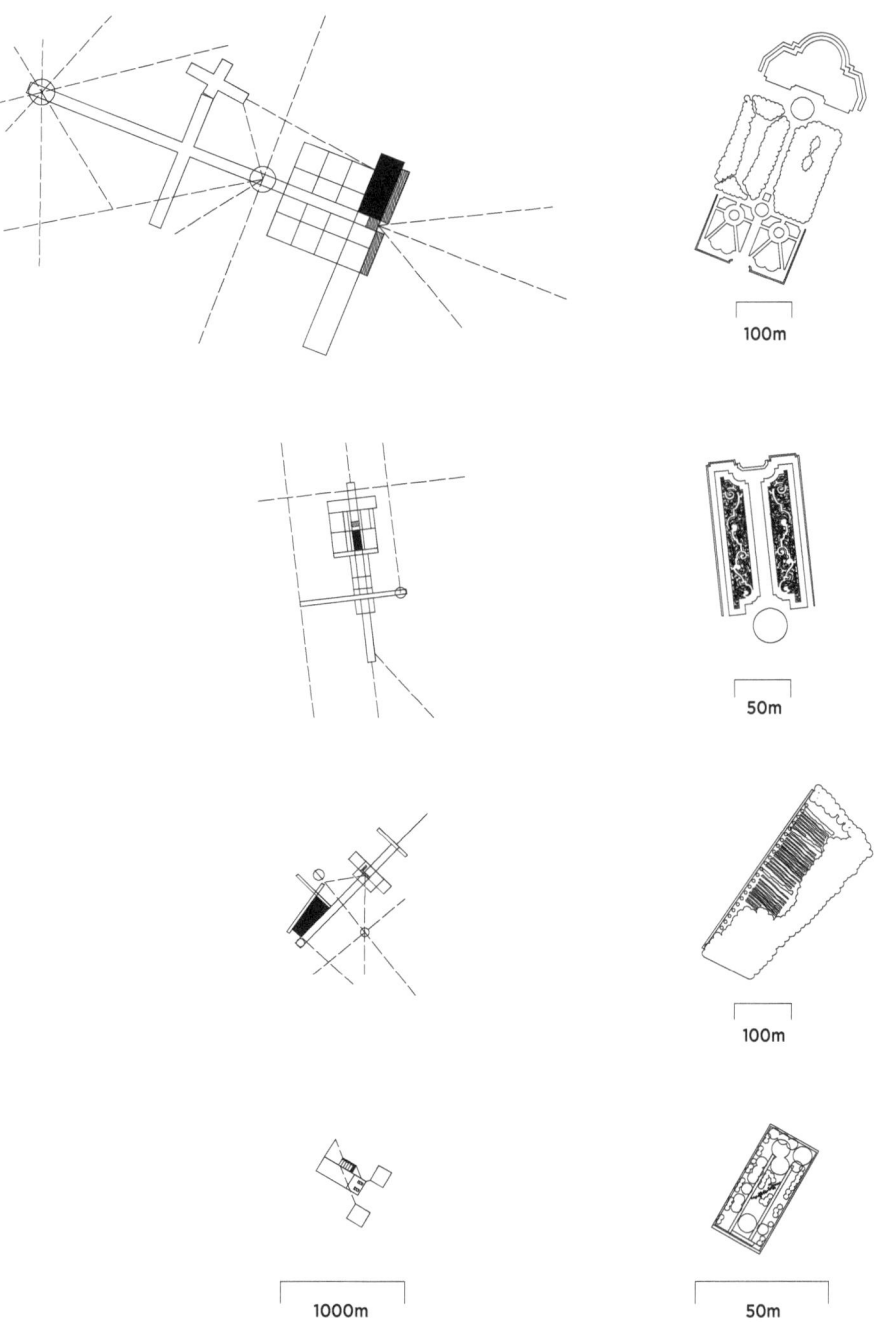

FIGURE 2.5

Parti diagrams (left) and component *parterres* (right) of a range of historic and contemporary French gardens: (from top) Château de Versailles, Château Vaux-le-Vicomte, Château Courances, Parc André Citroën.

Versailles, the *parti* is a cross, longer than it is wide, with the main axis aligned through the house, with a transverse axis perpendicular to it.

The term *parterre* refers literally to "a level space in a garden occupied by an ornamental arrangement of flower beds."[10] This definition is derived from *parterre de broderie*, the traditional hedged floral motif normally enclosed in a four-square division on a terrace.[11] The literal meaning of *parterre*—"on the ground"—describes how I use the term to refer to the detailed organization of spaces on a human scale, at eye level.[12] Taken together, *parti* and *parterre* are intimately related to one another in the French baroque garden as a way of dealing with scale. At the large scale, the *parti* is a relatively simple, crude figure, but this same figure divides up space at ground level into a series of smaller spaces, or *parterres*. The *parterre* accommodates different programs and their formal complexities, which come together like a mosaic to reinforce the overall territorial figure, the *parti*. Contemporary French gardens like Parc André Citroën also display this *parti-parterre* relationship, where intricate walled themed gardens are slotted into the bigger organizational figure. The relationship between *parti* and *parterre* is reciprocal because the detail of the *parterre* makes up the edges of the figure on the larger scale, even as the *parti* guides the location of such detail.

The *parti-parterre* relationship is "territorial," because, as French *paysagiste* and educator Michel Corajoud noted, "territories…have been historically subject to natural disturbances, successive occupations that have left traces, configurations, distributions…maintained…for centuries by having been confirmed by successive uses."[13] In territorial terms, the *parti* is a figure formed by time, by finer-grain edges and changes at the *parterre* scale. The edge can be comprised of hard landscape elements like paths, but more often it utilizes maintenance techniques that have different periodicities related to growth, the edge formed by repetitive actions over multiple iterations. Although the *parti* appears to be static, since it is made up of plants, it is a figure in time because plants grow and change along with the history of the site, its owners, and their management regimes.[14] The edge of the *parterre*, making up the boundary of *parti*, is a regulator of different growth patterns in the French garden, organized to envelop different land uses, each also with its own lifespan. When all these interrelated and overlapping time intervals are placed physically next to each other, the apparent static quality of the French landscape is revealed to be an illusion.[15]

Courances demonstrates this dynamic relationship between *parti* and *parterre* in an interesting way, because it has become simplified over time until it is now just "trees, grass and water," though with a lot of hedges in between. Taking *parti* and *parterre* respectively, I will examine two parts of Courances: the changes to the Allée d'Honneur (which forms the *parti*) that result from the garden's history; and the edges of the forest as *parterre*, for which I will develop a typology based on my observations. Despite the fact that it is made of living, changing trees, for the former I show how the *parti* of the garden persisted even as its spatiality and character on the ground changed. Different maintenance techniques negotiate the edge between different landscape types on the level of *parterre*, so for the latter I reflect on the interface between the garden and the park and their different time intervals. In both instances it is important to recognize, as Mariage reminds us, that the French baroque garden is really the ornamentalization of productive agricultural or silvicultural land use.[16]

BLURRED AXIS

Despite fluctuating in location, extent, and materiality over time, the overall *parti* of the French garden—and Courances is an example—persists on a territorial scale across its lifespan, as I have noted, generally comprising a cross made up of a main axis and a transverse axis. This is not to say that the French garden does not change over time—it does, and considerably; however, its change is generally within a small tolerance on the territorial scale of the *parti*. In the garden plants grow, die, and biodegrade, or are replaced, so the materiality of the edge is ephemeral. The persistence of a garden's geometry over time is miraculous, testament to its ongoing reinforcement by owners, gardeners, and managers across many generations, despite the garden's own inherent momentum toward change. The literature of garden design valorizes the designer as the originator of a garden. However, since the essence of a garden is change and growth, these conspire to vary it from the designer's intention, and render the

FIGURE 2.6

The Allée d'Honneur at Château Courances.

relevance of that intention negligible in the long term, visible only in the *parti*. Rather, it is garden owners who develop a garden over multiple generations. Any description of a garden's form over time is thus primarily a story of its owners. The persistence of the *parti* shows how—at considerable expense, and indeed often financial ruin—love for a garden moves across generations and different families. In relation to the overall *parti* of Courances, the changes in the Allée d'Honneur over 500 years are only approximately 50 meters in plan, but with considerable different vertical and spatial change in terms of experience over that time. The plane trees that currently line it are only half that age. Their intimate character is a result of the different planting arrangements and maintenance changes that have fluctuated in type and location around the axis's orientation and scale, of which the planes are only the most recent. By laying out the history of the allée, I will show how a dynamic relationship between plant growth and maintenance can inflect the persisting geometry of a garden and "personalize" it, give it a particular sensibility. In this process, the contribution of garden owners over long periods becomes clear, each

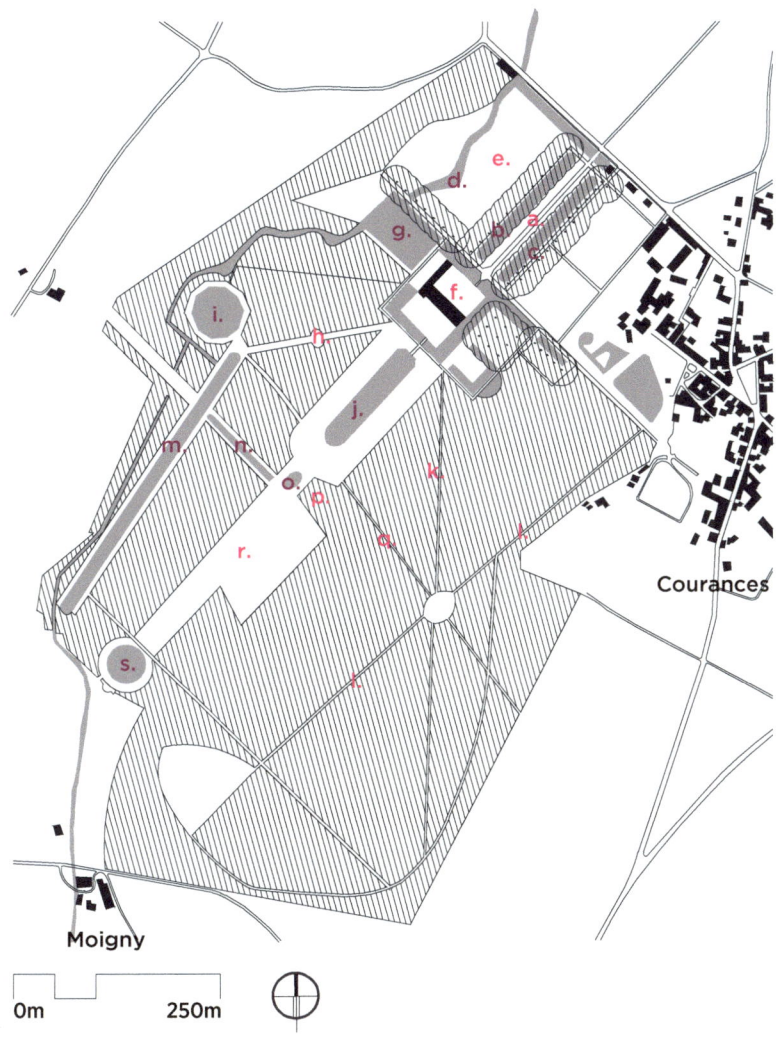

FIGURE 2.7

Plan of Château Courances garden and park.

a. Allée d'Honneur
b. Pièce d'eau des Platanes simples
c. Pièce d'eau des Platanes doubles
d. École River
e. Pré Bernay
f. Château
g. Salle d'eau
h. Allée de la Table
i. Gerbe
j. Miroir
k. Allée du vieux tennis
l. Champs-Élysées
m. Grand canal
n. Nappes
o. Dauphin
p. Fontaine du Roy
q. Percée du Miroir
r. Les Trois Grâces
s. Rond de Moigny

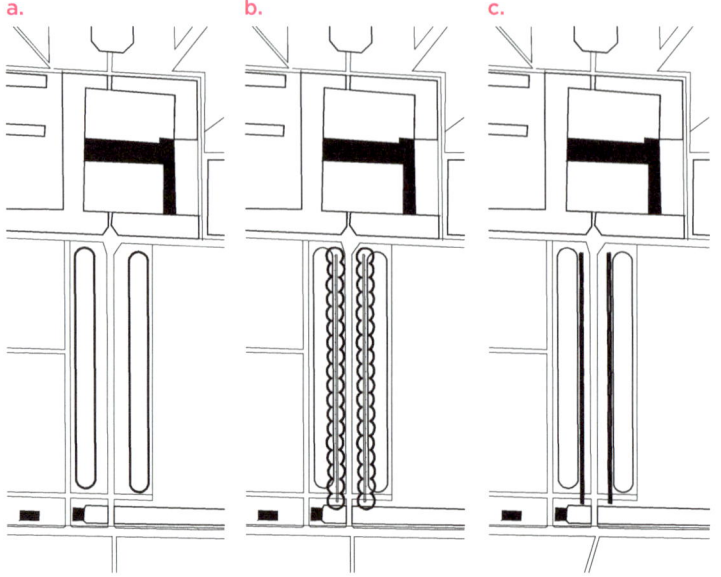
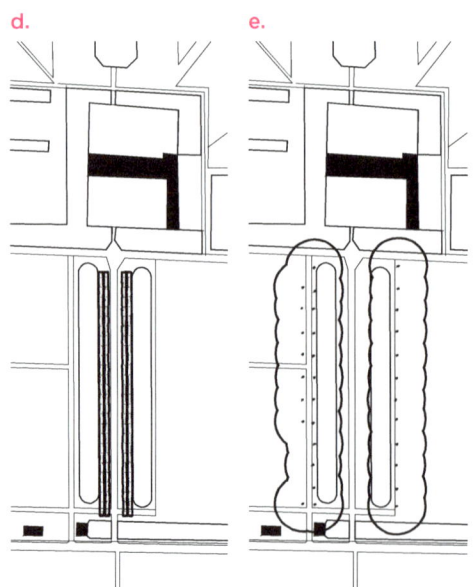

FIGURE 2.8

Changing planting configurations and spatial ordering of the Allée d'Honneur over time: (**a**) 1548–1622 Clausse (two current canals along the Allée d'Honneur); (**b**) 1643 Gallard (palisade of *épines* [wall of spines] below cypress trees); (**c**) 1645 Gallard (higher canopy of cypress in the palisade was removed); (**d**) 1756 Catherine de Gallard (*contre-allées*, or two rows of trees on each side of the allée); (**e**) 1782 Marquis de Nicolay (plane trees, current).

handing to the next a living baton over generations in a race to ensure that an idea, a *parti*, lasts despite being made of dying things: plants proceeding inevitably, as we too do, from natality to mortality. This provides an unusual metric, but one that shows how people and plants grow and change together and leave traces, the *parti*, of that growth.[17]

Since they are privately owned, French gardens reflect social, political, and economic movements in which their owners played a part. The name of the château, "Courances," comes from the reign of Louis VII (1120–1180), when it was a *seigneurie* (feudal land) owned by Jean de Courances, whose family sold it due to "economic and demographic upheavals of the Hundred Years War."[18] It was bought by the Lapite family in 1460, and the seeds of the garden arose as part of a process of modification of an older medieval dwelling. The main axis of the current garden layout was commenced almost 100 years later, in 1548, when Courances was bought by Cosme Clausse (a minister to Henri II [1519–1547]), whose family owned it until 1622.[19] Mariage describes this general process whereby defensive medieval structures like moats and walls became ornamental, with the château centered on the axis. Cosme Clausse also established another château 7 kilometers away, Fleury-en-Bière, marking the other end of a productive agricultural territory.

CANAL

Mariage shows how land management, too, was ornamentalized in the French garden, and examines Courances in terms of its water management primarily for agriculture, with water features in the garden a byproduct. This focus on water features leads Françoise Boudon to call Courances a "French Renaissance water garden."[20] Valentine de Ganay, the current owner/manager of Courances, advancing Boudon's argument, suggests that the moniker "baroque" is incorrect when applied to the garden of Courances, as well, potentially, to other "baroque" gardens, which is why I have until now called them "French gardens," and will henceforth call them "French Renaissance gardens," since I agree with Boudon's thesis. As a Renaissance garden, Boudon argues, Courances was an early example, its principles drawn less from the language of the Italian Renaissance, as Mariage had argued, than from the water-management methods used in the hydrological engineering of the lowlands of "les Pays-Bas," or the Netherlands. According to Boudon, Clausse's garden framework was largely hydrological, focused on redirecting and formalizing the river École north of the château, including the creation of the two current canals along the Allée d'Honneur, the one on the northwest side (the *pièce d'eau des Platanes simples*) joining with the moat to create the *pré en l'île*, or "island meadow," which became known later as *pré Bernay*.[21] In support of her French Renaissance water garden model, Boudon suggests that the garden arose through an expansion from the earlier moated manor, and that canals aligned to château grids were generally planted with allées of trees.[22]

In 1622 Claude Gallard purchased Courances from François Clausse,[23] who was forced to sell it due to numerous debts—an example of the toll the development of a garden can take on its owners. Gallard commenced major construction works in 1627: first on the château itself and its drive, the *avenue d'arrivée*, as well as further developing the dominant northeast-southwest axis in the garden behind the château, creating the Allée d'Honneur and the Rond de Moigny to join Courances to the adjacent village of Moigny. As in the defensive model described by Mariage, during this process the garden moved from a medieval organization to a characteristic French Renaissance arrangement where both château and garden are on the same long axis linked into a territorial organization of agriculture and towns, establishing the current *parti*.

Gallard further deviated the École and created a basin called Gerbe, between Clausse's *Grand canal* and the *Salle d'eau* next to the château, the other edge of the *pré en l'île*, which Gallard renamed the "*pré Bernay*." Mariage's description of French Renaissance water-garden operations like these at Courances convincingly shows that the territorial *modus operandi* of the garden is linked to an ostentatious but still economical hydrological strategy, demonstrating a very innovative and synthetic approach to landscape. The ornamental water mechanisms of the French Renaissance water garden in this period were obviously still governed by basic hydrological principles concerned with direction and flow of water, so the garden is a modification of, not a replacement for, existing natural systems. Although I am focusing in this section on the Allée d'Honneur

FIGURE 2.9
Contemporary example of a palisade from Versailles.

in the southeast, these pools and canals also represent a shaping of the park into a garden in the northwestern quadrant of Courances, which I will discuss later in the chapter in the context of the way maintenance practices mediate the transition from park to garden.

PALISADE

The planting of the Allée d'Honneur was also developed by Gallard, a horticultural innovator who built a new nursery onsite in 1643.[24] He established an edge treatment along the canals comprising a palisade of *épines* (or a wall of spines) below cypress trees.[25] A palisade is quite different from the avenue format in use since the seventeenth century, and has different spatial and programmatic implications in terms of the relationship between the allée and the agricultural or territorial context.

Boudon notes that the higher canopy of cypress in the palisade was removed in 1645, on the assumption that it was dead,[26] so the palisade may have been a hedge of crab apple (*Malus* spp.) along the inside of the canal with no canopy above: the opposite of the current configuration, where the trees are on the other side of the canal, with no hedge beneath them. Spatially, the two configurations of the Allée d'Honneur are very different: in the seventeenth century the hedges would have been more than 50 meters apart and no more than 3 meters high, whereas now the trees are 30 meters high and 70 meters apart. The location of the hedges on the inside of the canals made the canals address the *pré Bernay* and excluded them from the visual space of the allée, reinforcing their land-management role as supplying water for agriculture or draining it, rather than as garden features.[27]

CONTRE-ALLÉE

While the palisade of cypress disappeared, a drawing attributed to Catherine de Gallard from 1756, together with another from the end of the eighteenth century, features *contre-allées*, or two rows of trees on each side of the allée. *Contre-allées* were commonly made of *Tillia* spp. pruned into continuous vegetal structures. These palisades were elevated on the top of trunks, forming a parallel interior on each side of the avenue and an open space between them. With clear trunks, a continuous canopy, and little visible lateral branching, these kinds of *contre-allée* are visually permeable at the base, their form closer to topiary than to an avenue.[28] While the *contre-allée* was located between the entry road and the canals, and maintained the relationship the canals had to agricultural land use like the palisade, the *contre-allée* would have had very different spatial effects, since it would have been visually and physically permeable, allowing some sideways engagement between the allée and the adjacent fields.

ALLÉE

The current configuration of the Allée d'Honneur results from the plane trees that were planted in 1782 by the Marquis de Nicolay,[29] who bought Courances in 1768. Although the family was decimated by the French Revolution in 1794, Courances was returned to the family in 1798. The economic and labor upheavals of the French Revolution no doubt

FIGURE 2.10

Contemporary example of a *contre-allée* from Parc de Sceaux.

changed the way the garden was maintained, as the relationship between feudal labor and the aristocracy also changed.

Located on the outside rather than the inside of the canals, this new configuration created a very different spatial effect from the plantings that had preceded it. The allée became wider and made the canals ornamental, an edging of the allée rather than simply functional, as they had previously been, draining and separating the adjacent fields. The trees are also spaced much more widely, changing the allée from a walled space to an avenue. The change of species from lime trees to plane trees was accompanied by a change in maintenance. While lime trees were commonly spaced closely in rows, and pruned to create a continuous hedged surface, the plane trees were allowed to become fully grown trees, with thick trunks and branches.

Although they were planted in 1782, the current "romantic" form of the plane trees which Hobhouse and Taylor, Scully and Cribier describe is the result of political and economic changes in the almost 250 years that followed, which caused the trees to be left alone as maintenance ceased. Baron Samuel de Haber bought the property in 1872 and began extensive renovation of both the park and the château, which had been abandoned for forty years and was so derelict that a tree was said to be growing in the dining-room. Haber converted a part of Courances, adjacent to the château, to an English garden with the help of Hippolyte Destailleur, who both worked on the garden and restored the château, as he later did at Vaux-le-Vicomte. De Haber's daughter married the Marquis Octave de Béhague, and Courances returned to aristocratic ownership.

In the twentieth century, Berthe de Béhague inherited Courances from her grandfather, De Haber, and with her husband, Marquis Jean de Ganay, commissioned landscape designer Henri Duchêne in 1899, and later his son Achille in 1914, to work on the garden. The Duchênes were responsible for returning the *jardin anglais* to its "proper" French form in the area of the garden called "La Baigneuse." Berthe's sister, Martie de Béhague, acquired the domain of Fleury-en-Bière, uniting the two properties under single ownership as they had been in Clausse's time. Parts of the château were occupied by a Luftwaffe commandant during the Second World War, and munitions were stored in the park; then, between 1944 and 1955, it was occupied first by American troops and later by General Montgomery.

OLD TREES

Successive changes in ownership, and therefore management, conspired to ensure that the plane trees were neglected at key points during their growth. The most recent marquis, Jean-Louis de Ganay, suggested that they were not pruned for a hundred years:[30] from the period after the garden was seized from the Nicolays in the late eighteenth century until the Duchênes renovated it at the end of the nineteenth century. This condition was reflected in photographs of the garden taken in winter 1860 by Eugène Cuvelier, discussed by Dominique Planchon-de-Font-Réaulx. These photographs show a garden that has become overgrown, with edges bleeding into one another, since the trees had not been shaped for a long time. The current character of the allée results from working with the

FIGURE 2.11
Plane trees along the *pièce d'eau des Platanes simples* in winter.

forms of the trees after they have been allowed to grow naturally, "wildly." Current pruning is ameliorative rather than directive, since there was no pruning at key points in the trees' development. After a hundred years of growth, pruning attempts to create a recognizable and healthy tree form from otherwise aberrant plant material. This aberration is an inherent part of their character, producing, as Pascal Cribier says, "enormous horizontal branch[es], which should have cracked thousands of times but which resist, defying everything in the laws of weightlessness."[31] Paradoxically, this neglect allowed the planes to develop the long, wavy form that might have been expected in an English garden but is rare for a French garden.

According to my *parti-parterre* model, at a territorial level[32] changes in the Allée d'Honneur over the last 500 years have not altered the *parti* significantly, but have continued to reinforce it. On the *parterre* level, however, there have been significant dimensional, organizational, spatial, and qualitative effects on the allée as a whole. Since there has been little change in the hard landscape, these effects result from plant growth. Dimensionally, the allée has changed width by at least 20 meters on the ground, and much more at canopy level. The changes in plants have reflected social and economic changes in society in France generally, but also in the function and role of the canals in relation to adjacent land uses. The space of the allée has changed from a walled interior, focused on the château, to one where the relation to the adjacent fields is filtered and open. However, most critically for the allée, and the contemporary interest in Courances, the allée gained qualities with little or no plan change: the same qualities that caused it to be described in a certain way by particular garden authors, like Hobhouse and Taylor, Scully and Cribier. While many of these qualities have resulted from human decisions about species selection and spacing at installation, plants have not been mute or cooperative and, as aberrant individuals, have had their own effects, such as the death of the cypress in the palisade in the seventeenth century and the wayward growth of the planes in the nineteenth.

TIMED EDGE

While gardeners and garden historians visit them because they are beautiful, many French gardens continue to be part of a larger productive territory. I discovered the scale of this territory when I rode 15 kilometers from Fontainebleau to Courances via Fleury-en-Bière, the other property that has always been allied with Courances.[33] The current owners have declared that they wished they had the château of Fleury but in the garden of Courances, since it is a much more sophisticated and epic building in terms of scale. Fleury is walled, and the road to Courances tracks along the park until it ends at a defensive corner with a small tower, overlooking a field and a nearby motorway, which the road crosses. Between Fleury and Courances, fields of crops line either side of the road, edged

FIGURE 2.12
Turret on the corner of the walled garden of Château Fleury-en-Bière, overlooking the agricultural landscape between it and Château Courances, the historical territory of the gardens, again in possession of the contemporary owners.

by small hills covered in forest. This 7-kilometer-long strip of agriculture reveals that the relationship between the two châteaux is productive, and that even while gardens and buildings may be ornamental, they sit in a landscape of seasonal growth and harvest, and much labor. The calibration of these two modes—garden and agriculture—is a space between production and aesthetic ambitions, situating the château amid a landscape with which the garden negotiates. Valentine de Ganay, who is currently converting 500 hectares of this territory to organic agriculture, continues this approach.

Thinking of the garden as located *in* the park is important, because it provides the key to the simplified qualities and austerity that Hobhouse et al. admire at Courances. The French garden was first and foremost a land-management tool, and indeed was seen as such by garden writers at the time: Oliver de Serres called his treatise on gardens (1603) "The Theater of Agriculture."[34] As in the English landscape garden that would follow it, detailed or finer gardening during this time was generally undertaken in walled potagers, using tools like secateurs and forks to produce fruit and vegetables. To form the larger landscape as a garden required the appropriation and adaptation of agricultural equipment, and techniques for operations on a larger scale. Consequently, the qualities admired by Hobhouse et al. reflect the history of Courances across its 500 years in relation to both the history of France and the garden owners discussed in the section above, and changes in labor practices and mechanization, particularly since the French Revolution.

During medieval and Renaissance times, a feudal relationship with laborers was required to develop and maintain the garden and its owners, making local labor cheap and available. Although the cost still sent some owners, like the Clausses, broke, compared to contemporary gardening costs it was possible to sustain a large amount of maintenance.[35] Nonetheless, because of political disturbance, the rest of the garden, like the Allée d'Honneur, also suffered long periods of neglect during years of abandonment and fluctuating ownership. When parts of Courances became a *jardin anglais* in the nineteenth century, the style of the garden was more naturalistic and less maintenance-intensive, so that by the time the Duchênes renovated it in the early twentieth century the labor foundation of the French garden they were reinstalling had changed, so they focused on smaller, detailed *parterres* around the château, and used forestry techniques in the park.

The interruption of World War II meant that labor was expensive by the time of the current ownership regime, so Jean-Louis de Ganay had to develop an approach to maintenance based on mechanized agricultural equipment that was available on the farm to deal with the garden. Trained as an agriculturalist, Jean-Louis brought an economic, pragmatic view to garden maintenance, which, Valentine de Ganay argues, enhances the garden's qualities, because "when you don't have money you have to have good ideas." Its simplified form suited the "modern" style of the time Jean-Louis was living in, which Valentine calls "minimalist." Ironically, classic French garden elements like the palisade were well suited to the tractor as the literal "driver" of maintenance. With pruning arms (called *lamiers sécateur taille haie*) attached to the tractor, the wall of the palisade can be pruned once a year, and the lawns of the various allées cut regularly with a tractor-drawn mower, so that detailed hand pruning, also with machines, was required only for corners or inaccessible places. The "grave symphony of grass, trees, water" that Scully described is revealed to be a hardware operation, more like industrial electronic than classical music. Considered in square meterage of garden—or, rather, linear meters of edge—maintenance is highly economical in its current form, with considerable effect gained from concentrated bursts of mechanized activity. Despite the industrial character of the processes used, however, the qualities that Jean-Louis desired, says Valentine, were more romantic: the use of lawn rather than gravel for paths for its sensuousness, and allowing trees to have an individual character rather than cutting them into hedges.

The interface between garden and park is a balance between aesthetic quality and economy of management. Behind the château, the whole of the park at Courances is productive forest for harvesting trees. The garden is its inverse, the long lawns spacing out or separating patches of forest. These in-between garden spaces, linear paths of differing width, appear to be organizing the forest because of their compositional relationship to the château and main axis, and the qualities of plant material that compose their edge, which make the garden look as though it was subtracted from the forest, when it is in fact the other way around: the forest is organized around the garden. This is because, proportionately, the garden areas are smaller than the forest, so that they appear to be embedded in it.

This garden/park edge is about time, because it is made up from plant growth. For the park, the aim is consistent: ongoing growth of trees. Valentine acknowledges that tree replacement of this "old skeleton" is the biggest issue facing the current managers. These trees keep maturing, and any maintenance attempts to ensure that they are as consistently tall and straight as they can be. Once the trees are growing, and beyond the zone of competition from other species, the park is left to its own devices, with little in the way of maintenance. On the other hand, on the edge of the park, where the forest meets the garden, control of growth is necessary

FIGURE 2.13

Transition from garden to park along the
Allée de Moigny.

to, on the one hand, exhibit the sense of design and fineness that brings the forest into the language of the garden, but on the other, practically, to restrict and order its otherwise unconstrained growth. This sense of control is inherently linked to people's experience and expectations, which mark the nature of the garden as different to the nature of wilderness.[36] Geometries of trees and ordered walls of leaves exemplify this mark, as well as pragmatically obscuring the interior of the park, rendering it garden rather than park mass.

By analyzing that edge between garden and park here, I aim to demonstrate how garden elements that are architectonic transcend those categories because they involve time, and that their manipulation redefines the terms of landscape design practice.

Between 1661 and 1669, Louis XIV's minister Jean-Baptiste Colbert established policies for the systematic organization of the forest and its edge in relation to the territorial policies of France, the king reserving the right to fell logs from any forest in his kingdom to build ships for his navy. These forests were divided into two types: forests for general harvest (called *taillis composé*) and forests for more important timber species (the *grande futaie*).[37] Mariage describes how, to ensure that logs met the requirements for naval use, their planting arrangement was specified in law, including spacing, relationship to the edge and the corner of the palisade, and pruning. This system reveals that during this period the productivity of landscape and the aesthetic of the garden were inseparable, though Rumelhart, disagreeing with Mariage, questions whether such systems appeared in the parks of French gardens or only in larger woods. Such systematization nonetheless provides a precedent for a typology of edges in the French garden that I will describe in relation to Courances, fluctuating between ornamentality and production, each with different management intervals.

Timber production occurs between the axes of Courances with a hierarchy of edge types that influence the visibility of the forest as a productive element, rather than the edge of a mass that defines the garden. Continuing from the argument that the Allée d'Honneur creates the axis from growth, the edges of the garden and park are another manifestation of growth forming a line, this time reducing in intensity of maintenance

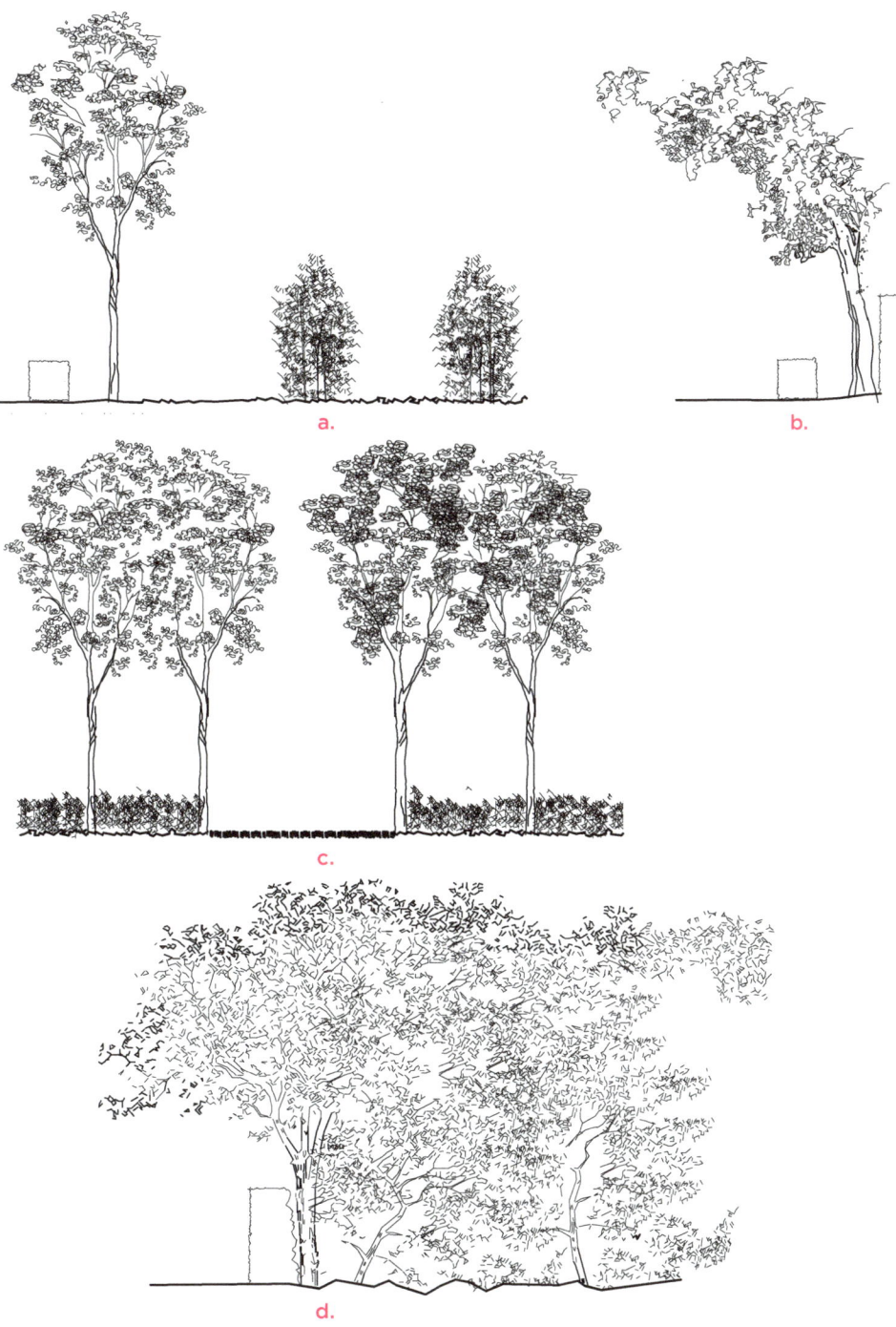

FIGURE 2.14

Sectional typology of treatments along allées between garden and park: (**a**) new plantation with hedge, allée, and forest; (**b**) thickened palisade; (**c**) mown path through forest; (**d**) regular palisade.

as one moves from the garden to the park, away from the axis. This pragmatic production logic becomes more economical and the trees themselves become more visible, but an edge of formality still prevails. The edge is 80 percent garden close to the axis and 80 percent forest furthest away, though at all times the garden is still a park, and vice versa. In the following description I will proceed from the main axis to the edge of the unadulterated forest.

I introduced the palisade as the earliest incarnation of the Allée d'Honneur, but I will develop it here in terms of the gradient between garden and park/forest, noting nonetheless that it is not strictly a palisade, because Jean-Louis did not believe in cutting trees into hedge forms. I developed this typology by finding glitches in the system, holes in hedges to crawl through and see what was on the inside, attempting to take improbable photographs on both sides and through a hedge. There are four components to the edges: path, low edge, high edge, and forest. The path is really the interior of the allée, the continuous surface of the line, and is generally, but not always, grass. The low and high edges both articulate the edge of the forest and are often, but not always, in the same plane, with the lower addressing the allée and the garden, and the upper part of the forest. The low edge is generally a hedge and the upper either a hedge or a row of trees. When I talk about forest I am referring to a realm that regenerates due to a natural process, its own kind of logic, that can be intervened in though activities such as pruning and weeding, but in general simply grows as a natural system.[38]

THICKENED PALISADE

The Allée Moigny, the main axis immediately behind the château, has the most convoluted or articulated palisade configuration, which I call a "thickened palisade." It is thickened because, rather than comprising

FIGURE 2.15
Thickened palisade treatment along the Percée du Miroir, called by Valentine de Ganay "the Champs-Élysées," with hedge and palisade separated and trees in between.

simply a single plane, its upper and lower layers are separated. Adjacent to the grassed surface of the allée is a low hedge (approximately 1.4 meters high) of box. Behind this a row of trees appears in the body of the higher hedge, all pruned so that the green crown of foliage starts at a consistent level. Valentine attributes this approach of revealing trees between hedges to the Belgian garden scholar René Pechère, who wrote a preface to Ernest de Ganay's book on French gardens. Behind these trees in turn is another hedge of laurel, approximately 2.5 meters tall, which marks the edge of the forest. The thickened palisade has all the components of the normal palisade, but with a different arrangement. In the normal palisade, the row of trees forms part of the forest and looms above the lower hedge, which is between 1 and 2 meters high, while at Courances the row of trees is inside the hedges, making this row part of the garden rather than the forest. In terms of maintenance, while the first hedge can be cut with a tractor, the second is obscured by trees, and would therefore need to be cut by hand, though still with a power tool. This level of maintenance reflects the fact that it is closest to the house, compared to the forest, where there is little point in using such intensive maintenance. With all components of the regular palisade, the separation of the lower hedge from the palisade running between trees gives the space in between the sense of being a garden bed, in the sense of a Victorian border. In describing this area as "maintenance-intensive," I am arguing that more maintenance reveals greater care, and generally areas with greater care are smaller, since it takes longer to do more of such fine work. As the distance from the house increases, so the intensiveness of maintenance decreases; or rather, it becomes more mechanized. This represents a gradient of both fineness and laboriousness, which graduates from house to garden, from garden to forest.

REGULAR PALISADE

The majority of the edges to the allées are regular palisades, with a hedge along the allée and forest canopy above. While the classic historic French Renaissance palisade featured pruning at both levels, the lower hedge and the trees in rows above, at Courances clipping tends to be restricted to the lower level. Correspondingly, a sense of classic palisade depends on the relationship between the lower hedge and the canopy above. Along the main axis, and at areas of focus like the Rond de Moigny, the hedge surface and the canopy above are distinct from each other because both the face of the hedge and its top are clipped, and the forest then intrudes into the allée, arching over the hedge. As one moves away from the main axis and into the park, into what Valentine called the "Champs-Élysées," the palisade form is governed entirely by the reach of the pruning arm fixed to the tractor. This causes the hedge to bulge out at the top, and gives the allée the quality of a tunnel. Since the top profile of the hedge is left to its own devices, the hedge and the forest blur into each other. Additionally, since the hedging is governed by the tractor arm tool, while areas like the Rond have a single species of hedge, in areas with less attention the forest edge has been pruned in such a way that the hedge is made up of diverse species with numerous different leaf types, all responding with profuse branching and leaf production to the disturbance by the tool.

NEW FOREST

Replanting of the forest alongside the *Grand canal* demonstrates clearly how the formation of the garden edge is a device to regulate the differences in growth between gardens and forest. On the bank of the canal a palisade is being developed, with a low hedge meeting the lawn and a strictly spaced row of poplar trees behind it, similar to the others in the garden. However, the way the vegetation is being managed on the forest side of the palisade gives clues about the fecundity of the forest when the priority is growth. On my most recent visit to Courances, the forest was being cleared selectively with brush-cutting equipment. Walking along rows spaced 1 meter apart, the operator was cutting all vegetation down to the ground in order to reduce the competition between trees and regenerate spontaneous vegetation.[39] While growth would obviously be profuse during the summer, the intensity of growth in the forest compared to the strict control of the garden reveals an economy that arises due to the difference between the productive forest as an area and the garden edge as a perimeter. The edge of the forest is a line that is navigable for farm vehicles, where growth is controlled to maintain an edge, a perimeter of deliberate

FIGURE 2.16

Regular palisade treatment, with hedge below with its top pruned and trees from the forest behind arching over, along Rond de Moigny.

FIGURE 2.17

Regular palisade on the Percée du Miroir, bulging out beyond reach of the tractor pruning arm.

FIGURE 2.18

Installation of new forest and palisade along *le Grand canal*, with hedge along lawn beside the canal, a row of trees, then gridded forest planting beyond.

ornamentality, thought of in lineal meters to be cut. On the other hand, the forest is a mass, an area thought of in square meters. Allowing plants to grow requires them to be left alone, which means that all plants, not simply the desirable ones like the plantation trees, will grow. Seen in these terms, the row is not simply a formal predilection but a trope of economical maintenance. Keeping trees in rows allows an operator to simply walk the gap between them, removing everything between with a brush cutter. This dynamic relationship between the perimeter as controlled edge and the forest as an area of (relatively) unbridled growth demonstrates the dynamic relationships to change and time in the maintenance of the French garden.

ROW

If the hedge is the literal edge between the garden and the forest, then the row of trees in the palisade is an implied transition between the control of the hedge and the growth of the forest. Both are lines: the former, the hedge, uninterrupted; the latter, the row of trees, an implied line of dots, of tree centers. While both players in the palisade configuration, the hedge and the tree, reinforce each other, as we saw in the Allée d'Honneur, the row of trees is the fundamental formal unit of the French garden, but also its key management device. As with the palisade and the hedge, there are variations in the way the row controls the edge of the garden. As one moves away from the main axis, sometimes the hedge spans rows of trees. At other times there is no hedge at all, and a row of trees forms the edge between the garden and the replanted forest behind, maintained with the brush cutter in the forest and mowing in the allée. While the hedge provides a clear edge to articulate the transition between garden and forest, without the hedge the row requires a clear view of the tree trunks to make its implied line clear. To see a row requires a level of surface control below.

MOW EDGE

North of the Gerbe, relatively juvenile rows of trees planted on an east-west alignment make up the forest, and a path cuts across the forest to the École river, occupying a vacant row within the forest. The rigidity

FIGURE 2.19
Rows of trees without hedge defining boundary of forest on Les Trois Grâces.

of the tree grid makes the absence of a row seem like a deliberate path. The path surface is mown with a tractor and becomes a green sward, the edge of the forest simply regenerating natural vegetation lower than the trees, presumably cut like the other recently installed forest. Over time the forest's canopy cover has shaded the understory, reducing competition, thus requiring less active management. The mowing of the path also stops regeneration of woody vegetation. The combination of grass surface and clear tree grid makes the edge still seem ornamental despite the wild vegetation below, the grass providing the indicator of care that the hedge provided to the palisade.

PATH

At the periphery of the garden, deep in the park, the gradient between palisade, row, and forest disappears into something approximating wilderness, with only an opening on the ground surface indicating geometry or use; however, while the mown path had a grass surface, here only bare ground and an absence of trees indicate a passage. Here there seems to be no planting; instead, plants respond to each other in relatively uninterrupted ecological ways. Wilderness tends to imply a landscape untouched by human hands, though studies of indigenous land practices reveal that most "natural" landscapes were manipulated in some way for human need. Defining wilderness as a place where, on balance, natural systems are allowed to self-organize without intervention is a more scientific, less culturally skewed model. However, to my colonial eyes, used to landscapes apparently unmodified by people, where European plants are invaders, the idea that this forest is wilderness seems untenable. Despite the fact that it is a weedscape covered in ivy and other "alien species," a footpath wanders through this natural forest, as though one is deep in the wilderness. At the furthest literal and metaphorical distance from the axis, the path inverts the relationship of the palisade, moving through a

FIGURE 2.20
Mown path between rows of trees at periphery of garden between the *Salle d'eau* and the Allée de la Table.

FIGURE 2.21
Regenerating forest, or "wilderness," with a path made by feet.

forest mass that is setting its own rules through ecology, the human visiting rather than calling the shots, except insofar as to do nothing is still a decision, an action.

CONCLUSION

Landscape architecture has tended to treat hard landscape elements as "design" and planting as something that simply "renders" the hard landscape geometry, perhaps amplifying it with an offset avenue of trees. French Renaissance gardens like Courances demonstrate that plant maintenance can define territory as much as architectural elements, and that reconfiguration of those elements due to variations in maintenance can produce nuanced and spatially complex landscape forms with little hard landscape articulation.

The landscape conspires to change everything over time—trees, people, topography—making them disappear or transforming them beyond recognition. An old building looks old, but it is still the same building. Because a garden is made up of living things, an old garden generally still looks like a contemporary garden. However, the magic of an old garden is that something living recognizably persists in the face of constant change that seeks to make it unrecognizable. If you will excuse the pun, I like to say that, considering all the forces that conspire to "take out" the silent tree, every tree that survives is really a "vic-tree." Consequently, the survival of the planes in the Allée d'Honneur for 350 years is remarkable. At Courances, this persistence is the *parti*, but it is made up of changing things: at the front of the château the old planes that form the Allée d'Honneur; at the rear the *parterres* of the park, their growing edges crafted in time.

Courances is the first case study that I use to build my argument and model for the viridic because it shows that plant material can have a duration not dissimilar to architectural form. With the French Renaissance garden well recognized for its architectural qualities, this case study is important because it shows that plants can indeed have form, like architecture. However, at the same time, it shows that while architectural form is relatively consistent, plant form fluctuates, and this gives the *parti* a dynamism that contemporary architecture aims for rhetorically but is rarely able to deliver in practice. The viridic, then, is architectural form that can persist despite the ephemerality of plants, but form to which those plants give a dynamic quality. Although the *parti* is recognizable in its form, and the same as it was in earlier times, it is not exactly so, and never has been. Made up of growing plants in different configurations and at different stages of growth at different times, the *parti* of Courances has fluctuated considerably. If the *parti* is quantitatively much the same in terms of dimension and extent, then the growth adds qualities to this metric.

At the same time as the viridic describes an architectonic material, then, this dynamism is due to growth, which requires maintenance. Correspondingly, a regular and ongoing maintenance practice is inseparably linked to any of the architectonic qualities of the viridic. If one of the aims of this book is to break down the polarization of form and process by showing form as a process in relation to growth, Courances is important because of its very formality, because this formality results from a process of formation by maintenance.

At the edge of the garden, where it meets the forest, this formality allows the formal and the informal to coexist in dialogue, where the difference between each is a gradient of maintenance. The straightness and consistency of the forest *parterre* makes mechanized maintenance possible, thereby allowing for a large extent of garden. Even as these maintenance acts occur, they allow the forest to regenerate in an unfettered way without the entire landscape returning to forest. The change that a garden must endure is physical, but the catalyst for such change is diverse, as we have seen at Courances: it can include the political, the social, the economic, and the technological. These changes are reflected in changes in maintenance practice that have also contributed to its fluctuating figure.

The ordering of vegetation and the corresponding systematization of maintenance processes in the French Renaissance garden demonstrate how, "as always in the sixteenth century, there is no clear separation between the useful and the decorative."[40] In the cultural practice that is horticulture, the manipulation of plants for interchangeably aesthetic, utilitarian, or productive reasons has involved bringing them into regular organizational systems that both formally and practically indicate their appropriation. Processes are spatial and exist within some boundary system, whether defined through geology and microclimate or human predilection. While we may choose to relegate the compositional systems of the past to the past, in the landscape, where contexts are constantly in flux, it is important to remember that such systems persist because of processes that work, which cannot be separated from the form those processes have been given. For the viridic, seeking to keep plant material within the language of landscape architecture, territorial or strategic effects of vegetation are about regulating systems of maintenance that control a territory in a dynamic way.

If you asked landscape architects and garden enthusiasts about the "baroque" (but, rather, French Renaissance) garden, their general response would be to call it "formal," contrasting it to the "informal." The formality in composition, and emphasis on pruning and shaping, in the French garden has caused it to seem highly manipulated and, indeed, to be manipulative to plants. Calling the French garden "unnatural" and opposing it to the English "wild" garden is common in garden writing, even among fans of the French garden like proto-modern American landscape architect Fletcher Steele: "He [the French] has studied and experimented with his plants... for their aptitudes. He uses plants. He does not allow them to go their own way. As a consequence... the French horticulturalist has no equal, though you never forget that he is French."[41] Steele is right to say that French gardeners "use" plants, and this use is what makes them a valuable precedent for landscape architects. However, when he says that they do not allow them to "go their own way," he is incorrect, because plants, like people, have evolved by adapting to stresses in their environment. If we assume that growth is the natural condition that Steele is discussing, forces that stimulate growth are also natural. The assumption that manipulation is unnatural ignores the role of predation and disturbance in nature, which causes intense growth of shoots through apical cell division, called *traumatic reiteration*.[42] As I will argue in chapter 4, pruning, simulating predation, catalyzes these responses for productive or ornamental reasons.

I would argue that the intense maintenance of the French garden is in fact an active collaboration between people and plants. The acts of control by the gardener in the French garden are ecological; not static acts, but constant engagements with plant biology. It is ironic that the seemingly static form of the hedge, with its "controlled" plants, results from the stimulation of growth by maintenance activity. Courances shows us that for the viridic, the dynamic is used to create the static.

CHAPTER 3

ARCHITECTURE
with PLANTS

FIGURE 3.2
Period photograph of the Honey Locust Allée at night by Balthazar Korab (Courtesy of Korab Image).

T HE REDISCOVERY OF THE BAROQUE was part of the historicist strand of postmodernism. But landscape-architectural theorists and historians also rediscovered modernism during the postmodern period. Complaining in 1985 of a perennial absence of theory in landscape architecture, Steven Krog noted: "the strength of early modernist landscape architecture theory goes largely untapped, yet its reinvestigation could help provide one starting point for determining how to design the contemporary landscape."[1] Landscape architecture being always slightly out of step, always slightly uncool, the interest of modernist landscape architects in the baroque allowed the formal similarities of both to be converged and assimilated unselfconsciously into a postmodern landscape-architectural practice that failed to recognize that the appropriation of the baroque by modernism was not just stylistic: they could also be paired because they shared a similar totalizing essentialism.[2]

Garrett Eckbo was the best-known of the modernist landscape architects investigated during postmodernism, but Dan Kiley was the most admired. While Eckbo incorporated the diverse, and often divergent, compositional languages of modern art and architecture, easily combining the orthogonal and the biomorphic, Kiley, at his most pure, was a grid man. In Kiley's hands the orthogonal acquired an almost abstract quality, like the work of Russian painter Kazimir Malevich, where the rectangle was a *Gestalt* figure as much as it was a geometry. Kiley's grids were generally grids of trees, their debt to the baroque allée openly admitted by Kiley himself. The language of grids he used directly resembled the ubiquitous structural grid of modern architecture that freed the ground plane: a Mies van der Rohe trait acknowledged by Kiley. Despite its derivation from these two influences, Kiley's skill with planting design to enact the lessons of modern architecture was, and continues to be, miraculous.

The most admired of Kiley's projects is the Miller Garden, the setting for a house designed by Eero Saarinen in 1957.[3] Located in Columbus, Indiana, an industrial town for tractor manufacture, the Miller House and Garden joined numerous other sites in a town that is a site of architectural pilgrimage. The Millers commissioned numerous buildings from modern architects, demonstrating how the patronage of design can affect the character, reputation, and economy of a small town. They have since passed away, and the Miller House and Garden is now under the care of the Indianapolis Museum of Art (IMA), open to the public for guided tours that generally focus on the building by Saarinen and the interior design by Alexander Girard. The house is very much a *Gesamtkunstwerk*, a total work of art, still filled with furniture and art from the time when it was built. The tour guides carefully stage-manage the process of navigating it, showing rooms and furnishings to give a picture of how the Millers lived there. Despite the garden being the focus of landscape architects who understand the design in terms of how it organizes the site, I was struck by the tour's focus on the interior.

On my visit, the garden was out of bounds, ignored in favor of the luxuriance of the house's paradoxical modernist opulence. I had come in particular to see the famous Honey Locust Allée, two rows of *Gleditsia tricanthos* which ran along the western edge of the house, edging the transition between the house and the grassed meadow below. A simple but sophisticated configuration, these trees provided what has been called a "grille" when viewed in elevation from the interior, as well as creating an external corridor from one garden feature to the other. Or so I thought. When I visited, the old trees I was expecting were gone, replaced by new juvenile trees.

The Miller Garden is often cited as an example of how plants can be used for architectonic effect, shaping space. Since plants are alive, I had expected that the trees would now be old, and their spatial effects would be more sophisticated as their qualities had changed and deepened. At the same time, as a horticulturalist, I recognize that plants can be affected by old age, and catastrophes can happen. After almost sixty years, it did not seem unreasonable that the trees might have needed to be replaced. I was disappointed by the lack of trees, though still excited by the experience of the Miller House. I decided I would just have to accept that the spatial effects I had read about were real, and that I had simply missed them: that my timing was wrong.

The Miller Garden is a bridge between the old gardens of the baroque, discussed in chapter 2, and the modernist use of plants. In this chapter I reread the Miller Garden from a plant and maintenance perspective. I start by examining the architectural way in which the Miller Garden, and particularly the Honey Locust Allée, has been considered, the dominant narrative of contemporary readings of the garden which saw it as the operationalization of modernist architectural principles, and I attempt instead to heed Elizabeth Meyer's call that "we must move beyond analyzing [Kiley's] gardens through the exclusive language of de Stijl or Miesian spatial theories."[4] I consider the architectural view of treating plants as "architectural analogue," and continue by examining the models of Kiley's contemporary James Rose, who, I argue, has been the foremost historical theorist in reconsidering plants as a unique type of landscape-architectural material. Since I am arguing that plant form is actually growth, I find that while growth is implied in Rose's models, it is not explicit, so plants are still treated as architectural analogues by Rose, even as he theorizes them.

Searching for an account of the Miller Garden based on plant form as growth rather than simply as architecture, I reviewed photographs to see how the garden had changed, and was surprised to discover that regardless of which year one looked at it, the allée seemed to be constantly in the same state: static, endlessly mature. By digging deeper, and talking to the gardener on the project, I discovered that the trees had been replaced three times since their initial installation, and always by mature containerized trees, which contradicts many of the claims that the garden is a "maturing" icon of planting design. Reviewing the extensive archive of documentation about the Miller House and Garden in the IMA, using historical correspondence and photographs of the garden throughout its lifespan, I then show how constant gardening action was required to keep the allée in its desired architectural form, despite claims that it was unique because it was living architecture, so contradicting these claims. Advancing my definition of the viridic, in the conclusion I argue that the Miller Garden exemplifies a key problem in dealing with plants in the predictive way that landscape-architectural practice does in the professional office: that subsequent maintenance actions are always aimed at returning plants to the initial predictions of growth assumed in the design. In contrast, gardening operates by learning from ongoing observation and developing better performance in order to achieve the same effect.

ARCHITECTURAL ANALOGUES

The Miller Garden is the perfect landscape-architectural plan, with its "interlocking and spiraling point grids" of trees enclosing some spaces and simultaneously edging others.[5] The design broadly divides the site into three parts: the house setting, the meadow, and the river landscape. The geometry and type of visual experience is different in each part, though in this chapter I focus on the house setting and the Honey Locust Allée in particular. Related tightly to the planning of the house site, Kiley noted: "the house was designed in functional blocks. ... So I took the same geometry and made rooms outside using trees in groves and allées."[6] While Kiley's debt to the baroque is acknowledged and clear, his site planning at the Miller House is not axial but "spiraling," with the house at the center of the spiral, causing it to disappear among vegetation. Rather than locating the house at the end of the entry road, a tight allée crosses the site and the house is located alongside it, at the allée's center. Symmetrically across the drive from the house, two rows of trees create a central space for it. The line of the drive and of the house-tree space creates a cross-figure which separates four compartments, each with its own design; all, except the pool, based on regular grids of trees and shrubs. The entire house and garden complex is edged by Kiley's famous "baffle hedge," with two parallel "dashed lines" of hedges, resembling dashes, alternately in front of and behind each other.

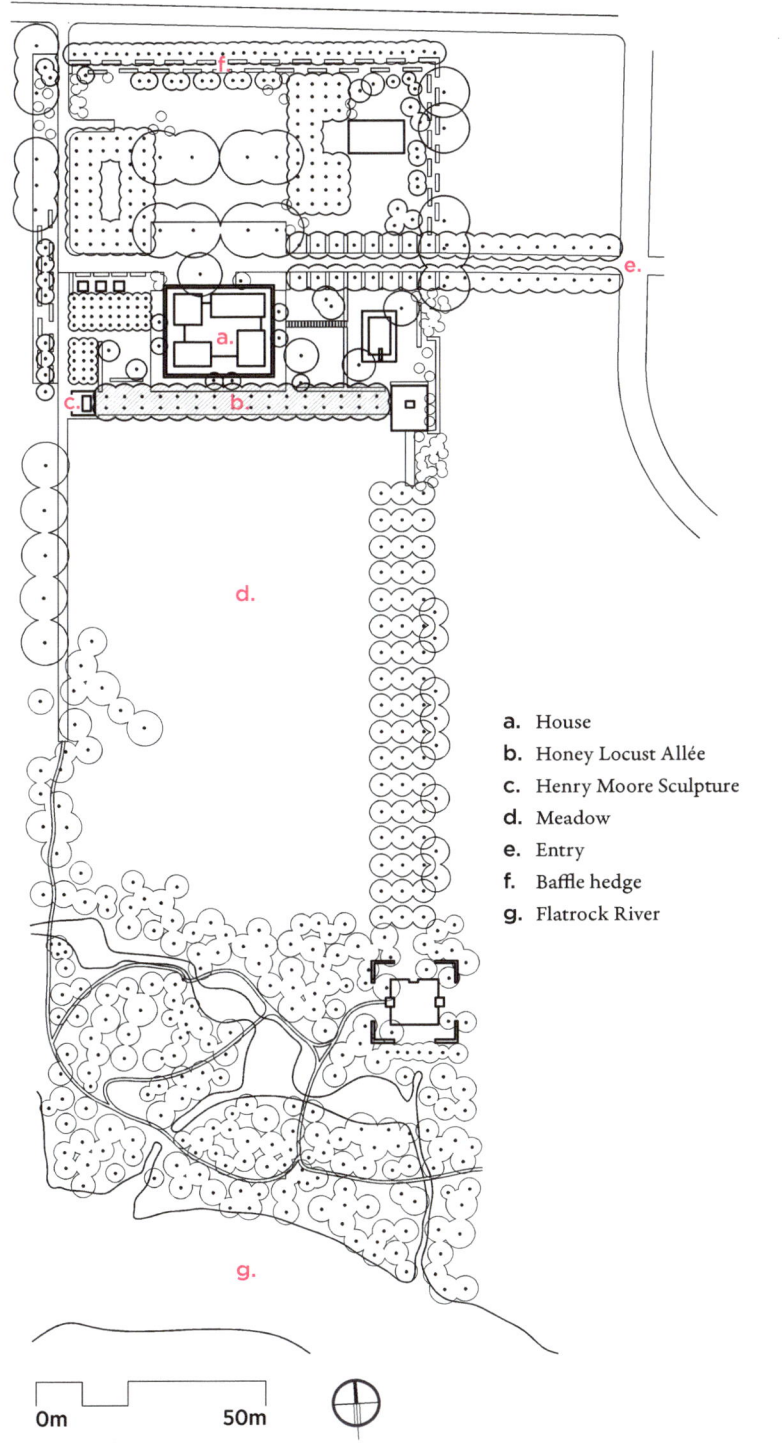

FIGURE 3.3

Plan of the Miller House and Garden.

FIGURE 3.4
Period photograph by Ezra Stoller from the living room through honey locusts to meadow below (Courtesy of ESTO).

Each tree mass shapes or addresses a space, but also constitutes an edge to another space, since each space is separately defined. Circulation moves in the gap between the spaces, so that the planting of one space provides one side of a corridor and a different planting the other, creating interesting material adjacencies and juxtapositions. Changing placement and spacing, and varying density of foliage through hedging or understory planting, also allows views through trees from the house, with each side of the house addressing a different space and a different screen through which it sees that space. Since the grids of planting are so dense, and come so close to the house, the house becomes immaterial: the walls disappear, and the house is an interior facing outward.

Perhaps the most photographed dialogue between inside and out is the view from the living room in the direction of the meadow and river. The glazed edge of the house sits on a plinth, while foliage from a

FIGURE 3.5
View down the Honey Locust Allée from the Henry Moore sculpture, mid-1990s by Marsh Davis (Courtesy of IMA).

weeping tree provides irregular filigree to the rhythmic planting of the Honey Locust Allée. The Honey Locust Allée, "the garden's best-known element"[7] and the focus of this chapter, runs parallel to the drive, on the other side of the house to the west. The allée crosses the site, with a Henry Moore sculpture at one end and a fountain at the other.[8] The Honey Locust Allée provides access to another allée, of three rows of trees this time rather than the conventional two, which links the house to the river, passing alongside the meadow. Even though the allée is for circulation, it forms a buffering strip between the house and the meadow, a filter or "grille" of trunks to the view down to the meadow.

Most scholarship about modern landscape architecture attempts to demonstrate its formal relationship to the compositional, and particularly "spatial," characteristics of its modern architectural counterpart. This is particularly true of the Miller Garden, widely regarded as the most significant example of modern landscape architecture, including by Kiley himself, who said: "I consider the Miller residence my first essentially *modern* landscape design."[9] While Kiley described the Miller Garden as a modern landscape design, his protégé Greg Bleam goes further and argues that it constituted "the ideal climate to translate Mies van der Rohe's spatial concepts into the garden,"[10] because "the architect [Eero Saarinen] allowed Kiley the freedom to integrate the house with the surrounding garden using a shared geometric order."[11] The "shared geometric order" of the garden suggests a substitution of plants into architectural elements, which treats plants as an analogue to architecture.

Introducing the idea of the analogue in chemistry, Alexander Shulgin said: "In the letters and arts, something is an analogue of something else if it is similar to it in function but different in structure or origin. The parent stem, analogy, was a Greek word that quite simply signified an agreement or correspondence between things that were in other respects different. And analogy can imply that if two things are alike in one way, they may be in another."[12]

Hilderbrand argues that plants allowed a redeployment of modernist principles with different materials in the Miller Garden: in modern landscape architecture, "the garden receded from view … [however] because the material aspects of the garden—fundamentally plants and planted forms—were not to be discarded entirely for new substitutes, the works of modernism changed not what they were, but how they were employed."[13] While it was pioneering in its methods, I would argue—like Bleam, but unlike Hilderbrand—that the modern garden was really modern architecture using other materials: plants. The garden as analogue shares the Miller House's compositional systems, where "the garden's design derives from the architectonic order of the house … rectangularly configured spaces defined by hedges, allées, and walls."[14]

As well as architectural descriptions of the garden, the plants in it are also described using names of architectural elements. According to Bleam, Kiley described the Honey Locust Allée as a "balustrade" in front of the platform of the house.[15] In a similar vein, Meyer refers to the allée as "a perforated wall" created by "the trunks of trees [which] if spaced close enough together [suggest that a] window existed between each tree

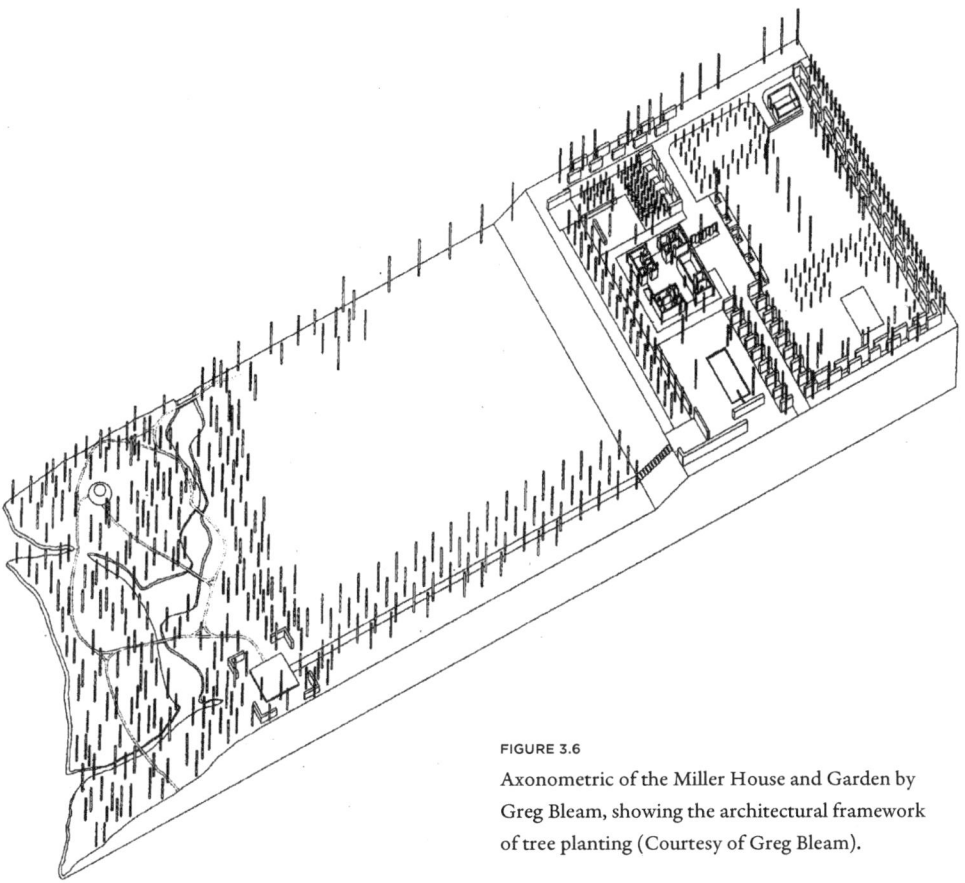

FIGURE 3.6
Axonometric of the Miller House and Garden by Greg Bleam, showing the architectural framework of tree planting (Courtesy of Greg Bleam).

column."[16] This type of description is common, and underlies Bleam's drawn analysis of the Miller Garden, where he argues for his reading of it as derivative of Mies van der Rohe's Barcelona Pavilion, using regular cylinders in isometric view to represent trees, which then appear as columns. It is ironic that while landscape architects argue that Kiley was adapting Mies van der Rohe's ideas for landscape conditions, Constant argues that the Barcelona Pavilion was actually doing the same thing, but for architecture, its "challenge [lying] not in the visual extension of space, as numerous interpretations of the Pavilion have claimed, but rather in the conceptual boundaries of the discipline," moving out from architecture to landscape architecture.[17]

Shulgin's definition of the analogue as "similar in function but different in structure or origin" makes the Honey Locust Allée an analogue to architecture because most descriptions of it utilize architectural elements and models, with the use of plants providing a minor difference

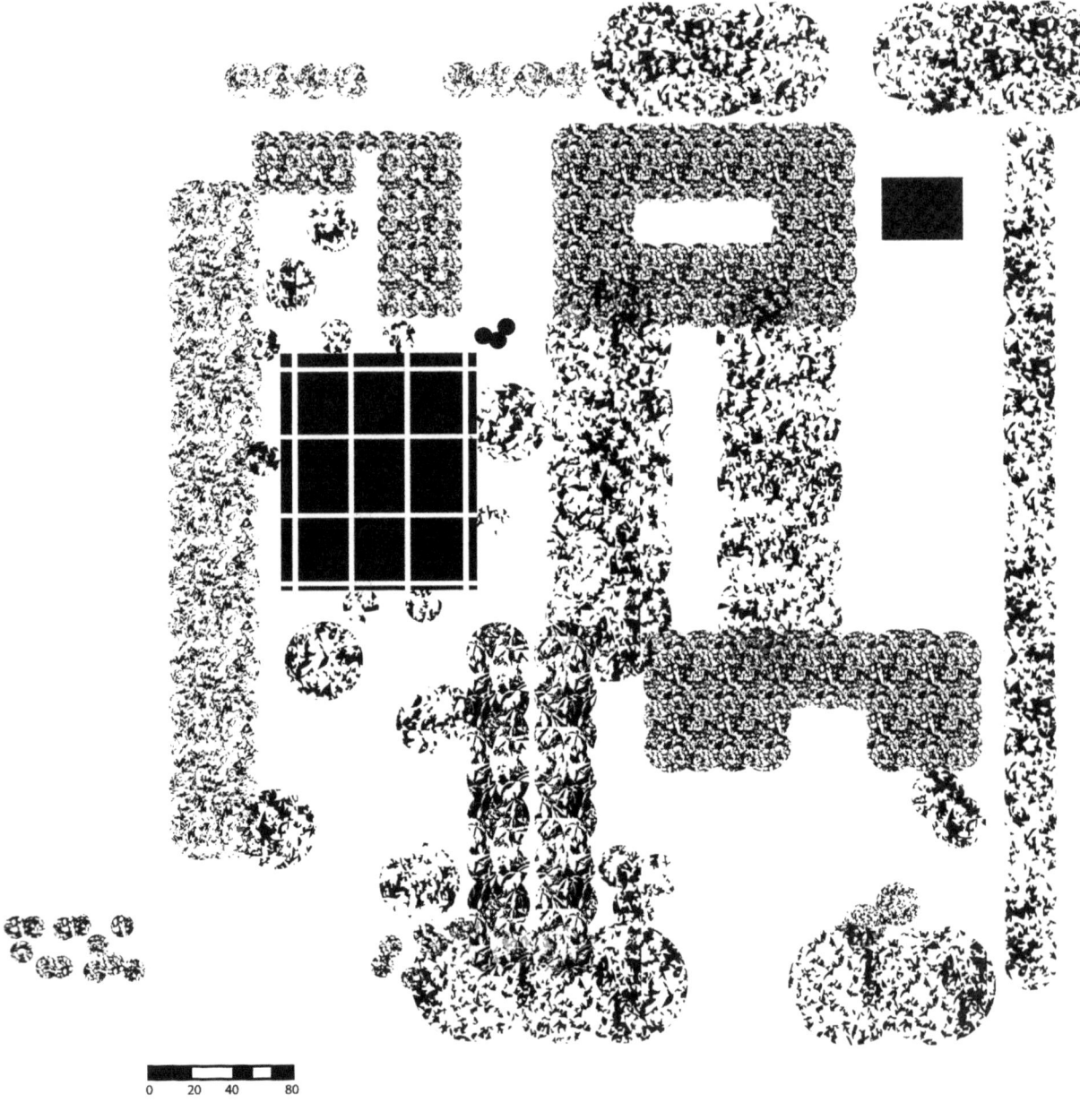

FIGURE 3.7

Drawing of the Miller Garden by Elizabeth K. Meyer, emphasizing the contribution of leaves to the qualities of the planting (Courtesy of Elizabeth K. Meyer).

in "origin." In contrast, however, Meyer argues that "landscape space is qualitatively different from architectural space even when the same spatial principles are deployed,"[18] so that "a tree ... is not simply green *poché*, to use the Beaux-Arts terminology for the rendering of the mass of a thick wall."[19] In drawings that accompany Meyer's discussion of the Miller Garden, these qualitative differences are shown by illustrating the contribution of different leaf types to the qualities of the canopy, which inflect the ubiquitous architectural spatial definition that Meyer nonetheless continues in her talk of "ceilings" and "walls."[20] So too does Frederick Gutheim in his assertion that Kiley's "plant material itself is boldly structured,"[21] its status as plants secondary to its architectonic effects. The consideration of leaf qualities by Meyer represents a desire to consider plants as a point of difference from the implicitly inorganic descriptions of the garden as architecture.

When plants are acknowledged in descriptions of the Miller Garden, it is because, as Brooks says, they "shape spaces [and] compose relationships of solids and voids rather than orchestrating complex floral combinations or bloom sequences."[22] By contrasting the serious architectural work of space shaping to the seemingly trivial floral work of the traditional garden, Brooks demonstrates that specifically biological aspects of the plant, such as ecology ("floral combinations") or seasonality ("bloom sequences"), are regarded as less important. I argue, however, that both the leaf effects that Meyer discusses and the space shaping mentioned by Brooks result from the process of growth and the change that accompanies it, the process of being alive, which is implicit to the use of plants as architectural analogies but is unrecognized in discussion of such effects.

TAXONOMY OF PLANT FORM

The treatment of plants as architectural analogues was novel to landscape historians and theorists during the postmodern period, because the use of plants as a form that shaped space was an innovation of modern American landscape architecture. Treib discusses Gabriel Guevrekian's Garden of Water and Light at the Exposition Internationale des Arts Décoratifs in 1925: "the design showcased inert rather than living materials, upsetting the traditional balance that had almost always favored vegetation."[23] In the external landscape, the new formal and spatial models of modernism became powerfully abstract design generators, so that Robert Mallet-Stevens's concrete trees shared more with the emerging French painting style of cubism,[24] seen in the round rather than projected onto the surface of the painting, than they did with organic trees *per se*. Indeed, while the Exposition was an important precursor to American modernist landscape architecture, Treib quotes Fletcher Steele, who attended it, on the French *paysagistes'* "utter lack of interest or understanding of plant life and the myriad ways it might reinforce their ideas and lend them a charm now usually lacking."[25] With the rejection of the baroque axis, the picturesque view, the triviality of gardening in the Gardenesque, modern American landscape architects like Kiley, Eckbo, and particularly James Rose sought to hinge their new model on the difference plants offered to modern architectural models of form and space. Rose saw plants as important and unique for landscape architecture: "plants are to the landscape designer what words are to the conversationalist."[26]

While the American modernist landscape architects favored plants, their use of them as analogues for architecture seems contradictory to their interest in them. Although the modernist form-space dialectic had an inherent interest in movement, which could be regarded as a type of change, such movement was present primarily as flexibility of location for the user, freed from the fixed plan, free from typology, an experiential subject in the thrall of space. Even while it was animated by people, the form-space dialectic was static, fundamentally uninterested in change or process, even though change as growth is implicit to any idea about plants shaping space, since the way in which they do so arises from the process of growth.

James Rose acknowledged that form was a process when he said that it was *produced*: that landscape architects should use "science to produce organic form rather than producing mere camouflage."[27] Science for Rose was the tool for working with the form of plants, a way of catalyzing their formal "production." Despite advancing architectural models of form and space, Rose nonetheless recognized that "plants, rock, earth and water are the major materials of landscape," the difference between modern architecture and landscape architecture pivoting around this material difference.[28] Just as contemporary readings of physics opened up structure to architectural experimentation, the use of science to articulate and direct natural systems by landscape architecture similarly reflected the role of technology in modernism generally.

Even while plants were an analogue for architecture, they nonetheless had specific and unique formal properties, which came from their nature as a material that allowed them to inflect the form-space dialectic. For Rose, plants were interesting because, for example, "when plants are used as specimens rather than in mass, fewer plants are required for the same control and division of space."[29] Steering away from the Gardenesque, where plants were "stuck in a "design" at the last minute to provide enclosure or frame "a picture,"[30] he sought to "lift plants out of their little niches in an eclectic ground pattern and use them as organic structural parts of the landscape, [so that] forms will appear which are expressive of plants as a material,"[31] allowing them to be used "for their own sake."[32] Separating out the plant allowed "the use of all sides of the plant... as a design element, instead of only one side in massing."[33] To speak of plants having a side is difficult, because they are irregular, but by speaking of them like this Rose shows the process of negotiating the modernist form-space dialectic to landscape architecture. Nonetheless this was an acknowledgment, even a celebration, of the formal complexity of plants resulting from the growth process. Rose sought to separate out the plant from the mass, "because [the mass] was a negation of [the] individual potentialities produced by the scientific method."[34] Liberated from these associations and conventions of usage by historic garden styles, he was directing attention to the plant—to *a* plant, an individual or specimen, because "all plants have definite potentialities and each plant has an inherent quality which will inevitably express itself."[35] Standing on its own, arguably more like a sculpture than a living thing, the plant's formal, and thereby space-shaping, properties could be seen and articulated.

Plant form is synonymous with growth habit, the characteristic shape of a species that nonetheless varies from one specific plant to another. Different stages of a plant's development also have different habits: a tree, for example, has the form of a tree only after it has been a seedling (a stalk with a few leaves), a sapling (a green and whippy, unthickened trunk, without branches), a juvenile (with branches to the ground), until it finally becomes the tree we recognize it as, its form for the longest part of its adult life. To speak of a particular habit is to prioritize one particular stage in the plant's growth over another, freezing the tree at a certain stage of its development. This is also a representational issue, because planting plans generally show trees as simply a circle that reflects the plant's characteristic size at maturity, suggesting that a tree's growth is a uniform expansion from this center. I argue that this treats growth as uniform extrusion.

Representation of plant forms is an important part of Rose's book *Creative Gardens*.[36] In *Creative Gardens*, Rose developed a drawn taxonomy of plant forms to articulate their effects in relation to the form-space dialectic of modernism.[37] While I have argued that plants were an analogue for architectural elements in modernism, for Rose their main difference was "[their] sense of transparency,... of visibility broken by a succession of planes."[38] Rose's theorization of transparency in plants is reminiscent of that of Paul Scheerbart's theorization of glass, described in his novel *Glasarchitektur*, discussed by Reyner Banham, which Bruno Taut tested at his Glass Pavilion in Cologne in 1914, while Rose tested his theories with physical models.[39] Colin Rowe and Robert Slutzky considered transparency in modern architecture "an inherent quality of substance—as in a wire mesh or a glass curtain wall or it may be an inherent quality of organization... one might, for this reason, distinguish between a real or a *literal* and a *phenomenal* or seeming transparency."[40] Rowe and Slutzky's qualification is useful in discussing the transition in Rose's taxonomy table, where "the individual plant is a 'specimen'; through spacing it becomes: fenestration; hedges; baffles; tracery; clumps; canopy."[41] Rose's progression mirrors a transition described by György Kepes: "Transparency... implies a... spatial order. Transparency means a simultaneous perception of different spatial locations. Space not only recedes but fluctuates in a continuous activity... as one sees each figure as the closer, now as the further one."[42]

Rose's initial typology of "specimens" is broken up into a series of habits based on the visibility of the trunk and branching, where types like "Columnar," "Pendulous," "Weeping" indicate that branching and the trunk are very visible and are drawn as lines, whereas names like "Round," "Oval," "Horizontal," and "Broad" suggest that the mass of green leaves obscures the branching, causing the overall form to be drawn as solid. Exceptions to this division are "Spreading," which straddles both, since spread suggests branching, but also the mass form, "Irregular," that might otherwise be conventionally called "sculptural," and "Picturesque," where a leaf canopy sits among the branching structure. Despite massively different heights, both a 40-foot willow and a 3-foot prostrate yew are in the same "Weeping" category, suggesting that the habit is the same regardless of height. Rose also usefully includes sizes and spacing, as well as a figure, which makes the table look like a tree version of Le Corbusier's *Modulor*.

Rose's diagram of plant habits reveals a contradiction in his model. An experiential subject is implicit in any model of space in the form-space dialectic, since a sense of enclosure presupposes a person present to experience it, as does transparency, which presupposes a subject looking at, or through, something. For the "Weeping" type, the subject is a viewer looking either over the 3-foot yew or up at the looming 40-foot tree, where neither is in fact transparent, and the effects of the "Weeping" shape are entirely different. Nevertheless, one gets the sense that this table is Rose's attempt to give an account of plant form that was, and continues to be, pioneering. Since Rose makes claims about transparency, the figure is not just for scaling but is implicitly experiencing "phenomena" in Rowe and Slutzky's terms.

Rose's first table of plant habits of specimens closely corresponds to Rowe and Slutzky's definition of literal transparency, the quality of an individual plant's leaves; while his second table, entitled "Spacing," where plants are aggregated together, corresponds to their definition of phenomenal transparency. In fact, both operate in a phenomenal manner. Since their definition of literal transparency is truly "literal," only plants that have 100 percent leaf cover, where the leaves are translucent, could really be described as literal. In every other instance, transparency refers to the gaps in between foliage. A continuous cover of leaves creates what is referred to as "texture" in planting design textbooks. Since

Columnar

| 40'+ | 20-40' | 12-20' | 6-12' | 3-6' | 1-3' | Tracery Columnar |

Cryptomeria
Ginkgo (fastigiata)
English oak (fastigiata)
Canaert red cedar
Swedish juniper
Lawson's cypress
upright privet
Paul's scarlet thorn
hybrid yew
Hicks yew
truehedge columnberry

Pendulous or Weeping

| 40'+ | 20-40' | 12-20' | 6-12' | 3-6' | 1-3' | Tracery Columnar |

willow - elegantissima babylonica
English weeping beech
Niobe willow et al
weeping mulberry
weeping cherry
" mountain ash
" flowering dogwood
weeping forsythia
- hemlock
willow-leaved cotoneaster
glossy abelia
weeping yew (baccata repandens)

Round or Oval

| 40'+ | 20-40' | 12-20' | 6-12' | 3-6' | 1-3' | Tracery |

Norway maple
Sugar maple
cucumber magnolia
white birch
horsechestnut (glabra)
American holly
flowering dogwood
star magnolia
rose of sharon
little-leaved holly
boxwood
dwarf hedge yew

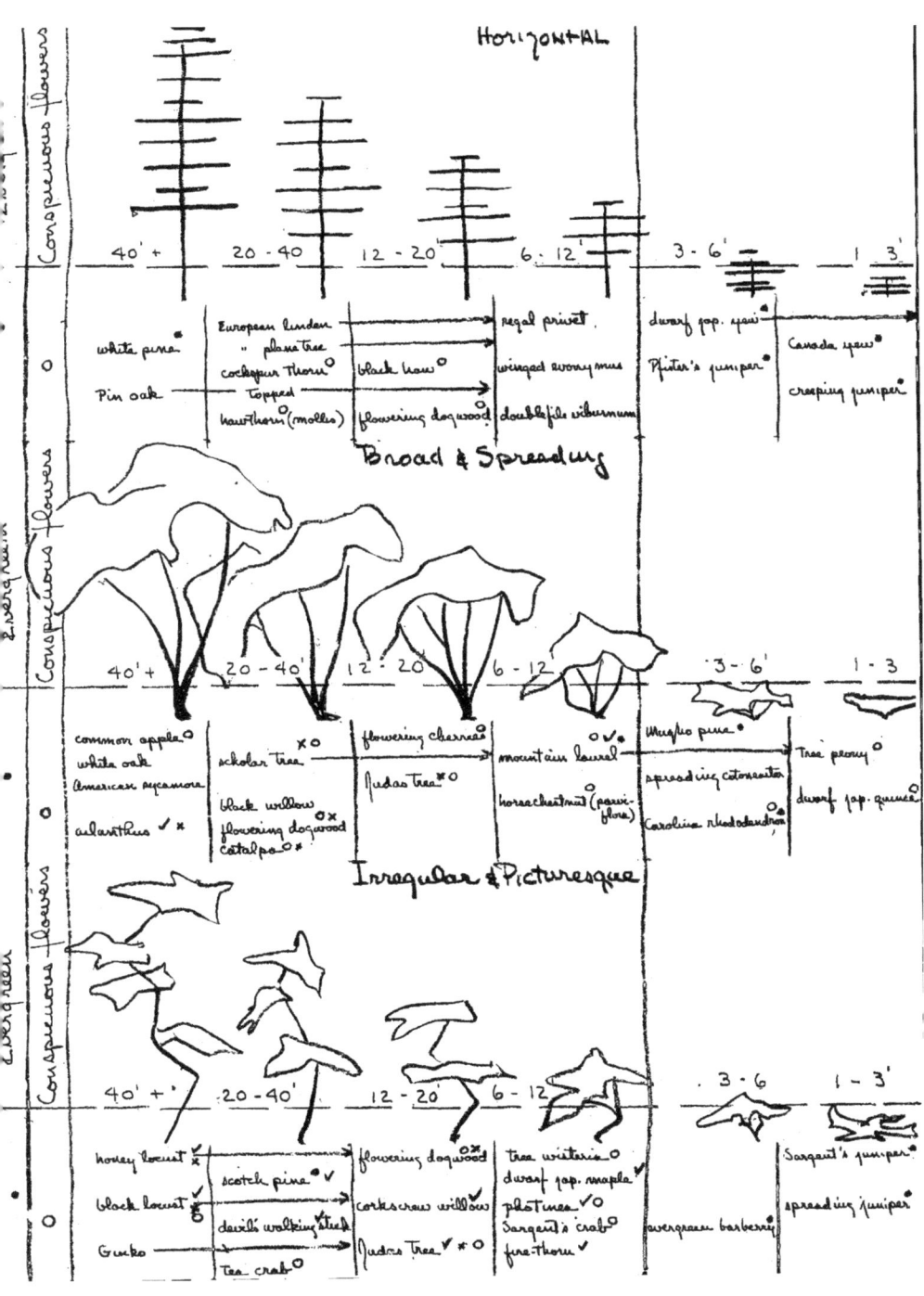

FIGURE 3.8

James Rose's taxonomy of plant forms, from *Creative Gardens*.

a plant's texture is made up of layers of leaves on top of one another, the transparency corresponds to architectural materials like shingles or thatching rather than the modern materials, like glass, that provided the literal transparency in modernism. Depending on seasons and time of day, leaves can indeed have lovely qualities of translucency, as when, for example, mid-morning light comes through new leaves in spring, perhaps making them lime-colored. However, this was not Rose's interest. When Rose was describing plants as transparent, and exploring this quality in drawing and model, he was really talking about gaps in foliage rather than translucency.

The arrangement of gaps made by leaves is like a moiré, where two identical patterns are superimposed and shifted slightly. Moiré refers to textiles and their weave, where the effect of the superimposition creates a pattern whereby every layer is different, greater than the sum of its parts. The concept of the moiré is useful, because it describes how the gaps between leaves compound layer over layer, such that the form of the leaf is submerged by the mass, and a new texture emerges. Thought of as a moiré, leaves can indeed be literally transparent *en masse*.

In the "Spacing" table Rose places the individual plant forms next to each other, and considers how form and spacing interact. As the gaps through foliage and trunk increase, the quality of transparency is more phenomenal: the gaps in the individual plant, and then in groupings, combine to produce different aggregations of gaps. Interestingly, in many categories of groupings Rose uses similar names as he did for individual plants, such as "Picturesque" or "Spreading," suggesting that the effect of the individual is amplified, or at least maintained, when it is aggregated.

The interrelationship between the two (the individual and the group) is best shown in his category "Tracery," which is made up of plants that were in the "Irregular" category as individuals. Where individuals were shown as clumps of leaves interspersed along limbs, when repeated they create a camouflage pattern, with series of masses across a screen of vertical trunks. In terms of transparency, one looks through large gaps in foliage at branching that provides a second level of larger gaps, appearing as bars across the whole gap. In this example, the result is somewhere

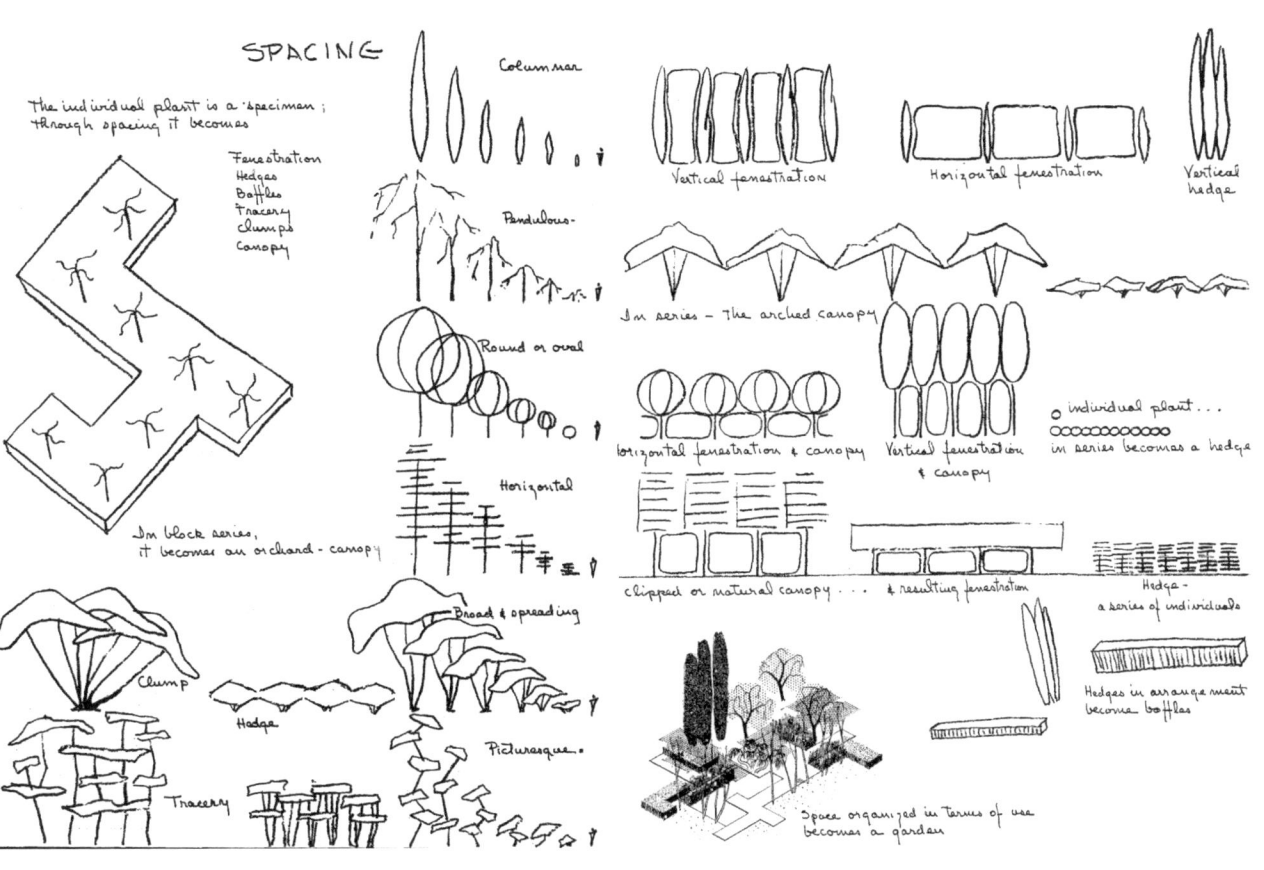

FIGURE 3.9

James Rose's taxonomy of plant "Spacing," from *Creative Gardens*.

between literal and phenomenal transparency, since the qualities of the leaves act like a moiré, providing literal transparency, while the trunks imply phenomenal transparency.

Since Rose was exploring landscape implications of modern architectural principles in his transparency studies, his investigations were in service of the spatial opportunities they presented. Correspondingly, it is not surprising that his second table includes versions of a spacing model called "Fenestration," based on the architectural term that describes "the arrangement of windows in a building,"[43] further supporting my argument that plants were an analogue for architectural elements in modernist landscape architecture. Fenestration is an investigation of phenomenal transparency because it concerns the effect of wide spacings between individuals, and the proportion of the height of the plant to the size of the gap.[44]

Coming after types like "Tracery," where portions of trunk and leaves are separated and visible, the "Fenestration" category utilizes plants that are covered by leaves rather than with visible branching. An example of this category, which also appears in Rose's earlier models, is the cypress form, which is the most architectural type, analogous to the column. The difference between "vertical" and "horizontal" fenestration relies entirely on the spacing between the columnar plants, where the vertical comprises gaps between columns significantly smaller than the overall height of the column. The horizontal, on the other hand, is where the gap is almost twice the height of the column. Describing these plant arrangements as vertical or horizontal relies on the figuration of the gap rather than the plant that figures it, which is of interest purely as a tool of spatial implication. When columns are adjacent to each other, without a gap, Rose annotates them as vertical hedge. Considering that Rose was a colleague of Kiley, it should come as no surprise that the terms used in his typology were also used by Kiley to describe his work at the Miller Garden: he calls the trunks of the honey locusts "columns."

When Rose combines trees from his "Broad" category, he calls the arrangement "Horizontal fenestration & canopy," where the canopy has coalesced and gaps between trunks are visible below. As he develops this series, he adds maintenance and shows the joined trees as clipped, in a clear resemblance to the baroque palisade. Rose's taxonomy reveals a methodological approach to landscape that was also present in the baroque: in Colbert's policies and the French garden treatises of Boyceau et al. This proves that baroque and modernist landscape architecture shared not just stylistic similarities, but also a systematic way of thinking about landscape.

A difference between the two is the role of maintenance. There was an acknowledgment in the baroque garden that maintenance techniques and tools were the key to mobilizing a plant-form language, and a valued part of the process. While Rose may have arrived at a similar formal or spatial outcome, he was distinctly uninterested in the act of gardening. Despite plant form being the result of growth, the work of gardening to achieve it seemed to frustrate Rose: "with plants the struggle is endless and results in victory neither for the plant nor the man who clipped it. If the plant should win the design would be lost; and if the man should win he would succeed only in preserving something false from the beginning."[45]

Considering that landscape architecture in a contemporary sense did not exist during the baroque, the spatial interests it shared with the modernists came from two totally different directions. The qualities of the baroque garden resulted from the process of gardening, whereas for modernist landscape architects they were the result of a theoretical and representational investigation appropriated from modernist architecture.

Without a discourse of space, spatial effect and gardening action are inseparable in the French "formal" garden. The "formal" garden was always a work of gardening. While modernist landscape architects were interested in spatial effects and uninterested in techniques, the use of techniques over time was still required to make the plantings perform in the desired ways. This is particularly true for the Honey Locust Allée, since if it were not for gardening, the celebrated architectonic effects would never have evolved.

SENESCENT ALLÉE

Architectural qualities dominate most of the accounts of the Honey Locust Allée. However, the horticultural story of the trees since installation is very different to these accounts, and has implications that undermine the way the design has been read. Whereas in the design account there is a muscularity, a certainty, about the trees, the horticultural account reveals that this celebrated effect has been very difficult to maintain over time. This alternative account concerns growth, change, and numerous people who worked hard to ensure that Kiley's aims continued to be realized, including other landscape architects, but also gardeners and property managers.

The stories of those who maintain famous gardens are rarely told. However, it is their work that ensures that gardens celebrated by visitors and writers are true to the designers' plans. While a photograph captures a garden at a particular moment, it is work over a long period of time that guides plants into the state that the designers envisaged. The back story of the Honey Locust Allée at the Miller Garden was told to me by gardener Ben Wever,[46] and is substantiated by documents held in the IMA archives. This story is informative because it inflects the dominant narrative about the Miller Garden as an icon of plant use and design, and shows that there were inherent problems with both the design and the realization of the allée. It inflects the narrative by showing that numerous horticultural and botanic factors must align to ensure that plants perform consistently enough, without too much change, to achieve the static effects of the architectural analogue that Rose theorized and Kiley designed for. From Wever, however, we learn that significant maintenance was expended to keep the Honey Locust Allée in the "mature" state that critics describe, since it was installed three times: replanted twice after its initial planting in 1957, once in 1986, and again in 2006. Over the years, progressive removal and replanting of individual dead trees eventually necessitated the replanting of the entire allée when it became too discontinuous. In view of such fundamental replacement, I argue that there were only short periods of maturity, or architectonic performance, among much change; and, furthermore, that this desire to maintain a static effect contradicts the interest in plants for which the garden is celebrated, since growth and change constitute the key difference between plant rather than inert materials.

FIRST INSTALLATION, 1957

The horticultural story of the Honey Locust Allée begins at the earliest concepts for the garden design, and shows that the use of honey locusts was by no means a *fait accompli*. An early letter, in September 1955, from the Office of Dan Kiley about the planting strategy notes 36 common honey locusts (*Gleditsia tricanthos*) in the tree schedule.[47] Miller may have questioned this selection, perhaps because of the thorns on the common honey locust, because in a letter written in November 1955 Kiley was adamant about the honey locust, which he now specified as the "thornless" variety: "After considering many possibilities for the west allée we are recommending the Honey Locust as the only available tree that will lend itself to horizontal training. It also has a delicate branch growth that will not inhibit the view to the meadow." It is interesting that at that time the celebrated view through to the meadow was secondary to the horizontal branch structure which does not feature in later writing about the allée. Despite Kiley's assertions, a handwritten note from Miller on the letter says: "Enquire about Honey Locusts."[48] Perhaps to disqualify Miller's suggestions, or demonstrate that other options had been considered, Kiley again stated that "*all other possibilities*" (emphasis added) other than the honey locust "were either too heavy (Horse Chestnut) or too stiff (Sweet Gum) or too messy (Plane Trees) or too low-branched (Lindens)." A follow-up letter from Kiley's office in December 1955 sought to demonstrate (and presumably argue for) the qualities of the honey locust, directing Miller to an allée at a nearby hillside nursery, showing their similar "foliage, shape and structure" to the thorned variety.[49] Considering how celebrated the Honey Locust Allée has become, it is startling to realize that had the Millers had their way, it might not have been this species that was used, and the architectonic effects that have inspired many landscape architects might never have been realized. While this species was worth fighting for because of these effects, the plant selection was not without its issues.

As well as showing that the trees developed well initially, a photograph taken by Kiley's office probably less than ten years after installation is interesting because it is taken from behind the fountain at the south end

FIGURE 3.10
View along the Honey Locust Allée by Office of Dan Kiley, taken from behind pond at south end, from approximately the early 1960s (Courtesy of IMA).

FIGURE 3.11

Photograph of the Honey Locust Allée in winter, early 1970s, with characteristic form, before regular replacements (Courtesy of IMA).

of the allée rather than from within the allée. The photographer might have chosen this inconvenient position because he was seeking the view that the allée was designed for and would become well known for later, but was not yet present because it was obscured by lower leaves. However, problems with the performance of the allée date from within twenty years of its first installation. In 1975, O. D. Hungerford sought quotes from a plant pathologist for the Honey Locust Allée,[50] and in 1977 he continued to worry about its condition.[51] He noted that five trees were being replaced, while another nine were so "disfigured and unattractive" that they might require replacement later. Asking boldly: "Why have these trees failed?," Hungerford suggested that the poor drainage of the terrace and the high lime content in the soil had weakened the trees, and made them susceptible to other problems like borers and bugs. While proposing amelioration of soil conditions as trees were replanted, Hungerford suggested the alternative of replacing thirty trees as an option in order to "achieve Kiley's original intent for the locusts, i.e., two rows of trees of about equal size and height." The desire to return to the original form of the allée reflects the fact that all the replacements along the way had caused it to be uneven, making wholesale replacement the best option to retain the original architectonic effect. In the end the allée was replaced piecemeal: the Millers approved the replacement of ten trees in 1978,[52] and a further four later on in the same year.[53] Two more trees were replaced in 1983.[54]

I could find only one picture, an undated color print presumably from the early 1970s prior to the numerous replacements, showing a consistently sized allée, its form clearly visible because the picture was taken in winter, so there are no leaves. However, in both a photograph by Balthazar Korab, which appears to be from the late 1970s, and another from Kiley's office (1980), the cumulative effect of the numerous replacements is obvious. If one looks along the allée, north to south, the different ages of the trees are perceptible in the different trunk thicknesses, only a few substantial original trees remaining, with many smaller trunks in between, and the canopy at one end has low leaves despite pruning to lift crowns, revealing the youth of some trees.

Reporting on the honey locusts in 1980, Hungerford noted hopefully: "good health is returning to the Locusts. Best guess is that they are

FIGURE 3.12
Photograph from late 1970s along the Honey Locust Allée with mixture of trunk sizes showing replacements by Balthazar Korab (Courtesy of Korab Image).

FIGURE 3.13
Photograph by Office of Dan Kiley taken in 1980 along the Honey Locust Allée, also with mixture of trunk sizes showing replacements (Courtesy of IMA).

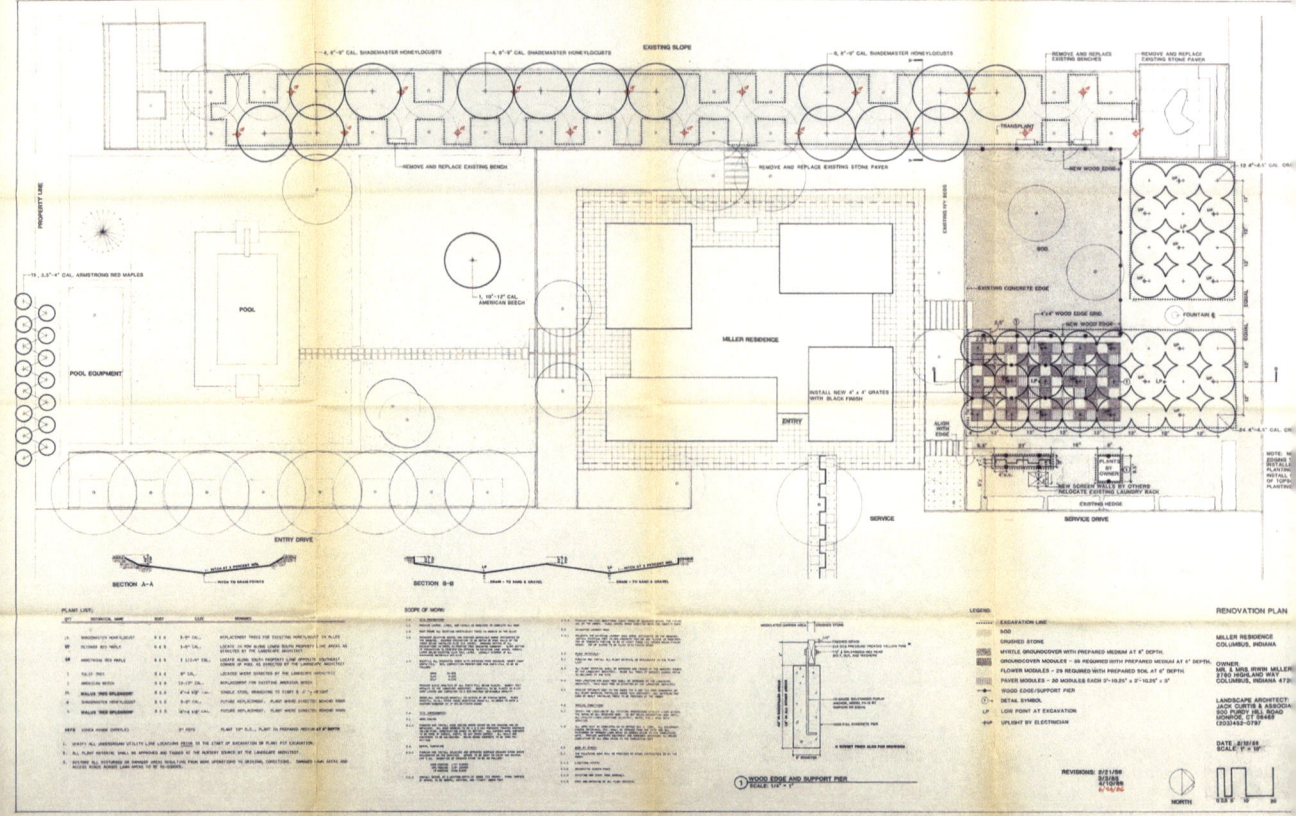

recovering from three *very* cold winters 1977–78, 1978–79 and 1979–1980,"[55] clearly deferring wholesale replacement for the time being. However, five years later the honey locusts were again flagged as an issue for discussion by Jack Curtis, leading to a more extensive replanting in 1986.[56]

SECOND INSTALLATION, 1986

The substantial scale of the replanting can be seen in Jack Curtis's plan of the proposed works.[57] It involved fifteen new trees at the north end of the allée and along most of its edge to the meadow, as well as earthworks and resurfacing of the terrace. While the trees were being set out to be planted, it was noted that some of the "new" trees retained (trees that had been recently replaced) were "not exactly in line but [the contractor] will do his best to locate the new trees to create a *reasonably* uniform allée,"[58]

FIGURE 3.14
Jack Curtis's plan showing trees to be retained and replaced in the renovation of the Honey Locust Allée in 1986 (Courtesy of IMA).

FIGURE 3.15
Photograph by landscape architect Meg Storrow of retained trees augmented with new trees during the renovation of the allée in 1986 (Courtesy of IMA).

perhaps because the line had moved during the numerous replacements. The work was superintended onsite by landscape architect Meg Storrow, and her picture of the soil profile clearly shows the layer of limestone fill that was used to build the terrace.

Photographs taken by Jack Schmeckebier in 1986, after the works were complete, show replacements bought at a larger trunk size, and the existing "new" trees merged to quickly return the allée to its characteristic form, such that Felice Frankel's photographs, taken within three years of replacement (1989), appear indistinguishable from the first allée's incarnation fifteen years earlier, confirming what Ben Wever told me: that "the allée always seemed mature." However, within just ten years after the original allée had been replaced, there were again problems with the honey locusts. In 1997, five or six of the trees were identified as being

FIGURE 3.16
Detail photograph by Meg Storrow of the existing soil profile of the terrace during the renovation of the allée in 1986, showing layer of limestone fill that was believed to have retarded the growth of the honey locusts (Courtesy of IMA).

FIGURE 3.17 (below)
Photograph by Jack Schmeckebier of the allée within six months of reconstruction in 1986 (Courtesy of IMA).

FIGURE 3.18 (opposite)
Felice Frankel's classic photograph of the allée taken in 1989, three years after reinstallation, included in Walker and Simo, *Invisible Gardens* (Courtesy of Felice Frankel).

problematic, with issues arising from the more free-draining mix used for the replanting in 1986.[59] In 1999, head gardener Jim Shearn reported that the trees were again under stress.[60] A tree survey undertaken listed 40 percent of the trees as in either fair or poor condition, many with girdling roots, where roots begin encircling the main stem, restricting uptake of water and nutrients, a sign of poor root development.[61] Trees continued to be replaced: two more in 2004, this time with a 12–13-inch diameter, three inches larger than the original trees, perhaps to obtain the effect more quickly.[62] Throughout this time the trees were constantly sprayed for borer and treated with fungicides.

THIRD INSTALLATION, 2009

Coinciding with the transfer of ownership of the Miller House and Garden to the Indianapolis Museum of Art, the allée was again replaced wholesale in 2009, with landscape architect Michael Van Valkenburgh responsible for extensive works throughout the garden. During this time, the entire soil profile was replaced to address the long-running issues with the limestone fill. Wever told me that the initial detail used at the edge of the allée, a huge concrete edge, ensured that excavation of the allée meant that the bank to the meadow did not have to be disturbed. It is ironic that a photograph of the house taken by Ezra Stoller when young honey locusts were first planted and another, current photograph of the Honey Locust Allée on the IMA website taken sixty years later should so closely resemble one another, the former in black and white and the later now in color: two rows of healthy small trees that can be looked through from the house.

From his experience in the garden, Wever cited three main causes for the problems of the allée: (1) the soil condition of the allée terrace; (2) compounded by ecological effects arising from the spacing of the honey locust trees; and (3) the fact that the trees are a monoculture. The soil issues arise from the original fill material, a crushed local limestone, used to make the terrace. High in calcium carbonate, this material made the soil alkaline, with a pH much higher than neutral 7. Both Wever and Shearn before him observed that the trees developed dense, shallow fibrous roots in the soil profile immediately adjacent to the surface, rather than sending down deep roots. Combining the shallow root penetration, seen in Storrow's photograph of the soil profile where roots do not penetrate through the fill, with the concrete edge where the allée met the meadow bank on the west, Wever described the trees as "bonsais" because they were effectively containerized.

The allée is made up of 36 trees, in two rows of 18, 9 feet apart, a spacing rigorously repeated in each subsequent replanting. The close proximity of this spacing has created a problem due to competition between trees, even while that spacing has also, ironically, created the desired architectonic effects: the "balustrade,"[63] "a perforated wall" made by "the trunks of trees [which] if spaced close enough together [suggest that a] window existed between each tree column,"[64] or a ceiling where "the tree canopy's lower surface [is] defined by a tree's branches and leaves."[65] The closeness of the trees means that they have to grow tall to compete for light, as they would in a forest, leaving dead limbs below that need to be regularly removed. Since the allée was generally planted with trees that had a trunk diameter of between 5 and 10 inches, their advanced condition forced them to compete immediately, though Wever is pruning the most recent iteration (2009) to lift the crowns in order to force them to grow tall rather than wide, since the trees are smaller than they were in previous replacements. For the mature trees, pruning comprised either dead-wooding or clearing crossed canopies, both caused by close spacing. Because lower limbs are shaded by competing high limbs, they can die off, necessitating their removal, lifting the lower edge of the canopy and creating Meyer's "ceiling." Trees can also grow into each other, interfering with each other's growth, so that some trees die off because they are outcompeted. Wever maintains that 40 percent of each replacement of the allée was in turn replanted over time, with 10-inch trunk diameter replacements at Mr. Miller's request, as is evident from the IMA archive; this will be difficult now that the garden is owned by an institution with limited funds. The density of the trees also made it difficult to achieve consistent shaping where the allée met the two massive European weeping beeches close to the house, which shaded the honey locust trees on all sides, causing them to grow taller and thinner, and angle away from their taller neighbors. When I asked Wever what

FIGURE 3.19

Photograph of the Miller House by Ezra Stoller shortly after construction, with young honey locusts in the foreground, almost identical to the recent replanting in 2009 (Courtesy of ESTO).

FIGURE 3.20

Photograph of the Honey Locust Allée taken after the 2009 replanting, the third installation, an iconic image from the IMA website for the Miller House and Garden (Courtesy of IMA).

spacing he would have used, he says he would have doubled it to 18 feet. Clearly, though, such spacing would have reduced the effect that Kiley wanted, since there would have been only nine trees on each side. This configuration would also have mitigated the effect that Wever himself likes best, also discussed by Hilderbrand: the graduation through the grille of trunks down to the meadow.

While the architectural effects were assured by the dense spacing, this spacing has negative consequences when it is combined with soil issues and species selection. The combination of the height of the trees with the shallow root system meant that the trees were unstable and prone to infection. Wever's description of the honey locusts as a monoculture would apply to any avenue which relies on consistent tree-planting for effect. Because the trees were close, and the same species, pests and diseases could spread quickly through the canopy. Treating these problems is hard because working in a canopy with such density is difficult: for example, it is impossible to cover an entire tree with spray. Combined with the collapse of the trees, pest problems were a significant contributor to the wholesale replacements of the allée.

Despite the fact that "[Kiley] appreciate[d] the need for careful maintenance, without which [his] work could never achieve its promise,"[66] his landscape analogue for architectural elements, his fenestrated wall and green ceiling, came at an ecological cost which was nonetheless vital to the delivery of his design. That the much-admired, mythologized Honey Locust Allée should be made of failing, early-senescent trees is an irony not lost on him. Despite his reservations about the way it was implemented, and the immense amounts of activity and money needed to maintain it, he still regards it as his favorite space in the Miller Garden, after virtually a whole lifetime spent there as a gardener.

Architecture of significance is preserved. Preservation seeks to maintain a work of architecture in the state in which it was when it was first built, before the vagaries of time or disrespectful owners and occupiers modified it to accommodate their lifestyle.[67] In contrast, plantings get better with time, as they reach the "mature" state the designer envisioned for them when eventually they "grow up," deferring perfection to a later time, but not indefinitely. Similarly, "Kiley's magnificent planting concept" for spaces like the Honey Locust Allée is described as a "component that has steadily improved with age,"[68] as it reaches its oft-described "maturity."

Writing in the early 1980s, Gutheim commented that "a quarter century later, the planting [of the Miller Garden] has matured."[69] Hilderbrand tells us that this was because the Millers were so private, their house and garden not receiving significant exposure until "at a point in the early 1980s... the Miller garden emerged [as an] already *mature* landscape."[70] When the garden did emerge, it was "*mature* without being old, as though it had magically defied time and change."[71] Since it had been in sight for so long, growth was *assumed* to have occurred, such that plants had finally reached maturity.

The emergence of the garden as mature corresponds with Alan Ward's celebrated photographs of it taken in the mid-1990s, which, on first examination, show the allée resplendent, grown, *architectural*. Looking more closely, with some knowledge of the history of the allée, we can see that it was in fact quite discontinuous, with smaller trunks among the bigger, older trees, which are responsible for the overall effect, demonstrating that the photograph was taken after its first replacement. The allée did not improve with age; in fact it declined and ultimately died well before honey locusts normally should, and was replaced twice. As this analysis has shown, the description of the Honey Locust Allée as a growing architectural performance is rhetorical rather than real.

CONCLUSION

While I have been critical in this chapter of the idea of the plant as "analogue" to architecture, the Miller Garden and Rose's taxonomy are extremely important contributions to my model of the viridic. This is because, like Courances, they demonstrate that plants can produce architectonic form, thereby shaping space. As a founding premise for the viridic, they allow the plants to be thought of in a spatial design frame, rather than simply as something used in amateur gardening: in the first instance since, according to the modernist definition of form making space, Rose's taxonomy provides a useful expansion to the existing planting design category of "Form." In the second, the Miller Garden, aggregating plant

FIGURE 3.21

Photograph by Alan Ward of Honey Locust Allée when mature, but actually just replaced, in 1986 (© Alan Ward).

forms, shows how plants can create space. However, while welcoming the sophistication that this language of form and space for plants provides for the viridic, it is important for us to recognize that both of these aspects—form and space of plants—are secondary to growth, without which they could not exist. The difficulty of maintaining the architectural effect of the honey locusts at the Miller Garden demonstrates that growth cannot be taken for granted, and needs to be thought of not simply as the result of maintenance but as evolution of the desired properties over time. Failure to do this can mean that plants never meet the formal and spatial criteria envisaged by designers.

At the heart of the Miller Garden as an exemplar for planting design, and the Honey Locust Allée in particular, is a contradiction: the contradiction between the reality of growth and the desire for a static architectural effect. The use of plants as architectonic elements is novel, because they are alive.[72] Growth is a defining characteristic of being alive, which means that in reality living things change. In contrast, architectonic effects can arise only if plants perform consistently when they are mature, particularly in an allée, where the differences between individual trees can distort the continuity of the whole. In the Miller Garden, constant work and replacement of individual trees was required to ensure that the effect is perpetuated. If the allée is effective or valuable only during its maturity, what is it during the rest of the time? In waiting? If it is really only about maturity, does it matter if the plants are plants, or could they be outdoor columns? If it doesn't matter, then I would argue that the allée is architecture rather than a garden.

In his essay "The Meaninglessness of Gardens," G. R. F. Ferrari argues that "the elements of a gardener's art are lives," and that when we choose a plant, we are "composing with its life."[73] With life come significant implications, because "as far as the aesthetic arts are concerned, gardening is messy. It is fraught with unpredictability and it is never complete."[74] This essence of the garden, its lack of completeness, is the key to what a garden is, and its relationship to plants as living things. Correspondingly, Ferrari argues that the Japanese Zen garden of Ryoan-ji is not a garden at all, because the rocks that make it up are not alive.[75] If we use this criterion, and apply it to the allée at the Miller Garden and the architectonic claims made for it, the desire for ceaseless maturity ultimately demonstrates that the Miller Garden is architecture. While Kiley's planting design was novel for its creation of a landscape analogue for modern architectural principles, it did not go so far as to engage with the implications of the material, plants, in their own terms. For modern American landscape architects, landscape architecture was really architecture with plants.

CHAPTER 4

CHANGING ROOMS

I F MODERN LANDSCAPE ARCHITECTURE sought to apply architectural analogies to the garden, postmodernism was interested in what the garden meant. More than public landscape projects, during postmodernism, "gardens [had] special meaning. ... By making gardens ... we create our own idealized order of nature and culture. ... Gardens connect us to our collective and primeval pasts."[1] The relationship between "culture" and "nature" was a preoccupation during this period, and the garden was the archetypal space in which to explore it. This exploration was through "making," recognizing that the meaning of the garden in relation to nature could be understood only through the process of working in the garden. The garden's philosophical analogies were best understood practically. Modernism was focused on strategic formal frameworks to organize space around function, unapologetically top-down. In contrast, postmodernism was more interested in ground-level tactics, Michel de Certeau arguing that everyday practices represented a bottom-up mechanism from which strategic consequences emerged.[2]

FIGURE 4.2
The "henyard" in Sven-Ingvar Andersson's garden at Marnas, Sweden, when I visited it in 2010.

The idea that gardens are "made," rather than designed, fits this tactical approach, since nature (as ecology) is best understood by interacting with plants in the garden.

When I was a horticulture student, Anne Whiston Spirn's *Granite Garden* influenced me profoundly because it reread the city as an ecological system, articulating things like the soil profile of cracks in the pavement, and treating the mix of weeds and native plants like a natural ecosystem.[3] Later, after studying landscape architecture, I was excited to read Spirn's next book, *The Language of Landscape*, which she said arose from the question "Where is the art?" put to her by contemporaries in relation to the science of the *Granite Garden*. Attempting to find a bridge between that science and the "art" of *The Language of Landscape*, she used a linguistic model, since "both grammar and biological structure are products of communicational and organizational process,"[4] and semiotics is an interest for postmodernism generally in this period.[5] For Spirn, *The Language of Landscape* was a language of context, "a place where processes happen, a setting of dynamic relationships *not* a collection of static states," where to "guide such contextual expression is the function of the grammar of landscape."[6]

Continuing her linguistic analogy, Spirn developed this general grammar to make it more specific, speaking of "local landscape dialects [which] emerge out of dialogue with enduring contexts of place: traditional vernacular landscapes are a consequence of collective learning, trial and error, finding what works and repeating it, refining [it] through experience."[7] The trial and error in the vernacular landscape to which Spirn referred was the "making" that happens in the garden, seen as completely separate from landscape architecture during modernism. An emphasis on "making" gardens could be a critique of landscape architecture, as in Martha Schwartz's Bagel Garden in Boston in 1979, which Schwartz described as a "Dada-esque installation that questioned the absence of art in the profession."[8] A work of art is directly "made," like the garden, rather than represented in a scaled drawing produced by landscape architects. The similarity between making in art and in the garden has made the garden a popular site for artists, notably Derek Jarman.[9]

One of Spirn's case studies in *The Language of Landscape* was Sven-Ingvar Andersson's private garden at Marnas, Sweden. Like Schwartz's Bagel Garden, this garden could easily be regarded as a classic work of postmodernism, whimsical with its overscaled topiary hens wandering around their hedged "henyard."[10] However, as with Schwartz's bagels, much more is at stake with Andersson's hens than meets the eye. Andersson's garden was a study in change, and a place for exploring the dynamic between people and plants in the garden using vernacular garden practices, since it was Andersson himself who pruned the garden and aged alongside it. Indeed, the form of the topiary hens was conditional on Andersson's agility, and "Andersson foresaw a time when he would no longer have the strength to 'hold clippers or climb up ladders.'"[11] As a gardener, I found a lot of truth in his calibration of his own existence to that of the garden and the change that can happen over time when he said: "I have a definite idea of how my henyard will end, but a lot which lies between *now* and *then* is an open plan. … A lot can happen before the henyard becomes a hawthorn grove."[12]

I met Andersson at a conference in Copenhagen when he was a sprightly and dignified old man, but forgot to ask him about the progress of his hawthorn grove. It was only when I was next in Copenhagen, just after he had died, that I was able to visit the garden. Following directions from his daughter Beata, a colleague and I embarked on a train from Copenhagen to Lund via Malmö, riding the final 14 kilometers on bicycles. Unable to appreciate the scale of the garden or circulation systems, when we arrived we entered through a hedge at the north end, making our way through overgrown passages to the "henyard." Mindful of Andersson's projections about the hawthorn grove, I was surprised to discover that the hawthorns were still pruned into their characteristic hen shapes,[13] and that his predictions about the transformation of henyard to hawthorn grove had not occurred, seemingly undermining the way he had rhetorically used the garden to argue about change.

However, other parts of this garden—the henyard itself rather than the hens—illustrated his point better. I was familiar with the plan of the garden he had drawn; in my imagination, however, I had ignored the series of garden rooms that were also made out of hawthorn hedges, one

FIGURE 4.3

Sven-Ingvar Andersson with his hens in 2008
(Courtesy of Sven-Ingvar Andersson).

of which was the "henyard" that enclosed the chickens. While the chickens had not changed from the photographs I had seen, Spirn described to me how they had changed over the lifespan of the garden: starting off as egg shapes, becoming chicks, and finally growing into hens, the form they have retained, though Spirn suggests that Andersson may have been "reluctant to let the hens grow out into freely growing trees because the henyard with its hens had become the iconic image of the garden, reproduced widely in photographs."[14] And anyway, Spirn countered, the hens had changed, since "some died and were cut down, some skeletons were left in place. Sometimes the hens grew unpruned and rangy [and] Sven Ingvar's brother would complain when he left them unpruned."

Instead, the hedges defining the henyard and the hawthorn grove had grown into a myriad of different forms creating diverse spaces, pruned by Andersson to optimize emerging spatial characteristics. Rather than Andersson's hypothesis that the henyard would turn into a hawthorn grove being a correct prediction about what would happen in the garden, Andersson had actually predicted his own interests, and had been wrong. To my gardener's eye, the garden seemed like a study in the manipulation of spaces using techniques that revealed much about Andersson's changing curation of the space as a whole, and his actions in it. Andersson's interventions modified the strict form of the initial plan, creating spaces that are not immediately apparent in that plan.[15] In the end, the chickens stayed the same but Andersson himself changed, in relation to the plants as "actors and coauthors" that shaped the chickens at Marnas.[16]

Located in the middle of this book, the Marnas garden represents a transition between design as a representational, predictive practice and maintenance as a real-time practice, since both play an equal part. Since Andersson's character and his reflections on the garden are so important to understanding both the project and this part of the argument, I start by introducing him and describing how he talked about the garden before it had started to change as a result of his maintenance. Since this chapter is the hinge of the book, I will use Marnas as an opportunity to define the viridic in some depth by focusing on the nature of plants as material, and demonstrating an etymology for the viridic. Working initially from "medium specificity" in art, as theorized by Clement Greenberg, I directly

FIGURE 4.4

"Eggs" (at front) and young hens in 1970, three years after planting (Courtesy of Royal Danish Academy of Art).

appropriate Gottfried Semper's model of the "tectonic" in architecture for plants, discovering that his model for material generally, rather than the tectonic specifically, fits plants and gardening. Semper's model links the properties of a material with the techniques of manipulating it, thus suiting the relationship between plants and gardening well, leading me to coin the term the viridic. Since Andersson was ostensibly a modernist landscape architect, I continue to use architecture's language of spatiality, and Rose's reflection on it, just as I used it in discussing the Miller Garden. However, with the viridic as a lens to look at how these spaces arose through a combination of design and maintenance over time, I discuss three different spaces and plant forms that all share the same structure and plants, a viridic effect that can be achieved only through maintenance. I conclude by arguing that it is not useful (indeed, it is disingenuous) to separate design and maintenance in talking about plants, and propose that the viridic must bring together prediction, in the planting design, but also adaptation, through maintenance practice. In order to do so, however, the viridic requires a different sort of practice, for which Andersson provides a model.

AN OPEN PLAN FOR THE FUTURE

Sven-Ingvar Andersson fused modernism and postmodernism, practicing in Denmark from the 1950s, working with Scandinavian modernist architects like Arne Jacobsen on the Rødovre Town Hall (1956), and then internationally on a number of well-known public projects outside Scandinavia, including Karlsplatz in Vienna (1971) and Museumplein in Amsterdam (1992). He studied botany and biology at Lund University and landscape architecture at the Swedish University of Agricultural Sciences, then worked as an assistant to Professor C. Th. Sørensen[17] at the Royal Danish Academy of Fine Arts, School of Architecture, Copenhagen, teaching there between 1963 and 1994.[18]

Following Sørensen, Andersson continued a significant modernist tradition of landscape architecture in Scandinavia which had always contained elements of the folkloric that would later seem postmodern, such as Sørensen's use of a "Moon Gate" in his project at Stokkerup (1934), a

circular portal through a mound that created a transition between sea and land, though the ellipse was a more common figure in both Sørensen's and Andersson's work.[19] Indeed, Andersson's "Letter from My Henyard" was published as a comment on Robert Venturi's *Complexity and Contradiction in Architecture* in a Danish architecture magazine in 1967, using his garden at Marnas to illustrate it.[20]

The garden was an important part of Danish landscape architecture, which had previously been called *havekunst* or garden art, without the negative associations that gardening acquired in English-speaking landscape architecture later in the twentieth century. Like Eckbo later, Sørensen also produced prototypical garden plans in his series of a hundred gardens, but in his hands they were actualized by the occupants and their gardening activities, unlike Eckbo's completed spaces for outdoor living. In his own garden, Andersson continued a tradition of Danish

FIGURE 4.5
Andersson's 1956 landscape for Arne Jacobsen's Rødovre Town Hall.

FIGURE 4.6
C. Th. Sørensen's Stokkerup (Moongate) (1934) in Copenhagen.

landscape architects who used their personal gardens as laboratories, including the proto-modernist G. N. Brandt. In *The Coming Garden*, Brandt "gave his profession a new dimension by combining academic matter-of-factness with a craftsman-like understanding of both nature and the possibilities of the material and the conditions for health and growth of the plants."[21] Andersson's own work in his garden at Marnas used this "craftsmanship" in his pruning to develop an ecological argument over time.

Born in 1927, Andersson was given the property at Marnas in 1957 by his family for his thirtieth birthday, and worked on it for nearly fifty years until his death in 2008 at the age of seventy-nine. The garden shares with the family's holiday house a 3,000-square-meter plot, of which half is a meadow, on Dalbyvägen, a road leading from Södra Sandby, near Lund in Sweden. Originally set in a purely rural context, the property is now sandwiched between a major road on one side and a bicycle path with adjacent townhouses on the other, with a high-tension power line nearby.[22] The design of the garden can be simply described. It is divided in two by a line of buildings: the original house, and a newer guest house. The buildings create a roughly one-third, two-thirds division, with the smaller third enclosing a grassed area with a summerhouse. The larger part of the garden, a series of garden rooms enclosed with hedges, is the focus, because a single species—common hawthorn (*Crataegus monogyna*)—is used in multiple forms to create multiple effects. The complex of garden rooms is divided longitudinally into three zones. One of these zones runs continuously along the length of the garden: the henyard, with its hawthorn trees cut into the shape of hens, the main feature of the garden. The other two zones are divided in three to create an irregular grid, one strip thinner and at an angle. This network of rooms and the hedges that define it are spatially very complex, despite a simple-looking plan.

Gardens change over time according to a dynamic relationship between design and activity. Predictions made in the initial planting plan are reflected in plant spacing, while improvised gardening activity modifies resulting plant growth. Although the planting design of the rooms or compartments at Marnas follows a rigid and consistent format,

FIGURE 4.7

Photograph of the henyard commonly used when the garden is discussed (Courtesy of Royal Danish Academy of Art).

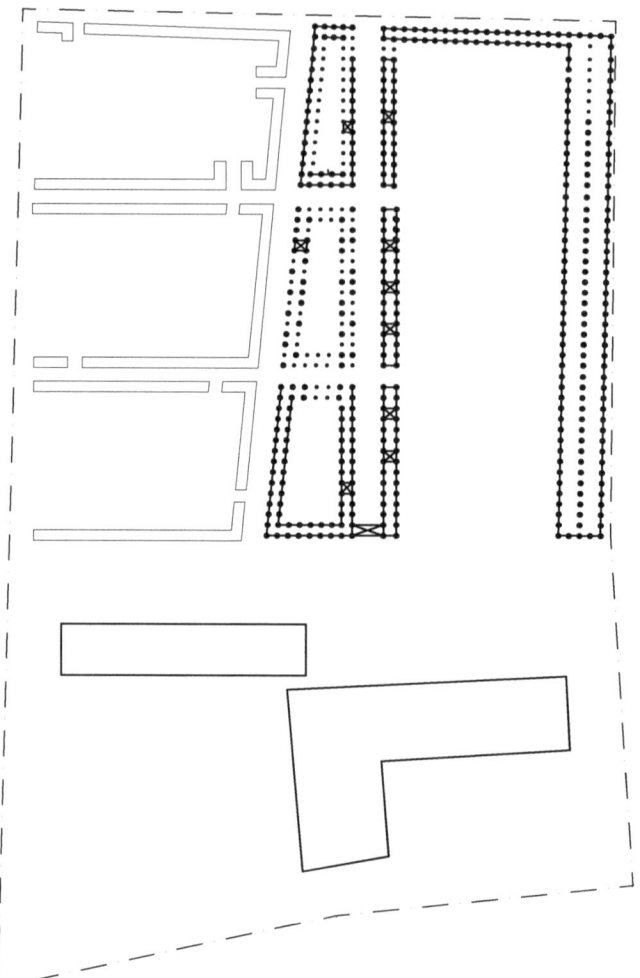

FIGURE 4.8

The hedges dividing the garden rooms are all planted at 500-millimeter spacing in double rows, but over time some plants have been removed (indicated with smaller dots) and others added or allowed to grow to fill gaps (indicated with crosses).

a.	Hønsegård (henyard)
b.	Hedgerow
c.	Løvgang (leafy passage)
d.	Passage
e.	Beatas have (Beata's garden)
f.	Solgård (sun court)
g.	Blomstergård (flower farm)
h.	House
i.	Outhouse and guest house

FIGURE 4.9

Plan of the Marnas garden.

Andersson always assumed that this rigidity allowed for variation between plants due to growth, according to his argument that "there are environments that are exciting because they permit a brilliant freedom against the background of a fixed feature in the landscape context or in the pattern of the plan."[23] With this principle in mind, Andersson set up the garden rooms to allow for transformation over time, but in the knowledge that "even if it just becomes a big mess, it won't be all bad. My confidence stems from two facts: the simple pattern of the planting [design] and the [plant] material, hawthorn."[24]

A planting plan specifying the location of plants is the result of a planting design process where the location specified is the foundation for subsequent growth, a kind of datum for each plant. While growth may take a range of different forms, the locations will not change unless a plant dies or is removed. Based on the plants' size at maturity, planting plans predict growth by specifying the spacing between them. However, the predictive model of growth used in the planting plan, which aims for a fixed-future mature condition, denies the very thing that makes such an idea unique: growth. Using an architectural drawing—the plan—forces a uniform projection of growth over time.

A landscape designer tends to see growth that varies greatly from the original prediction as a catastrophe. Growth cannot always be assumed, since plants are fickle and all different, as we saw with the Miller Garden, so changes should not only be both allowed for in the design and welcomed as serendipitous (which the *Oxford English Dictionary* defines as "the occurrence and development of events by chance in a happy or beneficial way"), but also cultivated through gardening. Andersson sought to balance design and accident in his plan for Marnas, observing that the design had a pattern that could "adapt to whatever serendipitous circumstances are introduced by myself and by time."[25] Since the plan of the garden does not change, it is the optimization of the serendipitous tendencies arising from growth through Andersson's gardening technique that has created the diversity of spaces in the garden, despite rather than because of the rigidity of the plan. Spirn recounts how Andersson described three actions in relation to plants in the garden: "What had volunteered, what to alter and what to leave."[26]

FIGURE 4.10

Hawthorn plants for garden "rooms" immediately after planting on March 5, 1964. All hedges were planted in one day, a public holiday (Courtesy of Royal Danish Academy of Art).

Andersson described the structure of the seven garden rooms as "a playground with a differentiated plan. Not with respect to traffic, but spatially."[27] By distinguishing between traffic and space, Andersson was acknowledging that while the circulation of the garden might appear simple and uniform, with clear corridors running between the garden rooms, the resulting spaces would be differentiated due to growth variation and his own maintenance. While the planting design for Marnas sets out a rigid structure against which change can occur and be registered, its consistency and rigidity create different microclimatic effects at the level of the garden room. The hedges were very closely planted (500 mm apart); their growth has had significant and varying effects on the plants themselves, and thereby the space they have created. These effects are produced by adjacent plants affecting the growth of their neighbors ecologically.

Andersson's side garden is relatively small, half taken up by the henyard, so the other six garden rooms have a premium on space, with a passage between each and hedges along each room edge and passage. While these hedges may have been small at the time of planting, they have become larger, and compress the spaces they edge. This compression has caused the hedges to shade themselves and their neighbors, in turn affecting their growth and the resulting shape of the hedges nearby. The hedges serve a dual function: they edge the rooms as interiors, and create a space between them for circulation. While Andersson was off the mark in his predictions for the henyard as a hawthorn grove, his concept of the way the passages would work approximates their current effects:

> In the in-between spaces between the rectangles lie many other possibilities. One immediately experiences them as the garden's negative parts, as the separation between those parts which mean something, as passages from the house out to the attractions and activities. But it could also be just the opposite: all the in-between spaces could be made into enclosed leafy passages. From the rectangles one could peek in at these wonders through openings in the hedges.[28]

A LANGUAGE FOR PLANTS

While Rose articulated a taxonomy of plant forms, I argued in chapter 3 that his taxonomy ignored growth, and the role of gardening in directing such growth. However, Andersson was interested in and involved with gardening, and its role in affecting the performance of plants spatially, as a landscape-architectural material. In discussing Rose, and now Andersson, I am developing a model of materiality unique to plants for landscape architecture, which necessarily must account for growth

Discussing Rose's and Kiley's work as research into plant material, Elizabeth Meyer suggests that landscape architecture should embark upon a consideration of plants equivalent to Clement Greenberg's analysis of modernist painters, "wherein artists sought to exploit the specific properties and logic of their medium,"[29] known as "medium specificity."[30] Greenberg suggested that under modernism, "what had to be exhibited was...that which was unique and irreducible in each particular art." Coined in his essay "Modernist Painting," the term "medium specificity" describes the taking "possession" of a "narrow area of competence" by "determining...through its own operations and works, the effects exclusive to itself."[31] Taking a reductive view, "Greenberg saw Modernism's acknowledgement of its medium as some form of materialist objectivity that this kind of painting shared with contemporary science."[32] Correspondingly, what became specific to painting was its raw materiality, its canvas, its frame, and the two-dimensionality that came with it, dislocating the role of the figure and the subject, making "the drumhead flatness of wall...a little fictive space in which so many figurative presences could be placed like actors."[33] The works that Greenberg used to illustrate medium specificity were interested in the immediacy of the painting as a material record of its making processes, such as those of Jackson Pollock.

If one were to immediately extend to landscape architecture this direct model—taking the outcomes of the discipline as they are, not what they represent—it would resemble architecture insofar as both make drawings, or simulations of a medium, as Krauss says.[34] For medium specificity, the buildings or landscapes that those drawings represent would be immediately rejected as representational figures, deferrals away from the materiality of the drawing; instead, perhaps, the technical drawing's conventions or marks would become its own graphic language, like the early drawings of Daniel Libeskind, perhaps cross-referencing each other, but at 1:1 scale.

On the other hand, gardening is nonrepresentational and immediate in the same way as painting, or even sculpture. If we take Greenberg's suggestion that we should "determine [gardening's medium specificity]...through its own *operations* and *works*, [and] *effects* exclusive to itself"[35] as a formula to examine the specificity of the medium, we end up with growth and its manipulation by gardening techniques.

The "works" of gardening are the same as the "work" of gardening, which, Ferrari notes—somewhat quixotically—"treats...the garden as the artwork that it is when it is an artwork."[36] This means that the "work" and "operations" of Greenberg's formula are the same: the practices of gardening, such as working with soil, planting, pruning, tending of plants, propagating. These are the "work," as in art*work*, because, as Ferrari argues, the garden is a composition with lives. This means that tending those lives and the physical work of the garden are the same. This is also a clue to the final part of Greenberg's formula: effects. The effect of gardening is clearly growth. When gardening is ineffective, plants die and there is no longer a garden. The similarity of Ferrari's idea of the garden as art to Greenberg's notion of medium specificity is even clearer, albeit expressed in more romantic prose, when he says: "there is something refreshing about a type of art that does not need to tease you with meaning in order to absorb you by its beauty."[37] Here he is arguing for the same type of directness that Greenberg locates in modernist painting.

Greenberg's and Ferrari's accounts apply to gardening rather than landscape architecture. However, while landscape architecture produces drawings, in a strict definition of medium specificity, the practice of landscape architecture that Andersson was pursuing in his garden at Marnas brings together the real-time actions of gardening with a reflection and judgment that come from landscape architecture. In discussing his garden here, as the bridge between case studies that rely on a practice of designing with plants and those that shape plants in a designerly way through gardening, I am arguing for a reformulation of landscape-architectural practice that combines the landscape architect and the gardener.

A model for such a hybrid practice might be the reformulation of medium provided by Rosalind Krauss, which focuses on the relationship between medium and memory, from her recent book *Under Blue Cup*. She suggests the aphorism "the medium is the memory," and insists on "the power of the medium to hold the efforts of the forebears of a specific genre in reserve for the present."[38] Krauss contrasts "Greenberg's specificity [which] is empirically tied to a physical substance" with her own approach in *Under Blue Cup*, which is "focused on the rules of the guild."[39] She argues that material is "a logical support [which] can substitute itself for a physical substance in founding the rules for a medium."[40]

Landscape architecture could be read as such a "logical support" for the activity of gardening, if one treats plant configuration as ecological. When Greenberg talks of "effects" of the medium, in the garden such effects cannot be separated from location. The location of plants in relation to each other creates a calibration between them with which gardening techniques (Krauss's "rules of the guild") interact. For example, as one plant shades another, it might be pruned to let in light for its neighbor. Configuration cannot be easily separated from technique in the garden, and as a discipline with configuration at its heart, landscape architecture offers a way of working with plant growth that is different from but also similar to gardening, if it is considered on the level playing field of ecological effect.

Krauss's idea of memory is similar to Gottfried Semper's notion of the tectonic, which could be adapted to landscape architecture to develop a type of "plant tectonics," which I am instead calling the "viridic." The contemporary interest in tectonics in architecture has been influenced by Kenneth Frampton's *Studies in Tectonic Culture*, which "seeks to mediate and enrich the priority given to space by a reconsideration of the constructional and structural modes by which, of necessity, it has to be achieved," calling the tectonic "a poetics of construction."[41] From this definition, the spatial ambitions of the discipline are aligned with how architecture is made. It is in terms of a similar alignment that I consider the idea of "plant tectonics" (though I give it a different name): to join space-making with gardening—using gardening to work with the change in plants due to growth to fulfill landscape architecture's space-making ambitions: ambitions which it has inherited from architecture, but where plants, I argue, inflect those ambitions uniquely.

Discussing Semper's contribution to tectonics, Frampton suggests that Semper's taxonomy was a challenge to Laugier's *Essai sur l'architecture*. Instead, Semper talked of "the tectonics of the frame" and "the stereotomics of the earthwork," exemplified by either *die Wand*, a screenlike partition of wattle and daub, or *die Mauer* [the wall], as a fortification.[42] Frampton says that the early Greek etymology of tectonics is *tekton*, which refers to the carpenter or builder; however, he later professionalizes the term, breaking its previous relationship to the trade of carpentry, because: "needless to say, the role of the *tekton* leads eventually to the emergence of the master builder or *architekton*."[43]

This professionalization moves the emphasis of *tekton* from the act of the carpenter as maker to the *tectonic* becoming an artifact, a representation of "constructionness," where the maker is anonymous: the result of the designer's decisions rather than the maker's techniques. When Frampton argues that Adolf Loos "embraced an atectonic strategy in that his spatially dynamic *Raumplan* could never be clearly expressed in tectonic terms,"[44] he seems to be arguing for a kind of modernism where the tectonic must be represented in a project. However, Frampton's version of the tectonic as artifact is quite different from that of Semper, from which he drew, in which the tectonic was one of a series of processes in a dynamic making relationship to the material.

The tectonic was one category in a study that Semper undertook to understand "the work as a result of the *material* used to produce it, as well as of the tools and *procedures* applied."[45] In this study he begins by defining categories of raw material which exhibit properties that lend themselves to certain uses. From these materials he extrapolates artistic categories that "require lesser or greater effort and technical procedures to make the raw material serve a definite purpose suited to its qualification." For example, he identified a raw material that was "pliable, tough [and] highly resistant to tearing" which was then allied to the art of "textiles." For Semper, "each of these technical divisions (e.g. textiles) has its own domain of forms whose production is the technique's most natural and most ancient task." If we compare this definition to Frampton's, we see that Semper's emphasis was on a dynamic tactile relationship, more like "the guild," as Krauss said, than Frampton's *architekton*. I am seeking the kind of fundamental relationship between plants and landscape architecture that the tectonic has acquired for architecture. However, since the tectonic is a particular material domain tied to the carpenter as a worker of wood, according to Semper's categorization, it is incorrect to speak of plant tectonics.

While logical names with a classical orientation might include derivatives of *hortus*, which focuses on the garden as a type, or *silva*, which concerns trees, neither denotes the quality of growth that, I am arguing, distinguishes plants as a material. In his history of the color green, Michel Pastoureau explores the Latin name for green: *virent*.[46] As in the English term "greenery," vegetation was *virentia*. Green also denoted growth in the Latin *viridesco*, a characteristic linked to the garden, which was a *viridarium*, and also to spring, which was *ver*.[47] Consequently, I am proposing a new term, *viridic*, in the place of tectonic, to refer to plant material in the sense of the word material that Semper used. In proposing that "[the] work [is] a result of the *material* used to produce it, as well as of the tools and procedures applied,"[48] he provides a plausible model for the *viridic*, which is a dynamic relationship between plant and gardener. For Semper there was a dynamic relationship between these three factors that can be neatly explained in relation to the hawthorns at the Marnas garden, which show how the viridic performs. While the materiality of textiles might seem self-evident, for Semper their essence was weaving and knotting, like the operation of molding for the plasticity of ceramics. Using this formulation, while the material of the viridic would seem to be leaves, it is in fact, as I have been arguing throughout, growth, the process by which leaves emerge. Andersson himself discusses this dynamic relationship between plant biology, human action, and resultant plant form when he observes: "the hawthorns permit enormous variation, from metre-high closely clipped to the freely growing 20-foot tree."[49] Correspondingly, there is no inherent shape to the plant apart from the way it is affected by external factors, such as the gardener.

When a branch is pruned, its apical meristem is removed. This makes it "bushier."[50] The pruning process is manipulated by spacing out actions in relation to growth periods and resultant desired growth. Particular pruning tools are used at particular times in relation to the growth period and development of resulting growth, as well as the volume of cutting required. Hedge clippers are used to cut new leaf growth rather than branches, cutting a mass of foliage at one time, resulting in the removal of many buds and much branching. Secateurs are used for smaller branches selected individually, as are pruning saws, but for bigger branches. Bigger branches result from choosing not to cut smaller leaves or branches at an earlier stage, in order to allow growth. This causes branches to thicken, requiring the use of a different tool and also a change in pruning aims and strategy: from working with a mass of foliage to working with individual branches. The tools used are linked to the times of activity in relation to growth between pruning intervals of particular apical meristems. The pruning tools thus represent moments in the growth story, because their selection is the result of timing decisions and previous guesses about future plant growth, in some cases necessitating a choice not to prune at a particular time, in the knowledge that at a later time a different tool will be required. This dynamic between the plant and the actions of the gardener using tools and procedures forms the base of this new Semperian category, the viridic.

In proposing the viridic as a category, I am adopting some of Greenberg's motives for defining medium specificity, but qualifying them on the basis of Krauss's suggestion that medium is memory. I am thereby linking the medium's specificity with the historic techniques of gardening, and the tools that have arisen from them. Since Semper's model came from an ethnographic analysis, it also refers to the traditions of manipulation ("the guild"), as we saw in the French garden, where form resulted from horticultural technique. Whereas in the French garden the technique is a system that is anonymous, in Semper's model the agent who wields tools and undertakes procedures is implied, as it is in Andersson's first-person description of the hens remaining hens only for as long as he can stand on the ladder holding the clippers.

FIGURE 4.11
Hawthorns as consistent and uniform mature hedges in 1982, prior to differentiation (Courtesy of Royal Danish Academy of Art).

PRUNED SPACE

If the viridic describes the gardener's direct intervention in the growth of material, then it could not be used to describe the work of landscape architects who, as Krauss argues, produce drawings. For spatial ambitions to result, configurative decisions must interact with gardening and cause growth, regardless of the representational nature of the drawing.

The Marnas garden is a useful case study for exploring the relationship between design and the viridic. Because the structure of the garden is uniform, insofar as it is comprised of a series of hedges of the same species planted at regular intervals, their subsequent differentiation demonstrates how spatial effects have changed due to the response of plants to pruning and resultant microclimates, in the kind of dynamic that Semper describes when he talks about the "style" of a material, in this case plants.

Being both defining elements for the room they enclose, and edging elements for the "in-between spaces," the hedges perform multiple spatial functions. The pruning of a single plant to perform both these functions demonstrates how garden maintenance can be used to transcend the planting plan predictions of growth made by plant location. It is also possible to look at the resulting growth from the density of the initial planting and see the effects that the plants have had on each other, not to mention the effects the changing plants have had on the garden rooms' functions.

In the discussion that follows, the resultant plant form of the garden rooms will be analyzed as the archaeology of previous growth and gardening moves over time, considering the plant morphology factors described above and the form of the plant as it was when I analyzed it. Wörle and Wörle state: "In a garden, a continuous coming into being and passing away can be observed. However, this innate dynamic also poses questions: when is a garden complete?"[51] The form of a garden at any given moment is provisional, because the garden is always growing. The gardener as observer is always linked to the analysis of a garden because s/he is also maturing while the garden is growing, and s/he and the garden are both at particular, ephemeral stages. This means that the experience of a gardener during a visit plays a significant in the subsequent shape of the garden.

Andersson makes an oblique observation in his "Letter" about manufactured products in late-1960s society that is pertinent to the way he saw his work in the garden at Marnas, noting that "our potential for shaping is [now] completely limited to combining finished things to form new wholes."[52] In contrast, the garden is a site of improvisation, unfinished and provisional, made rather of unfinished and unfinishing growing things. This is a paradigm shift from a view that the plant in the garden is an object at a point in time to one where the plant's shape at any time is a momentary instance in a continuum of active growth. The state of plants in a garden at any one moment relates to the previous actions of the gardener at a particular point in time, then the subsequent growth of the plants.[53] When the gardener returns, s/he reads this growth in relation to the plants' response, and acts again from the found condition. The pruned plant bears the scars of the previous actions, so one could speak of a plant's form as a record of those actions, but also, more importantly for design, as a record of formal decisions. In terms of the timing of actions in relation to the development of buds, it is possible to initiate a trend in the growth of the organism that, if left too long, can result in an undesired change. Such a trajectory in the plant's form may not be rectifiable according to the designer's original intentions. This may cause the designer to change the design in an interesting if unexpected way, serendipitously.

From this perspective, I will look at the garden as a record of Andersson's gardening actions in response to emerging conditions. From my observations of the garden I speculate on what happened, and when, from the evidence of the resultant plant growth, and the pruning actions on that growth. The three different areas I discuss show how the rigid planting has been affected by maintenance and by growth to demonstrate the role of gardening in giving Andersson his "differentiated plan" where one plant or planting has multiple spatial effects, guided by the action of the gardener, activated though the manipulation of plant biology, detailed in the introduction. The three areas of types considered—hedgerow, passage, and hedge (my names, not Andersson's)—reflect the progress of my visit from the north end of the site to the henyard, at the east, where a discovery in one part was checked against one element, then tested against the next element found. While these spaces and their sequence may not have been the most important to Andersson, the fact that all use the same species—hawthorn—and that each manifests it differently, despite similar planting configuration, means that comparison between them is instructive. As I will say in chapter 6, where I discuss site specificity in relation to the garden of poet Geoffrey Dutton, Druimchardain, if one accepts the premise that gardening is a real-time activity, experiences during activities like site visits can play a fundamental role in shaping inquiry and action.

THE HEDGEROW

The planting on the north boundary of the garden behind the henyard is a "hedgerow," a manmade structure comprising a "narrow belt of vegetation dominated by a variety of shrubs and trees separating one area of land from another."[54] According to its Anglo-Saxon etymology, *hega* means *haw*, from "hawthorn," the plant used at Marnas. The hawthorn is a common plant in hedgerows both in England and in Denmark. The word *hedge* is the same in English and Danish. Treib discusses the use of the hedge and the hedgerow in Danish landscape architecture: "the wind from the west blows strong and cold across Denmark; [something which] created the need for the hedgerow almost from the time of first settlement to comfort the people and protect the soil against erosion."[55]

Since it is our first area and element, it is worth unpacking the initial shaping process of the hedgerow. Removing the top shoot, known as the leader, with secateurs, results in the first side branching, creating a hedge. After reaching a certain distance from the plant, these side branches are then pruned back to a visible dormant bud. Once the plants grow into adjacent plants with too many branches to prune each plant individually, hedge clippers are used to work across the whole surface as a formal hedge.

While the planting on the north boundary is a hedge like the others in the garden, with the same spacing, it has a more naturalistic appearance due to changes in maintenance that allow it to self-regulate, developing a freely growing form. After strict initial pruning with hedge clippers,

FIGURE 4.12

Photographic elevation of the hedgerow, showing the rougher condition of the hedges at the back of the garden, which are clipped on the inside. The passage is entered from the first opening on the left.

an informal strategy has been used that aims to control the overall extent of the hedgerow and ensure that it remains dense, but is not formally consistent. Andersson anticipated this when he speculated about how high the hedges should be: "It's hard to clip them if they are over a metre and a half, but I would like to enclose the henyard a bit better, more for my own experience of the space than the need to keep the hens shut in."[56] Bulges in the hedgerow arise when woody branches have grown due to infrequent clipping. When a branch noticeably extends past the line of the hedgerow, it may be removed with an implement such as a pruning saw rather than hedge clippers or secateurs, which may take out the whole large branch and cut it back to the tree. Since this creates an opening for light, the adjacent branches and foliage grow into this gap. As this type of branch is removed, other bulges come into relief and gain visual dominance. This type of pruning is occasional, perhaps happening every few years, and might also be accompanied by a rough work-over of the hedgerow with hedge clippers to ensure density of leaves and re-branching for the next year. The same technique on the denser hedges is used: only the frequency is different. This allows plants to grow more and more diversely before the hedgerow is cut back again.

An early diagrammatic plan of the garden from 1967 also includes an elevation of the hedgerow which shows it as a firmly cut hedge, its top line kept level in opposition to the rising level of the topography, a question that Andersson also considers in his "Letter": "A position has to be taken on whether the tops of the hedges should follow the slope of the

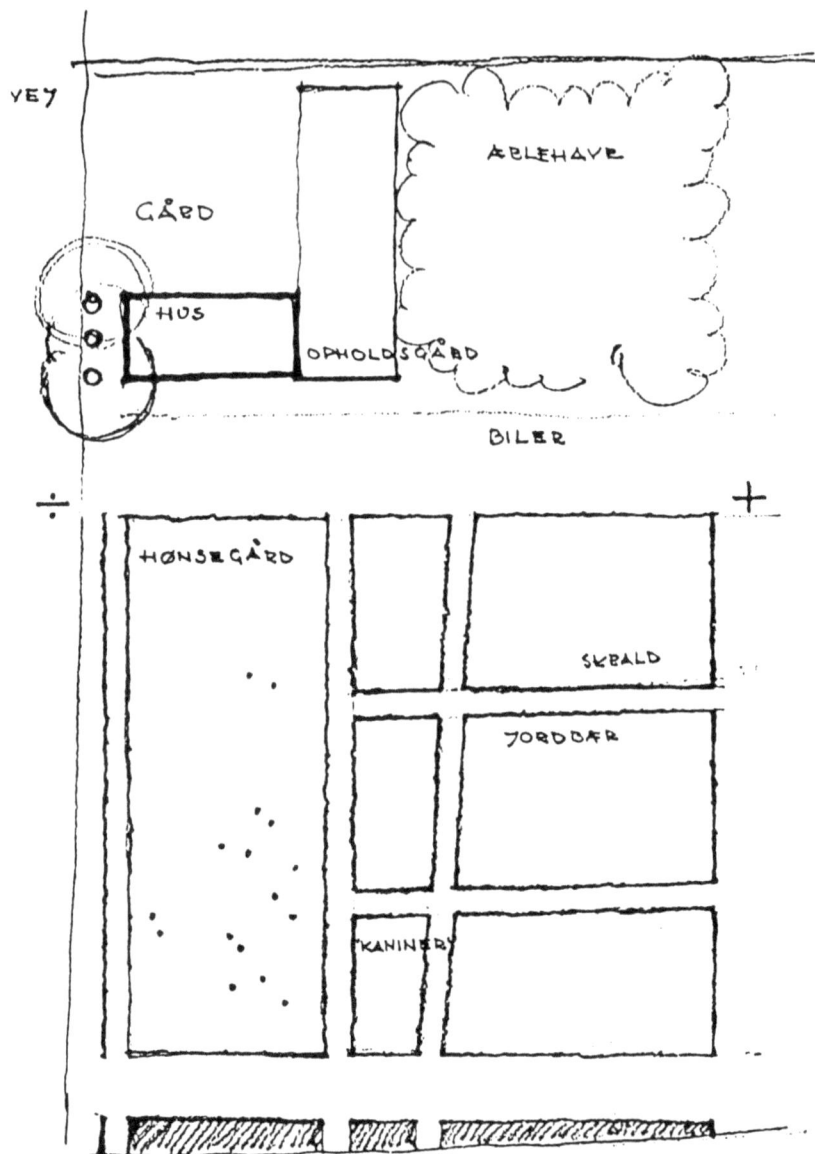

FIGURE 4.13

Early schematic plan (1960) shows the original intention for the rear hedgerow to be pruned level (Courtesy of Beata Andersson).

terrain or lie in a horizontal plane."[57] This rigidity is no longer evident, since the top the hedgerow has been allowed to grow naturally; Spirn suggested in conversation that this may be because there was previously a view of the meadow, now obscured by housing, removing the necessity to cut the top to retain the view.

Along Dalbyvägen, the hedgerows were planted in three rows at 500-millimeter centers, like the rest of the hedges, but each row is 1 meter apart, double the distance of the rest of the hedges in the garden. Due to the death of individual hedges within the lines, gaps arose, creating clear spaces. More space between the rows than along them has created an impermeable wall element outside the line, but also a room inside the hedgerow that is compressed but still accessible: a tight allée that emphasizes the length of this side of the garden, since the width is greater than the spacing. This contrasts with the plants along the north boundary, where the trees are at 500-millimeter centers, in two rows, also 500-millimeter, a grid rather than an allée formation. This difference in spacing suggests an intentional outcome, and indeed, when I discussed this element with Spirn, she directed me to photographs that show this interior of the hedge pruned open, creating an area that Andersson called the "leafy passage," demonstrating how changes in maintenance can transform a space completely.

While close spacing creates a mass of foliage quickly for hedging, the variation in spacing between rows causes plants to grow tall rapidly by stimulating competition between individuals. As plants grow, they begin to shade each other, which also suppresses side branching and emphasizes the growth of the top leaders. This competition has created a hierarchy in the hedgerow because as the trees have grown, some have pushed through to become treelike specimens while others have remained in the shrub layer. Where certain hawthorns have become mature, it is because they have "slipped through the net" of regular pruning, out of reach of the pruner. The density of the planting has meant that various individuals have been shaded out, have died, or are missing, with little effect on the overall hedgerow, which has begun to act as a self-regulating ecology. This interior effect is caused by pruning on the outside and the ecology of the planting density inside. The idea of pruning the outside of the hedgerow

to achieve an interior effect is interesting, creating a chaotic silhouette when light comes through it into the more open interior. Until my later conversation with Spirn, over a draft of this chapter, where she referred me to a photograph of the "leafy passage," I had doubted that Andersson ever intended that the interior of the hedgerow should be visited in the way I visited it.

This more casual pruning strategy has allowed the hedge to become a hedgerow, giving it a more diverse ecology than the other hedges. Other species have been allowed to colonize in the herb and perennial layer (a diversity common in agricultural hedgerows), including climbers such as ivy, and smaller flowering annuals. This is particularly true on the outside of the hedgerow, which is not shaded and blurs into the grassed strip behind. While the hedges that form the row were set out in the initial planting plan, it was gardening actions over time that caused it to develop into a hedgerow. Its character is the result of changes to the plants as a material, which were due to gardening rather than design, developing iteratively over multiple growing seasons.

PASSAGE AND ROOMS

Entering the garden from the north through one of two gaps in the hedgerow, one enters a passage, which runs alongside the henyard. If one inspects the plan and earlier photographs of the garden, it is difficult to appreciate the intricate network of spaces of which the henyard forms a part. Since a hedge encloses each garden room, a corridor develops between them. The use of a single hedge to edge one space and also define another in such tight dimensions is economical.

FIGURE 4.14
It is possible to get inside the hedgerow and examine planting locations, and how competition has caused them to grow.

FIGURE 4.15
The "leafy passage," the same space as figure 4.14, when it was still maintained as an interior inside the "wave hedge" (Courtesy of Royal Danish Academy of Art).

The hedges around the garden rooms define the rooms as interiors, each with its own internal thematic and pruning treatment. Since these rooms are adjacent, hedges form edges that define the passages with a different treatment on each side, derived from the treatment of the adjacent garden room. Even while the edges are inconsistent along their length, due to the different pruning regimes, the passages still have a spatial consistency. Proceeding from the hedgerow at the north, the henyard edge continues for the whole length of this passage on the east, finally deforming near the south end, while on the right each of the three different rooms has a different hedge treatment.

In general, a passage is formed from hawthorns that arc over the space, each having what is sometimes called in gardening literature "sculptural form," because their twisting trunks have been emphasized through pruning, leaving few lower leaves. These hawthorns are multi-trunked, allowing them to act together like a palisade wall, with numerous vertical trunks creating a visually penetrable grille or screen.

The first compartment along the passage, *Beatas have* (Beata's garden), is most affected by shade because it is behind the rear hedgerow, causing it to be sparse. It looks like a separate hedge, due to the disappearance of some plants in the middle row; however, it shares this edge with the hedgerow. The hawthorns have very thin and rangy trunks that act as supports for ivy, *Hedera helix*, to climb, leaving little trunk visible. The hawthorn is acting as a living climbing structure. The effect of the ivy changes the way one reads the hawthorns, compared to the other trunks that are not covered. Like a hedge, the ivy creates a surface, though as it grows and sags between trunks, it becomes curtain-like. The hawthorns that have become straggly due to the extreme shading in this part of the garden have been pruned by circulation as well as by the gardener. It is hard to imagine that this area was once a garden; however, earlier photographs, taken when the hedges were not yet grown, show its open character, with light beaming in so that the young Beata could grow plants. Perhaps Andersson allowed this change because the child grew into a woman, the space still scaled to her size as a child, no longer fitting the adult.

The second room, the *solgård* ("sun court"), has a more open interior without planting at either end. It is a seating area, slightly elevated by a step,

FIGURE 4.16

In *Beatas have* (Beata's garden) the hawthorns are thinner because they are heavily shaded, and gardening has emphasized this form, allowing ivy to use the trunks as support.

FIGURE 4.17

Beatas have in 1970, when it was still open enough to grow flowers (Courtesy of Royal Danish Academy of Art).

with a black cube for a seat. Because the room is open in the center, light penetrates into the interior causing the hawthorns to grow into it, arching from the passage. As in *Beatas have*, the hawthorns have numerous smaller trunks articulating the edge of the compartment, branching horizontally at 2 meters high, their form opposed to the low height of the opposite hedge along the henyard that allows light and views to come through to the center of the *solgård*. Below the hawthorns, privet (*Ligustrum sinense*) in irregular clumps is cut into tight balls. While the hawthorns in the first and second rooms have similar forms, the second room is more permeable, and defined by the trunks rather than a veil of climber.

As in *Beatas have*, the multi-trunked form of the hawthorns has developed as much from the resulting microclimate as it has through pruning intention. Early photographs show that initially all the dividing hedges in the garden were pruned the same, as hedges, which would have caused bifurcation of branches, but at some point these multiple branches must have been allowed to elongate. When the plants were allowed to grow further, and to get some length along the trunks, side branching may have been removed at this more mature stage using secateurs or a saw. As these trunks grew, selective removal of individual trees must have occurred, since the spacing is no longer consistently 500-millimeter. In general the pruning would pursue a strategy of retarding the development of small branches to keep trunks clear and leaves above. To prune for sculptural form is to deliberately choose to retain eccentric branch forms and remove consistent growth (the opposite of hedging), emphasizing the eccentric form emerging as the plant grows over time. Comparing the role of the initial planting plan and the gardening actions that followed, it is clear that both played a part. As a result of designing the garden room to be slightly larger, the hawthorns would grow into the gap due to phototropism, a hormonal desire to grow toward the light, but at the same time not close over it as the canopy does in the adjacent passage, revealing Andersson's canny spacing decisions, optimized through pruning.

The third compartment, *blomstergård* ("flower farm"), clearly demonstrates the deformation of the space and view as plants grow together and as geometries lose their rigorous form over time. The *blomstergård* is

FIGURE 4.18

In the *solgård* the hawthorns have been allowed to grow tall, but hedges of the adjacent rooms are kept low to allow views across.

FIGURE 4.19

The *solgård* as hedges were allowed to grow tall, before it had become shaded (Courtesy of Royal Danish Academy of Art).

FIGURE 4.20
Early photograph showing the hawthorns closely clipped to hedges along the passage which have since grown into a diverse range of plant forms.

FIGURE 4.21
Indicative section from henyard across the passage to the *solgård*, showing how the difference in spacing of the hawthorns in the passage and the *solgård* has created different levels of enclosure, resulting in different plant form.

edged by a high hedge comprised of different species, including notably beech (*Fagus* spp.) rather than hawthorns. This creates a distinct walled interior, the hedge pruned carefully to be dense and luxuriant, in contrast to the other two compartments, defined by the careful shaped form that allows views through the trunks. The *blomstergård* has an emphasis on foliage rather than trunks, and is closer in character to the henyard, which is also edged by foliage. This change of materiality—from trunks to foliage—affects the passage and begins to merge into the henyard, becoming a hedge which is stepped down to address both spaces. Over time, gardening activity has caused the end of the hedge to close the passage, varying from the initial planting plan. Wandering rows of *Buxus sempervirens*, also used to define the circular garden beds in the henyard, have been planted along the interior length of the compartment. As the *Buxus* have developed, they have grown into each other, and this in turn has affected the way they were pruned, the lines that initially shaped the hedges disappearing into a topiaried mass.

A long visual axis starts at the *blomstergård* which is cut into the hedge at end of the room in the form of a portal, then continues along the open middle *solgård* and into the back of the first room, *Beatas have*. Without any change to the planting plan configuration, the view axis has been created by being repeatedly cut into the hedge by Andersson. There is evidence that this view line developed over time, rather than in the initial planting plan, because the 1960 plan shows an enclosing hedge all around both the *solgård* and the *blomstergård*, while they are now open. The view gap in the end of the *blomstergård* demonstrates

FIGURE 4.22
The hedge surrounding the *blomstergård* includes multiple species and has been allowed over time to close off the passage, departing from the original design.

FIGURE 4.23
Inside the *blomstergård*, smaller hedges have grown together, making a general topiary mass.

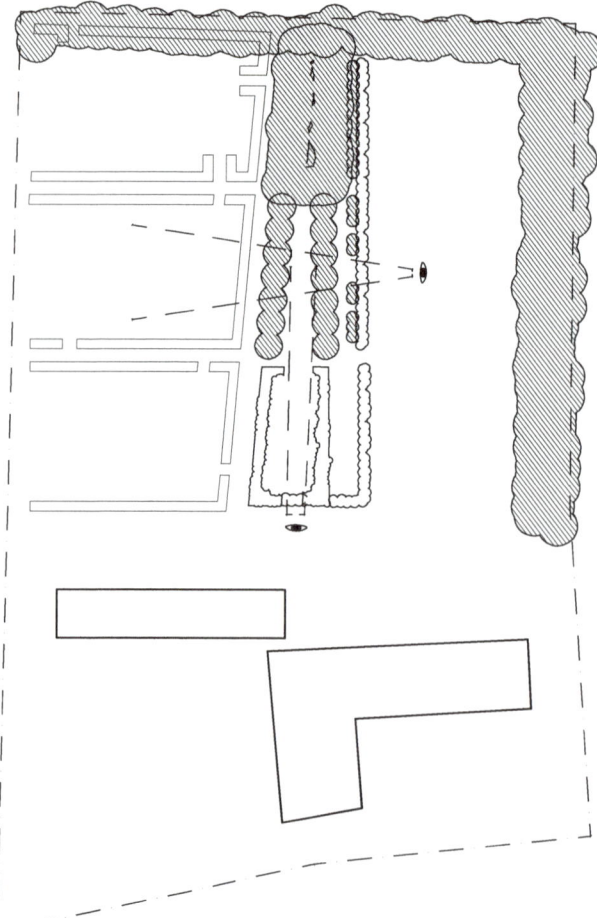

FIGURE 4.24

The hedge enclosing the *blomstergård* is the tallest in the garden and has been cut to provide a portal, by also manipulating the other two compartments behind it.

FIGURE 4.25

Plan showing the views through the various rooms that have developed through gardening activity.

how a major design axis in the garden has been developed and maintained over time with a combination of the removal of individual plants and a use of pruning possible only through gardening, with no change in plan.

THE HEDGE

The sophistication of Andersson's design is the use of plants both to define a particular space and to provide material and formal effects to other adjacent spaces. Pruning treatments in the Marnas garden differ depending on which side of the plant addresses which room or design relationship, with reference to orientation and circulation. Since the entire structure is provided by hedges, hedges are used to edge or wall rooms throughout the garden, most intensely in the henyard, and their surface pruning treatments are oriented to the space they address. Individual plants have multiple spatial effects depending on the way different parts of the plant were maintained in relation to the space each side of the plant addresses. Studying the group of plants that makes up the hedge between the henyard and the passage shows how one plant has been cut in multiple ways to serve a number of different spatial functions. When this hedge addresses the circulation space of the passage, it does so through transparency of trunks rather than a wall of vegetation, while on the henyard side plants have been regularly pruned with clippers to maintain lush foliage—a true hedge treatment.

The hedge that constitutes the edge of the henyard steps down, changing a number of times when it is viewed from the interior. From behind the hedgerow it begins as a consistent hedge of hawthorn, and as one progresses up its length toward the top of the henyard it gets greener as other species have colonized the hedge, such as beech, which has softer foliage. The paths that cross between the compartments penetrate the hedge, allowing access to the henyard, so that a third of the way along its length a stretch of hawthorn has been pruned to create an opening to walk through, which in turn then steps down to mid-chest height. This pruning maneuver creates interesting organizational effects for the room system. As the hedge steps down, a view across is possible from the henyard through the *solgård* and into the far compartment

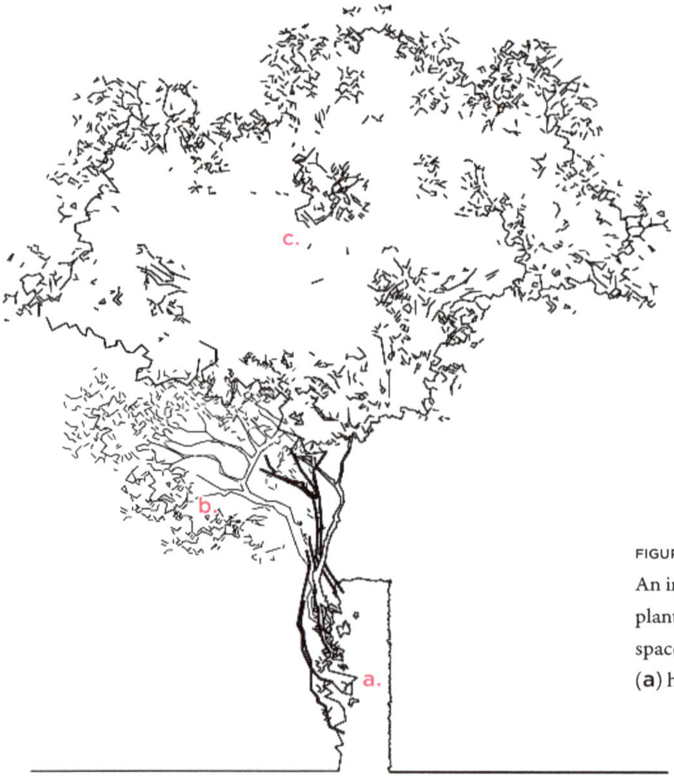

FIGURE 4.26

An indicative section showing how a single plant can have multiple forms according to the space a part of it addresses, and how it is pruned: (**a**) hedge; (**b**) shrub; (**c**) small tree.

FIGURE 4.27

Photograph from henyard into *solgård* showing how the hedge along the edge of the henyard has been pruned to allow views into the *solgård*.

in the furthest third row of garden rooms, each through a step down in the hedges between. Together with the long view down through the *blomstergård* to the other rooms, these views reveal the complexity of the spatial organization, and are made possible only by modifying the plants' form through pruning, without any change in consistency of plant location.

Hedging favors lots of small branches bearing leaves at the top of the branch. Each pruning cuts into these leaves and also into the small stems, which produce new denser shoots quickly. Over time some hedge plants can become too woody and may have to be cut back hard to prepare new dense branching, depending on how predisposed a plant is to shoot from latent buds. For the hawthorn, small side branching seems to develop easily from buds under the bark: even in old branches, with lots of small branch growth along heavier structural branching that provides the overall outline and support for the shape. This type of growth

FIGURE 4.28

As one looks from the path into the henyard from the passage, the hedge covers the entry, its carefully trained branching visible in silhouette from outside.

pattern occurs where the hawthorns in the hedge have been cut and trained to allow for access to the henyard from the path between *Beatas have* and *solgård*. As one views the hedge from the passage where it enters the henyard, the structure of the branching is dominant, with little density of leaves; this results in an intricate view of branching as light comes through the hedge from the henyard. This is because the hedge is shaded from this direction. As in *Beatas have* and *solgård*, the larger microclimate that results from the planting design decisions has affected plant growth and caused visual and spatial effects, which may not have been anticipated but were made the most of through subsequent gardening activity.

Another section of the hedge between the henyard and the passage further demonstrates that multiple spatial effects can be created by different methods of pruning a single plant. Where it faces the henyard, the hedge is lush and covered with leaves, and while it contains segments of other species, its structure is still a hawthorn plant from a single 500-millimeter-wide hedge. Since it is pruned with hedge clippers to produce a consistent vegetated surface, none of its branching structure is visible from the inside the henyard, which appears to be continuously green as a result of its orientation, a background to the overall room structure. On the other side, however, an entirely different result has arisen because of different spatial aspirations, but also because of the microclimate and the character of the adjacent space, *Beatas have*. Oriented to the passage, the rear structure of the same hedge is visible as a number of vertical branches, with side branching facing toward the light on the other side of the henyard. Since the structure of the passage is branching, in order to create a canopy with arching forms, it is clear that branches of the same plant have different results for different orientations. Both types of surface, green hedge and leafless branch structure, are present, but the material finish suits the character of each orientation. Much of the maintenance in the passage would be self-regulating, as its shading prohibits too much additional growth away from the trunks that drive upward to the light. On the other hand, the inside of the henyard is maintained so that there is always plenty of juvenile foliage through constant clipping, while the passage relies on woodier

mature growth. These two different vegetation treatments on the same plant are accompanied by a third: the full small tree emerging through the canopy where clippers cannot reach.

CONCLUSION

The range of novel spatial effects that result from intervention into the growth of a single plant demonstrate that the viridic relies on latent potentials, or trajectories, that reside in the dynamic relationship between the plant, expressed in its DNA, and the environment, which includes the gardener. Andersson admits that the range of possible growth habits of the hawthorns is not infinite: "But not beyond those limits which lie in being a hawthorn, which means that every single cell, whether it sits in the roots or in the skin of the fruit, has a predetermined number of chromosomes[58] with a particular set of genes, which can vary a little bit and give each plant its unique individuality, yet still ensure similarities in form and mode of meeting external conditions."[59] He describes plant form as a two-way process: the specificity of the organism, expressing itself outwardly as form; and the impact of the environment, in this case the gardener, shaping the organism, pushing into it. This difference could be said to come from two different directions (inside or outside the organism), on two different scales (cellular scale or organism scale), and in two different time periods (the life of the individual, versus the change of a species over millennia).

FIGURE 4.29
The foliage of the hedge on the inside of the henyard is lusher, and has been pruned to be dense without revealing branching, with a mix of hawthorn and beech.

FIGURE 4.30
The other side of the hedge in figure 4.29, along the passage, has less foliage and a more upright form due to microclimate and pruning, demonstrating how a single plant can have multiple forms.

For the viridic, these are the limits of "hawthornness," and how the different techniques of the gardener cause a species' propensity to be one way or another. Insofar as Andersson was using pruning to create certain forms, in his terms he was catalyzing latent genetic potentials through hormonal responses. However, even as there can be differentiation, a hawthorn is always a hawthorn, not an oak. This sense of a limited range of possibilities corresponds to the way Andersson saw the possibilities resulting from the pruning of the hawthorns at Marnas.

These trajectories call into question the accuracy of prediction and specification in landscape design, since there can be great variations between individuals of a certain species that give the plan a certain waviness compared to its architectural counterpart: one that the gardener, rather than the landscape architect, is better at directing. Without a practice informed by the idea of the viridic, particular formal or aesthetic effects cannot be achieved through design alone, since, while they are latent in the original design, without gardening they could easily be missed. Located at the center of this book, Andersson's garden is a useful balance between a strong design as a starting point and an ongoing practice that makes it different from the way it began.

PART II

GARDENING DESIGN

CHAPTER 5

A MOVING WORK of ART

SOMBRAL GRAZIELA BARROSO

WHILE MODERNISM in landscape architecture remains of historical interest in the development of the profession, the contemporary landscape architecture of "the process discourse" disavows its compositional nature. Reacting to architectural modernism, avant-garde postmodernism in the 1980s drew from other creative disciplines, such as film, to generate design via automatist processes that bypassed the compositional but nonetheless had a rationale. The most celebrated of these was Bernard Tschumi's Parc de la Villette, which combined grids, lines, and biomorphic strips to arrange park activities.[1] The utilization of design generation processes since La Villette has worked on the basis that an idea must be represented in a process that is additive, utilizing collage, superimposition, and hierarchy to create a composition in which these ideas are assumed to be embedded. As software with layers has become ubiquitous, this process has become automatic and increasingly quasi-scientific. While postmodernism looked to artistic methods to appropriate these techniques, this creative root has been sacrificed to technology in the process discourse which now imbues them with a scientific rationale, notably since the advent of parametric design and landscape urbanism.

FIGURE 5.2
The gate into the walled 1.4-hectare shade house
at the Sítio Roberto Burle Marx.

One might imagine that modernist landscape architect Dan Kiley, whose work was based on a functional diagram, would be a precedent for a scientific interest in design. It is surprising, then, that Brazilian modernist landscape architect Roberto Burle Marx is currently the most celebrated of all the modernist landscape architects,[2] since his work is so blatantly compositional. Both Burle Marx and Oscar Niemeyer were influenced by the biomorphic tendencies in Le Corbusier. Niemeyer said that Burle Marx "paint[ed] with plants."[3] Despite the process discourse's rejection of the compositions of modernism, Burle Marx is the exception, and I argue that this is because his apparent "organic-ness" seems in synch with the emergent organic language of biomimicry, parametricism, and ecological services. The process discourse uses ecology and its patterns to organize form, but regards form as an expression of process. The fact that Burle Marx is a precedent demonstrates that, regardless of the processes themselves, only certain types of formal outcomes are acceptable to the process discourse, notably the biomorphic. Even if many contemporary projects do not reflect this scientific interest, Burle Marx's characteristic chamfered polygons can be seen everywhere in celebrated contemporary landscape architecture, from Sydney to Copenhagen.[4]

Sima Eliovson has said that Burle Marx's gardens are "meant to create movement ... of people ... directed ... through plants."[5] Contemporary use of this type of geometry represents "dynamism," another analogy linked to the process discourse and the flexibility of natural systems. This same type of geometry also seems analogous to ideas in contemporary cultural discourse such as mobility and flows of information,[6] an interest that was also part of modernism, with its fetishization of vehicular movement, for example by the futurists. As the type of geometry that Burle Marx used has become common, its deployment follows the same rationale as the modernist functional diagram, but is described in terms of *flows*. The fact that Burle Marx had an interest in science (notably botany) suggests a scientific rationale for compositional decisions.

With an expectation of gaudy planting design and biomorphic ground pattern, I was surprised when I visited Burle Marx's own garden, the Sítio Burle Marx, to see that it was very much a garden, a collection of plants, rather than a showcase for his characteristic compositions. When

I saw a huge nursery and a myriad of small spaces set in forest, as a gardener I could appreciate his curatorial—or, rather, botanical—agenda, particularly in his large collection of aroids. Reading about the garden later, and interviewing people who collected plants with him and worked for him, I was struck by how literally experimental the garden was, even as it was obviously compositional in parts. While the increasing scientism in the process discourse may disavow the compositional in favor of the generated, the ecological rather than the aesthetic, it was clear that Burle Marx was able to maintain an interest in both without any cognitive dissonance.

In making a case for the viridic in chapter 4, I critiqued planting design convention because, I argued, it does not account for growth, the process from which all the qualities that concern planting design arise. The qualities of growth that are used for aesthetic reasons occur because of the practices of the gardener over time. At Marnas the plan was set down in advance; however, gardening modified the plants, but not the plan, as the plants grew. At the Sítio, as in the gardens in chapters 6 and 7, decisions were made at eye level, without a plan, on an ongoing basis, as an improvisatory practice; this has contributed to its being described as a laboratory, since such improvisation is a kind of testing.

In the context of the process discourse, it is not surprising that the idea that a garden can be a place for experimentation and learning, a laboratory, should gain prominence. Burle Marx described the Sítio Roberto Burle Marx as a laboratory,[7] saying that while he had made many gardens for others, he didn't have one because the Sitio was a laboratory, not a garden.[8] With this in mind, after describing Burle Marx and the Sítio, I look at the way he worked with plants there using an essay by the Sítio's previous director, Roberio Dias, as a form of evidence. Dias, professor of landscape architecture at the Universidade Federal do Rio de Janeiro (UFRJ) and director of the Sítio between 1995 and 2011, has written most extensively about the Sítio, calling it "a landscape laboratory." In a polemical fight with the managing authority, Dias argues that the Sítio is not a museum but a laboratory. Burle Marx was both an artist and a gardener, neither of which was mutually exclusive. Despite the fact that Burle Marx used the term, calling it a laboratory separates his botanical from his aesthetic interests, whereas both were actually united, part of a single practice. Sally-Ann Murray talks about a visit by Burle Marx to Durban in South Africa, where the local gardeners made their gardens into tropical extravaganzas *à la* Brazil, upon which Burle Marx was said to ask: "But why not use your own native plants?"[9] Undoubtedly Burle Marx's language of plant material came with the indigenous plants he used; however, the aesthetic qualities of those plants are still part of that language. One can test aesthetic ideas in the garden at the same time as one tests requirements for plant growth; indeed, keeping them connected is a key component of the viridic. Since the separation of the scientific from the aesthetic is a fundamental criticism I make of the process discourse, I am using the Sítio as an opportunity, perhaps even a proxy, to develop my critique, and for the sake of a broader discussion of the garden as a testing site, as much as to discuss the Sítio *per se*. As Dias rightly pointed out to me, to this end I am exaggerating the definition of the laboratory as scientific to make it a "straw man" (the creation of something to take down) to argue for the relationship between the scientific and the aesthetic, and the nature of the places where each occurs: a discussion that is valuable for developing the viridic as simultaneously scientific and aesthetic.

While he was not specifically interested in the scientific, Burle Marx was nonetheless interested, as a collector, in the botanical aspects of plants, and as a gardener, in the horticultural science required to make them grow, albeit by default. These "scientific" interests were in service of, rather than in opposition to, the aesthetic. Correspondingly, I suggest that the Sítio is a different kind of place in which tests are also made, but by the artist or designer: a studio. After introducing Burle Marx and the Sítio Roberto Burle Marx via Dias, I focus on the way Burle Marx thought about using plants in both his garden and his design. I explore the conventional language of planting design, and find that its way of describing Burle Marx's planting in terms of "color" and "contrast" is deficient. In defining the viridic as being about growth, I am also arguing that working with growth is a creative, not simply a horticultural, exercise. The Sítio demonstrates that the viridic comprises both. Correspondingly, I examine the aroids—the Sítio has one of the largest collections of this type of plant, and they feature prominently in Burle Marx's design—in terms of both the creative and the botanical. I use the model of "plant functional type" to look at biological properties in relation to the aesthetic qualities that plants provide. I conclude the chapter by arguing that a language of the viridic must merge the aesthetic and the scientific—since without an understanding of biology, any aesthetic use will be impossible, because the plant must grow to exhibit aesthetic qualities—and demonstrate how that link can be theorized in relation to a reinvigorated planting design. With this synthesis, I argue that the garden as a site for exploration of the viridic is both a laboratory and a studio, a space for the operationalization of scientific knowledge to achieve aesthetic aims.

LEARNING IN THE GARDEN

Roberto Burle Marx (1909–1994) was "an autodidact regarding botany, [since] his education had been in arts and humanities,"[10] who preferred "gardener" to "landscape architect."[11] Although he was born in São Paulo, Brazil, his father was from Germany. Roberto studied painting in Berlin between 1928 and 1930, regularly visiting the Berlin-Dahlem Botanical Garden, examining its collection of Brazilian plants. While at art school in Rio de Janeiro he was taught by modernist Brazilian architect Lucio Costa, seven years his senior and his neighbor during his childhood, for whom he created his first professional garden in 1932. Costa, who worked extensively with both Oscar Niemeyer and Burle Marx on Brasília, described Burle Marx as "a musician who makes music with plants."[12] Despite—or perhaps due to—working so extensively with architects, "Burle Marx [exhibited] a rare combination of artist and plantsman, having an architectural understanding, yet never being so dominated by structures that he forgets his plants in their endless variety."[13]

While his first nursery was at a small family farm in the Leme district of Rio,[14] Burle Marx acquired an 80-hectare property in the Barra de Guaratiba outside Rio with his musician younger brother Siegfried, the Sítio de Santo Antônio de Bica, in 1949, and lived there from 1974 until his death in 1994.[15] He gave 40 hectares of the property to the Instituto do Patrimônio Histórico e Artístico Nacional / Ministério da Cultura (IPHAN) in 1984.

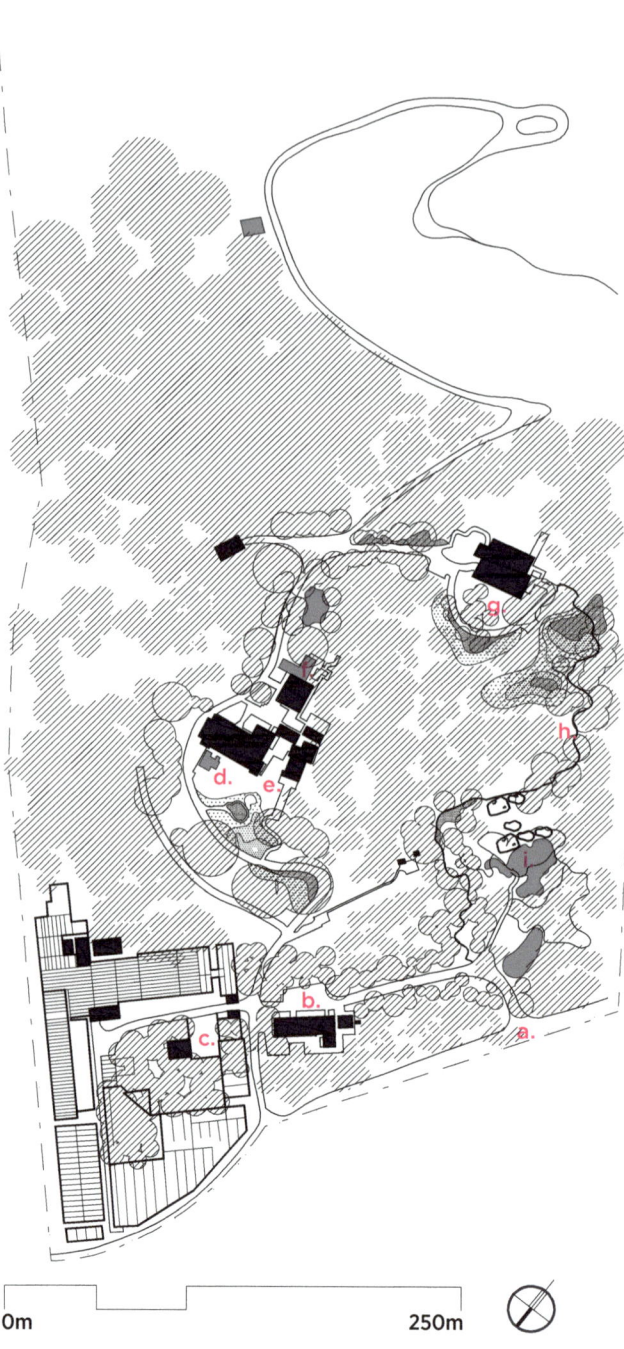

FIGURE 5.3

Plan of the Sítio Roberto Burle Marx.

FIGURE 5.4

The avenue from the entry to the Sítio to the administration buildings, where the tour commences, adjacent to the Lago, where it ends.

A visit to the Sítio, which is located on a hillside, comprises a circuit from the bottom to the middle of the site and back. Since the tour is the primary mechanism of raising funds for the garden, the importance of the route cannot be overstated, though its invention by previous director Dias was contentious, because it had not come from Burle Marx himself. The path features numerous instances of characteristic "Burlesque-Marxist" plantings, as Montero called Burle Marx's style of planting design.[16]

Before commencing the tour, the visitor drives or walks from the front gate along an elegant, informal paved avenue to the current administration buildings, which feature modern structures providing niches for bromeliads, reminding one that Burle Marx was an innovator ahead of his time, considering the current popularity of "greening" structures, like green walls and green roofs.

The first stop on the tour is the 1.4-hectare shade house, which, together with the garden, accommodates over 3,500 different species of plants. The Sítio is regarded as one of the world's most significant individual collections of plants, particularly due to its representation of the Araceae, Bromeliaceae, Cycadaceae, Heliconiaceae, Marantaceae, Arecaceae, and Velloziaceae families, in both the shade house and the garden. The Sítio has over 430 species of *Philodendron*. Burle Marx as a collector is commemorated in the naming of *P. burle-marxii*, as well as *Heliconia*, in *H. burle-marxii*.[17] In an inventory of the Sítio, Romão et al. show that "the collection organized by Roberto Burle Marx, preserved at the Sítio Roberto Burle Marx, totaling 106 families, 381 genera and 806 species, surpasses by several orders of magnitude the data available to the official collections, both American and Brazilian."[18]

From the shade house the road switches back up the hill. As one emerges from the forest, one crosses a succulent planting of different *Agave* spp. on a sunny bank to access the house complex and its chapel. The house complex comprises the original eighteenth-century farmhouse for the Santo Antônio da Bica farm, and its chapel, Capela de Santo Antônio,

FIGURE 5.5
Administration buildings with a prototypical "green wall" element designed by Burle Marx.

FIGURE 5.6

Numerous species of the family Araceae occupy the shade house.

FIGURE 5.7
A characteristic planting using succulents such as *Agave* spp. on a bank below the house.

both constructed of stone and lime cement, with ceramic tile roofs.[19] His father being Jewish and his mother a Brazilian Catholic, Burle Marx had a significant collection of religious art, making the chapel, restored with the help of Lucio Costa, an important part of the existing site. Burle Marx's house is next to the chapel, and its veranda edge to the garden is an important space in the garden's history, since beneath it Burle Marx enjoyed Sunday lunches with numerous guests and colleagues; recollections by participants of his spontaneous extemporizing provide much of the unpublished theory attributed to him. Beside the veranda is a lawn, with a pond and water feature which incorporates old stone elements, with plants growing on them, creating the feeling of a ruin. This area is the most photographed part of the Sítio in books on Burle Marx.

FIGURE 5.8
The historic chapel, Capela de Santo Antônio, next to the house where Burle Marx lived.

FIGURE 5.9
Burle Marx used to have regular Sunday lunches with colleagues, friends, and guests under the veranda of his house, Casa de R. Burle Marx, next to a faux-ruin water feature, the most photographed part of the Sítio.

Behind the house, edging the transition between its open, sunny slope, with its succulents, and the rainforest that extends up the hillside, is a large cantilevered concrete canopy called Cozinha de Pedra, or "stone kitchen." While the structure has had consistent problems, and was under renovation on both occasions when I visited the garden—in 2010, and then in 2015—it nonetheless constitutes a remarkable space. The roof structure changes into a pergola, Pérgula de Flor de Jade, that seems to surround buttressed tree roots, making the building complex seem like a prosthetic for the forest. Leaving the house complex, the tour returns to the road that switches back up the hill and moves into the forest, where the difference between garden and forest becomes difficult to determine, due both to the use of rainforest species like climbers, ground covers, and palms in a rainforest microclimate for ornamental reasons, and the naturalization of Burle Marx's collection.

At the top of the part of the garden visible to the public on the tour is Burle Marx studio or Atelier, which is now used as an exhibition venue for the Sítio. This building is clad with a reconstructed seventeenth-century Portuguese granite façade, which Burle Marx had rescued from demolition in Rio. From this point onward, the tour moves onto a path, called the "Trilha Trapézio," created by Roberio Dias while director for security, that also allows the tour to be a circuit, looping back to the beginning. This path effectively opens up parts of the Sítio that were never intended for viewing, with an elegant concrete stepping-stone arrangement. While the path was clearly Dias's invention, in my interviews with Dias he said he would respond to novel situations at the Sítio on the basis of his understanding of Burle Marx gleaned from working in his office. This is true also of the characteristic plantings on this route down toward the

FIGURE 5.10
Behind the house a concrete canopy that has had structural issues, Cozinha de Pedra, and pergola, Pérgula de Flor de Jade, reach out into the forest.

FIGURE 5.11
The road continues into a lush garden behind the house, the edge between the garden and regenerating forest blurred.

FIGURE 5.12

The Atelier, now used as an exhibition venue, marks the point at the top of the site accessible from the tour, which then begins to descend back to the entry.

path to the Lago (lake). Although this part of the tour was not created by Burle Marx himself, I nonetheless found it experientially the most dramatic and exciting regardless of authorship, though, as we shall see, the question of authorship would later be directed at Dias. Perhaps the most exciting moment on the tour is where the path switches back above the Lago and there is a view through the forest out of the site, edged by a large rock which was a major factor in Burle Marx acquiring the land, with another rock in the foreground on which lives a carefully composed collection of cacti, like a site-specific artwork.

The path finally arrives at the Lago, which I will describe in more depth later. Although it was reconstructed by Dias,[20] the Lago is one of the few planting designs at the Sítio that can be firmly attributed to Burle

FIGURE 5.13

Built by Dias when he was director, this beautiful path "in the style of Burle Marx," or "how Burle Marx would have done it," cuts through the back of the garden to the Lago.

FIGURE 5.14

Another characteristic planting using "correlated textures" installed by Dias on the return path.

FIGURE 5.15

Just before it reaches the Lago, the path provides one of the few views out from the Sítio, over a rock colonized by cactus, initially installed by Burle Marx.

FIGURE 5.16

The Lago, one of the few plantings definitively undertaken by Burle Marx at the Sítio, composed by eye from a truckload of species collected during one of his botanical expeditions.

Marx, who indicated exactly where these plants, a range of different species of aroid, should be situated as they were unloaded from the truck after one of his plant-collecting trips.

The idea that the Sítio is a type of laboratory is often discussed in the literature about it, including writing by Burle Marx himself, who claims: "This site [the Sítio] is the source of my experience in landscape architecture."[21] Imbert describes the Sítio straightforwardly as a "laboratory for the collection, study and growing of native plants,"[22] while Montero says that the Sítio had a didactic role for clients: "[Burle Marx] built up a pioneering laboratory which, as well as supplying plants for his gardens, provided the public with previously unknown species, stimulating a new demand"[23] As well as his botanical activities, Burle Marx "valorized" native plants, "enabling the transformation of a large part of [Brazil's] biodiversity into plant genetic resources."[24] His work might even be regarded as propagandist; Fraser argues that this arose from his lifelong belief in socialism,[25] shared with his frequent collaborator, Niemeyer. Burle Marx believed that "a garden must have didactic qualities. From a garden one can teach many lessons, and encourage people to live better."[26]

Dias's essay "O Sítio Santo Antônio da Bica: um laboratório paisagístico" is essentially a response to an argument as director with the managing agency, IPHAN, concerning the nature of the Sítio. There is more to this disagreement than there might seem to be on the surface. Parts of it concern provenance: whether the plants were endemic or not. Other parts concern the "look" of the Sítio: whether it does or doesn't look like other Burle Marx projects. Still other parts concern whether Burle Marx himself was actually involved in the newer parts. In essence, the argument between Dias and IPHAN concerns change, because the growth of a garden destabilizes ideas about authorship. Instrumental in suggesting that the site be preserved, Dias was clear that the Sítio was not a museum but a place of experimentation and learning, as Burle Marx suggested. For Dias, this means that—paradoxically—to preserve it was to allow it to continue to change. IPHAN, on the other hand, wanted to leave it as close as possible to the way it was when Burle Marx died, largely as a result of protestations from gardeners who continued to work there, who claimed that Dias was changing the site too much in line with his own intentions.²⁷ Dias, who worked with Burle Marx and talked with him extensively, ripostes that he "does things how Burle Marx did them."²⁸ In effect, he is arguing that the Sítio is a process or type of practice rather than a product, its physical condition simply the result of tests that were undertaken, many of which, according to him, have failed.

While Dias has called the Sítio a laboratory, I would argue with him fundamentally by suggesting that the artist's studio is a better way of thinking of both how the Sítio was used by Burle Marx and, more generally, of it as a model for the garden as a creative, testing space, not separate from but united with empirical testing.²⁹ I agree with Imbert when she says: "if Burle Marx is to be viewed as a landscape artist—one in control of the design and natural environment—his gardens should not merely be described as in 'resonance, harmony or contrast' with architecture, but as ecological systems."³⁰ In discussing the garden as an artist's studio, I am joining the ecological to the aesthetic, since without the ecological the plant would not grow, and there would be no aesthetic qualities.³¹

The concept of learning via testing is important to both the laboratory and the studio, so the definition of the garden as one or the other may seem trivial. However, I would argue that such a definition is key to positioning the acts of the gardener as not simply horticultural but creative; furthermore, it brings together the aesthetic qualities that plants exhibit and the gardener's work in growing them. When I talk about qualities, I am deliberately opposing them to prescribed qualitative criteria, preferring the definition "a distinctive attribute or characteristic possessed by something" to "the standard of something as measured against other things of a similar kind," because the former seeks to explore or articulate the specific nature of the thing, while the latter seeks to confirm its belonging to a preexisting category, such as texture, in the planting design context. This is not to say that the given quality may not fit into a category, only that it need not be limited to it. For example, a plant may have both texture and color, but another synergistic expression may better—and more usefully for design—capture it. The kind of aesthetics I am referring to are what Yuriko Saito calls "everyday aesthetics," the appreciation via aesthetic experience of the qualities of plants, and the application of judgments about such qualities in the selection and manipulation of plants according to the gardener's taste, in this instance that of Roberto Burle Marx. While historically aesthetics is tied to the philosophy of art and the idea of beauty, I am not exercising my own taste, only proposing that there is a relationship between plant qualities that arise from growth and a gardener's judgment about them. I agree with Saito, who argues in "Everyday Aesthetics" that treating art as the only subject of aesthetics "unduly limits the range of aesthetic issues by implying that only those related to art are worthwhile for theoretical analysis."[32]

GARDEN AS LABORATORY

The laboratory is a space of scientific experimentation. Epistemologically, this inherently ties the definition of the laboratory to notions of objectivity and an experimental model that precludes the personal judgment of the experimenter from interfering in the results. In this section I will explore Burle Marx's experimental model at the Sítio in the context of Dias's description of it as a laboratory. In his essay, Dias is quick to distance the experimental model of Burle Marx from the aesthetic characteristics of the plantings for which he is best known. Romão suggests that Burle Marx was operating at the Sítio in a scientific way, conducting "research traditionally used for genetic resources: sampling/introduction, multiplication, characterization, evaluation, conservation and use."[33] However, I will demonstrate that although Burle Marx's interests were botanical, and therefore had a scientific aspect, they were always also, and primarily, aesthetic.

According to Dias, for Burle Marx the process of learning at the "laboratory" of the Sítio comprised two stages: *getting* the plants and then *using* them.[34] The getting process involved collecting plants on his botanical trips all over Brazil. Landscape architect Oscar Bressane was a companion on some of these expeditions in the late 1970s, including one lasting over a month in the Amazon.[35] Both he and Dias discuss how everyone on these trips had a particular role: Brassane's being, he said, "a spotter," because he could see plants of certain types from a distance.[36] Part of the getting stage included a vetting of the plant by Burle Marx at the point of collection, and, Dias estimates, because Burle Marx had a good eye for what would survive, more than 90 percent did.

Since many of the plants Burle Marx collected (which Dias calls "trophies" of his travels) were not even known to science, and "were not accompanied by instructions, it was necessary to find out how to keep them alive and see how they behaved outside of their habitat over a reasonable time."[37] This was the "using" process. Bressane said that Burle Marx would "put a plant in the shade and also in the sun, in the wet and also the dry, to test what would grow," noting that plants they collected in the Amazon changed characteristics when they were moved from their native ecologies.[38] Here Burle Marx was developing ways of working with plants that he could use in his own professional practice, including acclimatization, maintenance, and propagation. Referring to the computer term, head gardener at the Sítio Marlon Souza describes the use of plants in multiple different places in the garden as "the backup," a term coined by Dias when he was director. In the final stages of "using" after the plant performance research, "aesthetic compositions were finally tested."[39]

I argue that Dias's description of the Sítio as "a high-quality generator of experimental knowledge" rather than a "museum for the purpose of exhibition" alludes to a scientism that renders Burle Marx's plant selections empirical, transforming Burle Marx from gardener to botanist, from artist to scientist.[40] This interest in science is supported both by his experimental model at the Sítio and by his botanical, and patriotic, interest in Brazilian native plants. His testing was a serious concern, botanical rather than aesthetic, so that his plantings are not tropical, they are indigenous, and just happen to look tropical because that was the nature of the environment;[41] however, "plants are [not just] culturally ... [but] aesthetically defined in Burle Marx's practice."[42]

Whereas in previous chapters I have concentrated on gardening techniques such as pruning and planting arrangement, at the Sítio, removal via weeding is an important gardening strategy. Raymond Jungles quotes Burle Marx on maintenance in the tropics: "In the tropics, garden maintenance is what you take out."[43] The term weeding turns the noun "weed" into a verb. A weed is "a wild plant growing where it is not wanted and

FIGURE 5.17

Anthurium salvinii collected by Burle Marx in the shade house, the first part of his testing process: "to get."

FIGURE 5.18

The second part of Burle Marx's testing process, "to use": the same plant, *Anthurium salvinii* (figure 5.17), in the garden after acclimatization in the shade house.

in competition with cultivated plants" (*OED*). The "wildness" in this definition explains why, in the 1930s, "the magnificent tropical plants of Brazil's jungles were considered weeds," and explains the shock caused by the fact that Burle Marx, as Director of Parks for Recife, "redesigned 15 squares for the city and put 'weeds' in them all."[44] Before the act of identification, a plant is a plant, subject to cultivation practices; however, once it has been identified as a weed, those practices change to practices of removal.

While it has been argued that "Burle Marx … [took] advantage of the phytophysiognomy of [species from] many Brazilian biomes, targeting a reduction of costs and work involved in the maintenance of the gardens,"[45] in fact this very quality makes the species invasive, so that weeding is the primary gardening activity at the Sítio. In an environment of continuous growth, like the tropics, to choose to grow a particular plant in a location is to deny another plant that location, to keep space for the desirable to exceed the spontaneous. Selection of plants is then an act of inversion, of stopping something else. Planting design is a balancing act, a balance between "fit" and aesthetics, where fit is the plant's appropriateness to the desired location. While other spontaneous or weed species may have a better fit, often our aesthetic or ideological (in the case of choosing native vegetation) desires compel us to choose less suitable plants.[46]

Weeding has "the illusion of perfectibility in the act,"[47] an appreciation of a moment of order in time that will soon disappear as plants grow and respond to changes in the garden. Indeed, in the Ecuadorean Amazon I heard local people refer to weeding of forest gardens in Spanish as *limpiar* or cleaning. This is probably a truer description of weeding, which, like cleaning, is actually directed at the restoration of order, even if that order is choosing one plant over another, "the necessary prerequisite to making the space [one's] own."[48]

A by-product of Burle Marx's enthusiasm for testing native plants, Dias says, is that "the collection started invading the gardens" because the plants had not undergone a long enough "vegetal probation."[49] He bemoans the fact that legislation for protection of native species means that indigenous plants which Burle Marx may have collected from the area and was testing, but had become naturalized, have acquired protected status despite the fact that the test may well have been unsuccessful, and might have led to the plants' removal if he was now alive to judge. Watching the Sítio turn into "a chaotic mess," Dias introduces another of Burle Marx's maxims: "A garden is nature ordered by man, for man,"[50] asserting that Burle Marx would have taken a much more interventionist approach.

That quote from Burle Marx demonstrates an intervention of judgment into an experimental process that is patently unscientific: even though the plant performs (passes its "test"), it has some other quality, perhaps aesthetic, that he chooses to emphasize, in his desire to order it. This judgment demonstrates Burle Marx's disinterest in the outcome of the experiment in botanical terms. About this, green wall designer and botanist Patrick Blanc is emphatic: "You have to forget the term 'botanist' as far as he's [Burle Marx] concerned ... he was what could be called a 'plantsman.'"[51] The plantsman collects plants on the basis of their subjective likes and dislikes. It is therefore no surprise that Burle Marx would abandon a plant experiment if it was necessary for the sake of the garden as a whole, rather than seeing it through to its full development.

Obviously Burle Marx would not "get," or collect, a plant that he didn't want in his garden in an aesthetic sense: would not put it into the experimental tests of "using" it in his garden if it had not met some design criterion or possibility in his own mind. It is impossible to separate the test of a plant's empirical ability to survive from its aesthetic qualities because it is through survival, through growth, that it gains those qualities. It is not surprising, therefore, that it was only after the performance tests that Burle Marx examined a plant's aesthetic qualities, because there is no point considering a plant aesthetically if it cannot survive. The willfulness of the gardener in relation to the plant is characteristically disinterested in a way that Ferrari calls political, because the gardener is interested in plant performance only insofar as it does the right thing for the overall garden's design, otherwise it is removed.[52] The scientist, on the other hand, would persevere regardless.

This brings into question what the tests are: are they for plants, or is the entire garden a test? Presumably both, since each plant is a test, and

FIGURE 5.19
Species that Burle Marx collected are both ornamental and have naturalized in the same space, only the figuration of planting pattern and maintenance demarcating which is which.

the site stages all the tests. Theoretically, this does not disturb the model of the conventional laboratory, because each plant can be an autonomous experiment simply located in the same space of the laboratory.[53] However, a garden is an ecological milieu, where plants interact with their environment and each other. Consequently, any plant/test is a factor in understanding any other plant in its sphere of influence. Therefore, I would argue, the ecology of the laboratory is a threat to any idea of experimental rigor, because it is impossible for any test to be autonomous, since tests interact.[54] This challenges spatial and temporal ideas of how a laboratory works, and shows that the analogy of the garden as a laboratory is not a neat fit. If we consider that the Sítio as a garden is both the physical location of the individual tests, the plants, but also the result of those tests, since it changes dynamically as all the tests interact, then we can see that this gives the garden as a testing site a unique and exciting status—unlike, for example, a conventional laboratory, which is simply a container for the processes and their artifacts.

Dias suggests that the garden's true nature is hidden from visitors: "People are generally stunned by the beauty of the gardens surrounding them, but may be surprised to discover that these vegetal symphonies were only provisional tests."[55] Even a major author on Burle Marx, Sima Eliovson, does not mention in her review of the Sítio that the garden is a place for testing, only that Burle Marx was a plant collector and that the formal house landscape "blended imperceptibly into the luxuriant vegetation around it," the testing space itself.[56] This separates the plants' performance in tests from their contribution to the garden as an aesthetic whole, emphasizing science over aesthetics. When Dias suggests that the random visitor to the Sítio would not know that it was an experiment, he is suggesting that the garden gives no outward sign of what was being done there, that the experiment and its outcome were somehow different, arguing that "the work triggered by Burle Marx is more than a product."[57] If we substitute "artifact," "something observed in a scientific investigation or experiment that is not naturally present but occurs as a result of the preparative or investigative procedure,"[58] for Dias's term "product," then we can see how vital some form of outcome is to an experimental process. The product is as vital as the process, because it provides the proof for any hypothesis.

Ultimately, I would argue that the Sítio is not a laboratory because it is affected by the tests that happen in it, which is not possible in the kind of science laboratories to which the term is inherently applied. Instead, the outcome of the experiment is the experiment itself.

If the Sítio is not a work of art, a botanic garden, a natural area, a monument to Burle Marx the man or, further, if Burle Marx was not really a scientist conducting laboratory experiments in an empirical sense, but nonetheless "he learned everything he needs to know from the site," then what is the Sítio?

THE GARDEN STUDIO

The Sítio is always a product and always an experiment, the two recursively interacting in complex ways. Burle Marx used science to guide unusual aesthetic outcomes through gardening in his vegetal studio. The activity of the user in a space is the determinant that identifies it: a cook works in a kitchen; an artist or designer works in a studio. Therefore the question of whether the garden is a laboratory or a studio hinges around what Burle Marx did there. In the previous section I demonstrated that even though Burle Marx was mobilizing science to grow plants, his ultimate decisions about whether or not to use plants were aesthetic. In this section I will show how the garden is really a workshop or studio, and then, building on the idea that the plant tests are at different stages and interacting, explore the garden as a living work of art that transcends existing planting design categories.

If we accept the idea that the whole garden is a test, then it is an enormously complex one, where the terms of reference are unclear and subjective, and individual judgment becomes important. In this sense the site is more like an artist's studio or workshop than a laboratory, though I do not mean to romanticize the studio. In a studio, tests are undertaken to develop a work through trial and error, a process of fine-tuning subjective judgment rather than the pursuit of an essentialist, scientific truth, as in the laboratory.

As well as calling the Sítio a laboratory, in his essay Dias also calls it a workshop, the trial-and-error, iterative making process being common to both. While I prefer the term workshop or studio to laboratory, in their book *Laboratory Life* Latour and Woolgar argue that the objectivity of the laboratory is not nearly as clear as science pretends, and that knowledge in the laboratory is "construct[ed through] slow, practical craftwork by which inscriptions are superimposed and accounts backed up and dismissed."[59] This emphasis on craft suggests that the Sítio is a workshop of practice, as a studio is for the artist.

The idea that Burle Marx was an artist with plants is pervasive, and discussed by almost all writers about him. Lucio Costa said that Burle Marx was "a painter, and he paints with plants also. He makes huge pictures with native flowers and plants,"[60] and as a painter he was for Walmsley "the Picasso of landscape."[61] Although Costa says that Burle Marx introduced to "his gardens the technique of painting," there are earlier precedents for this analogy. The history of landscape gardening is inherently linked to painting, since in the English landscape garden painters like Claude Lorrain were used to illustrate debates about the Picturesque within a discourse of taste in gardens. In the nineteenth century, Gertrude Jekyll also used painterly analogies in her discussion of planting design compositions, and in the early twentieth century Australian garden designer Edna Walling used watercolors to illustrate her garden designs. While Burle Marx did paint some of his garden designs, Dias says that his regular practice consisted of an overlay process on tracing paper, typical of landscape-architectural practice at the time.

This is reminiscent of the way an artist works in their studio. Describing the studio, Daniel Buren says it is "a private place ... presided over by the artist-resident, since only that work which he desires and allows to leave his studio will do so."[62] Allowed into an artist's studio, their private working space, one can see the process: work produced, provisional tests, half-completed artworks, all together in a space where they are not presented as they ultimately would be in an art gallery. Because of the transition from private garden to public museum, Burle Marx's explorations are visible in a way that he might not have countenanced in a professional project.

While Dias refers to "landscaped areas" and "plant compositions" in his description of Burle Marx's other projects, he calls the plantings at the Sítio "vegetal symphonies."[63] Perhaps the planting compositions that Burle Marx undertook in professional practice were complete for him because his work was representational: plants formed plan geometries for later installation rather than being installed directly without a plan as they were in in his "workshop," where he made decisions at eye level and in an iterative process over time. In the studio, like the gardener but unlike the landscape architect, the artist is interacting directly, non-representationally, with their work.

With the artist, Burle Marx, dead, perhaps the question is really what the studio looks like from the outside, without knowing what is being explored and at what stage such explorations are? For Dias, harsh judgment is required for the failed tests, which must go because "the remains of the tests that did not work are like the scribblings of their children that proud parents regard as masterpieces, foisting them on strangers."[64] Within the private studio these tests would not be seen, but now that the Sítio is a public garden, they are.

In the same way that Andersson's did in his garden at Marnas, Burle Marx's tests at the Sítio represented the accumulation of experience, as did his work on projects. He and his plants both developed over time. Dias says that Burle Marx was heavy-handed in his removal of plants, saying: "When I did that project I did not know the plant would do that."[65]

Autonomous of intention, author, or process, the garden test is still something with its own particular aesthetic qualities, which have arisen from the process but nonetheless exist in their own right. However, even as they exist in their own right, they are still a record of the process. Consequently, while the visitor might not know about the test, I would argue that they still see something in its outcome that they would not have seen if the process had not occurred. The visitor takes a garden as they find it at that moment in time, without expecting a clear explanation but liking it or not for what it is rather than what it means.

That Burle Marx regarded the Sítio as a workshop of change is evident when Dias notes that at the Sítio, unlike in many of his other gardens, "even in the most elaborately landscaped areas (such as characteristic plantings juxtaposing plant textures and colors, for example), he did not consider plant compositions [at the Sítio] as completed artworks."[66]

The incompleteness and ephemerality of the "vegetal symphony" gives clues to the real-time nature of the viridic, making the garden closer to a performance of music, which can also be described aesthetically, than to the art object that is a linear accumulation of a process of making in the studio but does not change on its own. The artwork produced in the garden as studio is composed of "lives," the lives of plants, as Ferrari says.[67] As living entities, the real materiality of plants is growth; this is why Burle Marx's work is so striking: because he seems to do such contrived things with plants that speak of growth not as naturalness but as artificiality.

Discussing what he calls "the time factor," Dias notes that in the Sítio, "experiments are untimed."[68] Certain plants seemed fine for many years and only later began to develop new characteristics that might be productive, frail, or sometimes disturbing. The tests in the Sítio are ongoing because many species collected have not been tested (for example, they are still in the greenhouses), or are not yet developed enough to ascertain the outcome of the test. Furthermore, some that are being tested are at different stages both individually and in relation to each other.

If we refuse to separate the performative characteristics of a plant from the aesthetic ones, then we have an account of plants that values them as relational artifacts at every moment of their growth. If each plant is untimed in terms of the overall duration of the experiment, it is nonetheless still at a particular stage in its growth, whether juvenile or senescent, or at any other qualitatively different stage in between. "The experiment lasts," Dias says, "while the plant is well and only stops when an insurmountable obstacle arises, such as death, or when the environment changes, making it impossible for the plant to live in that place... [in which case] we must transplant, but even in that other place we may consider that a new experiment begins for that plant."[69] Since, as I have been arguing, a garden as a whole is an experiment where each plant test interacts with every other, then the different growth conditions of each plant are also juxtaposed against each other. If we think of the garden as a moving work of art, then individual elements interact in dynamic ways, changing the work not just by degree, where plants get uniformly larger, but in kind, as Bergson would say, where the work is completely different over time.[70]

Despite the fact that any quality a plant has arises from growth over time, planting design tends to adopt a static painterly model, focusing on "plant selection" and the qualities of color, texture, and form.[71] Burle Marx is regarded as one of the greatest planting designers, rated highly for his work with "mass planting," "architectural plants," and "color contrasts."

In the conventional planting design texts, seasonality tends to be the only aspect that takes into consideration the fact that plants grow over time; however, all the other criteria rely on maintenance activities to retain their desired effects. At the Rio de Janeiro's Museu de Arte Modernas (MAM), designed by Affonso Reidy, Burle Marx made a "tight waving motif" in the lawn out of grass, with alternating green and yellow species, which, "although formally very striking... was actually a meticulously restrained gardening exercise that required the planting of seeds for two different grasses in a very precise pattern."[72] However, when I visited, only a slight ghosting within the otherwise uniform turf was visible. This shows that the planting design criterion "color" required constant maintenance to weed more vigorous green species out of the variegated yellow one, a key to the role of maintenance in ensuring that artificial planting design effects persist.

This maintenance approach is quite different to the one Burle Marx used at the Sítio. While the product of the test and the space of testing are united there, Burle Marx's "vegetal symphonies" in projects like MAM show that some characteristics that make them "moving works of art" are a result of a plant's form at a moment in time, relative to time as process, growth, and result—plant form—and thereby reliant on maintenance.

FIGURE 5.20
"Architectural plants," a dominant category of conventional planting design, feature in Burle Marx's work, such as at the Instituto Moreira Salles in Rio.

FIGURE 5.21
Using mass planting to create "contrast" is also a common feature of planting design celebrated in Burle Marx's projects, also at the Instituto Moreira Salles in Rio.

FIGURE 5.22
Wavy planting pattern of two different grasses at Affonso Reidy's Museu de Arte Modernas (MAM) in Rio de Janeiro, early in its installation (Sima Eliovson).

FIGURE 5.23

The same lawn (figure 5.22) in 2010, only a ghosting of the original pattern remaining as plants grew into each other.

This means that a plant's ecological role and effects will be different when it is young to when it is mature, as will its aesthetic or formal characteristics, both on its own as well as in relation to its neighbors, with which it forms a "composition." To use a tropical example: the juvenile leaves of many rainforest species are red when the tree is only perhaps 1 meter high, when it will have the appearance of a sparse shrub. These leaves might be the only color below the canopy. However, when a hole in the canopy opens, perhaps by design through the removal of a tree, the plant may shoot up to occupy it, changing from a shrub to a tree. This interlocking and blurring of form and time relationships ensures that, as Ferrari argues, "as aesthetic arts go, gardening is messy [since it] is fraught with unpredictability, and its work is never complete."[73] Burle Marx called this unpredictability "imponderables": "Sometimes the imponderables help and sometimes hinder.... We cannot preview everything.... You have to play a game. Sometimes you win and sometimes you lose."[74]

Considering planting design compositions as uncompleted artworks is a useful description of the viridic. At any given moment the gardener makes an aesthetic decision about the artwork as they find it, which will in turn affect how it is when they next intervene in it. Rather than incomplete, then, these compositions should be described as evolving. That Burle Marx's compositions were artworks is undeniable; however, these vegetal artworks redefine what an artwork is when it is not about completion: where art is an ongoing, evolving process.

AESTHETIC QUALITIES OF GROWTH

In Dias's essay, and during my conversations with him, he spoke of Burle Marx's "characteristic planting," often arguing that the Sítio was more about experimentation than such plantings: the "characteristic planting" at the Sítio being "in the style of Burle Marx" rather than by Burle Marx himself. It is interesting to interrogate such plantings in terms of ideas about him "painting with plants," and to see the relationship of such plantings to growth, which differentiates them from painting.

Modern paintings that are biomorphic, like Burle Marx's paintings and his planting designs, are often called "abstract," as opposed to art that is pictorial or figurative. However, if Burle Marx's plans as paintings were literally used to allocate plants, then they are not abstract at all, but figurative. Correspondingly, I would argue that there is much more going on in Burle Marx's planting designs than abstract painting. If one reads his writings (which were generally a transcription and translation of his lectures by his employees), he uses odd terms like "badly planned volumes" and "uncorrelated textures."

When I describe Burle Marx's mass planting arrangement to Dias as "monocultures next to each other," in contrast to the arrangements of contemporary planting designers who work with diverse perennial plantings, like Piet Oudolf, Dias provides a different rationale for the mass plantings, saying that Burle Marx believed: "people don't see one plant, they only see many." In these terms, Burle Marx's planting design decisions are based around an exposition of plant qualities, where massing "reveals" something that might not immediately be seen by the casual lay viewer. This gives planting design a didactic role, educating the eye of the viewer. The use of mass plantings figured biomorphically, like his, can lead one to regard such plantings as essentially flat; however, Burle Marx's planting designs were not flat. Dias described how Burle Marx worked in vertical layers: ground cover, shrub, and canopy layers. A "badly planned volume," a critique that Burle Marx used to describe a particular type of deficient planting design, is a relatively simple thing, where one layer obscures another from the viewer, rendering a plant invisible and therefore obsolete in the composition. Because plants grow, a good composition in volume at one point in time can become a bad one later.

The "uncorrelated texture," another of Burle Marx's planting design *faux pas*, is more complex, however, since it interacts with color. Leaf shapes feature prominently in his planting designs, which come together in multiples to create what others call "textures." Burle Marx would often use plants that had a similar growth habit—perennial plants with strappy leaves, for example—but where different species were of slightly different colors or heights. An uncorrelated texture, then, might be one where a plant's leaf characteristics might not be considered in relation to another adjacent species.

FIGURE 5.24

What Burle Marx called "correlated textures" at the Sítio, where plants of similar foliage type are placed with each other, even if their color varies.

The conjunction of "art" and "plant" suggests that the plants are a medium in a painterly sense *used* to make art. Plants are not passive, since they grow and change, so the idea that they can be simply applied, like paint, is misleading, as when Costa says that Burle Marx "had the plastic sensibility for disposing of masses and color, like a painter."[75] While, according to Dias, painting planting plans was not a part of his normal practice, nonetheless his use of color and masses in his planting designs was clearly compositional, organized with a form language characteristic of his time, and modernism generally. That said, there is something compelling and different in the way such compositions work with plants. Discussing Burle Marx's drawings on display at a recent exhibition, Imbert asks: "In the case of garden plans, how should one interpret color? As a legend indicating plantings and paving materials, or as an idealized representation? As a study in tension between opposite and complementary color combinations? Or is the plan another artistic expression of the garden, a posterior illustration of a never-to-be-encountered moment?"[76]

Leaving aside the compositional, it is easy to demonstrate how painterly approaches to planting design utilize the qualities that plants have due to their individual growth. While I have been arguing that the botanic/ecological and the aesthetic need not be separated in the garden, I will go further and argue that it is impossible to separate them in planting design, because any plant qualities that are used in a planting design have an evolutionary explanation.

The biology of plants singly and together forms the foundation of the ecological, in concert with their environment. If we take an evolutionary view, then the qualities of plants that Burle Marx consistently used reflect plant adaptations to environments. In order not to separate the ecological from the aesthetic, I will show how the plant qualities Burle Marx admired were responses to their indigenous environments, so that when we discuss particular aesthetic qualities we are also discussing the performance of those qualities, a performance that allowed them to succeed "ornamentally."[77]

Aesthetic qualities are the same as plant morphological qualities, be they the plant's architecture as "form," its leaf's shape and surface as "texture," or its flowers (or leaves) as "color," the basic planting design criteria. Despite morphology in biology being "the branch of biology that deals with the form of the living organism," whenever one is talking about plant form, one is always really talking about morphogenesis, "the origin and development of morphological characteristics," because morphology arises from growth. Interrogating the idea of morphogenesis, in turn, leads one to plant physiology ("branch of biology that deals with the normal functions of living organisms and their parts") because, if one assumes an evolutionary model, all morphological properties of a plant have a functional role that must have given them an evolutionary advantage.[78] This approach is called "Plant Functional Types" by Smith et al.: "those biotic components of ecosystems that perform the same function or set of functions within the ecosystem."[79] There are various ways of defining functional types; however, since I am interested in the particular qualities of plants that result from their physical characteristics, I would concur with Barbault et al. (1991), "[who] argued that functional types should be defined in terms of morphology and physiology...and represent 'plant growth forms.'"[80] Morphology, as physical plant characteristics, and physiology, as plant survival processes, are linked because the parts of the plant described by morphology have physiological effects—an idea implicit in evolution, which assumes that any characteristic a plant has must provide an evolutionary advantage. Beyond the scale of the individual plant, physiological processes of plants in an ecosystem become resources for other parts of the ecosystem—for example, decomposing plants become nutrients for other plants. Thus we can potentially talk about plant morphological characteristics of a particular family or genus having a functional role in an ecosystem.

"The clearest cases of the effect of function on the form of plants are in morphological adaptations to environmental conditions," though Shugart cautions against assuming simple ideas about optimization of function, since "in many cases, it is not clear what natural selection is optimising."[81] In this process, Shugart says, "pattern and process are mutually causal, with changes in ecosystem processes causing changes in pattern, and modifications in ecosystem pattern changing processes"[82] Violle et al. argue that the term "trait" should be used to describe "any morphological, physiological or phenological feature measurable at the individual level, from the cell to the whole-organism level, without reference to the environment or any other level of organisation."[83] Their model of traits expands Arnold's (1983) "morphology, performance, fitness" paradigm to plant ecology: performance traits are those which contribute directly to fitness, while functional traits are "those morpho-physio-phenological traits which have an impact on performance traits (and thus indirectly on fitness)."[84] Unpacking the term, morpho-physio-phenological refers to the relationship between morphology and physiology, discussed above, where physical plant features contribute to physiological processes, which in turn provide an evolutionary advantage over time, reflected in genetic characteristics. These functional traits can be correlated with qualities in planting design terms, and are visible in Burle Marx's use of aroids.

Clearly Burle Marx liked particular environments, such as tropical forest, in which he collected plants. That they also suited the climate of the places where he worked does not preclude him making aesthetic decisions that are also calibrated to the specific plant functional types of the ecological system he collected, like the aroids. Burle Marx had particular plant functional types that he liked, and used in both an ecological and an aesthetic way at the Sítio.

Burle Marx collected plants from the family Araceae. The 430 species of *Philodendron* account for more than half of the 806 species at the Sítio. While the aroids are distinguished by beautiful flowers in other genera, like the arum lily, the subfamiliy Philodendroideae are generally distinguished more on the basis of their dramatic leaves. In Deni Bown's book *Aroids*, she notes that "they are not the sort of plants you can be neutral about. Amongst the declarations of handsome and magnificent comes a multitude of comments that they are curious, weird, rather obscene, revolting or even terrifying."[85] Despite this, she contends that "these plants surely are more than redeemed by the beauty and astonishing variety of their foliage."[86] Aroids are easily recognized by their often large, heart-shaped leaves. A key morphological trait of successful plants in the rainforest is a high specific leaf area (SLA, measured by a single leaf area divided by its dry mass), which is influential on the main physiological factor of relative growth rate (RGR). A high SLA represents a larger relative number of leaf areas available for light interception, and hence photosynthetic carbon gain (literally plant biomass), therefore a high relative growth rate. The large and interesting leaves that Burle Marx uses to dramatic effect in his planting designs, such as at the Lago, all have a high SLA, but also persist in conditions that one would not imagine suited a rainforest plant.

Philodendron means tree-loving, and most aroids are climbers and epiphytes of tropical forests. Only 2 percent of light reaches the canopy floor of a rainforest, and the ability of some aroids to handle such low levels of light has made them suitable indoor plants. Aroids are present at every level in the rainforest, though mostly they occur below 5 meters, making the rainforest floor the richest area by far.[87] Mantovani notes of epiphytic aroids that plants of the same species in shade closer to the ground produced more leaves, whereas higher in the canopy leaves were longer-lived and more resistant: a conservative life strategy that, he argues, leads to the success of aroids in the canopy despite their lack of characteristic epiphytic adaptations.[88] This gives aroids a great deal of "plasticity" in terms of competition, allowing them to "make use of heterogeneity in time and space" by "[altering] allocation patterns, morphology or physiology in response to environmental variation."[89] Although philodendrons are called "epiphytic aroids," Mantovani suggests that they may have had a terrestrial origin, since they exhibit few epiphytic adaptations, and that they could be called mesophytes, plants that can handle both wet and dry conditions, or even hygrophytes, plants that like wet conditions.[90] This explains why the aroids Burle Marx used near the Lago can be the same as those used in the forest, able to handle both habitats. If we return to Burle Marx's two stages of testing plants analyzed by Dias—to get and to use—it is no surprise that the aroids feature so prominently. Quite apart from their aesthetic interest, they could be collected from deep shade in a forest and then used in full sun in the ornamental landscape, modifying their leaf production and attributes to suit the level of available water.

However, it was not simply the leaf shape or growth habit of aroids that interested Burle Marx, but also the color of their leaves. One of the most dramatic aroids used by the Lago is the purple-leaved *Calocasia*

FIGURE 5.25

A range of aroids at the Lago at the Sítio, plants from the family Araceae collected by Burle Marx which exhibited morphological characteristics inherently linked to his planting designs.

- a. *Colocasia esculenta,* var. *nigra*
- b. *Montrichardia linifera*
- c. *Philodendron brasiliensis*
- d. *Anthurium coriaceum*
- e. *Monstera deliciosa*
- f. *Cyrtosperma mercusii*
- g. *Anubias barteri*

esculenta, the result of an experiment conducted by Dias with botanist Herri Lorenzi, a specialist in Araceae.[91] Colored foliage on plants is generally admired, whether it be autumn foliage on deciduous trees, juvenile foliage on *Photinia* hedges, or leaves on rainforest plants like the *Calocasia*. This coloration is due to the presence of anthocyanins, which "accumulate[s] in young, expanding foliage, in autumnal foliage of deciduous species, in response to nutrient efficiency or ultraviolet (UV) radiation exposure, and in association with damage or defense against browsing herbivores or pathogenic fungal infection."[92] Young leaves in shade-tolerant rainforest species, like the aroids, are twenty times more likely to suffer damage from herbivores and pathogens than mature leaves. Leafcutter ants in the rainforest collect leaves that they store underground to feed fungi for agriculture; however, these ants prefer leaves with lower levels of anthocyanin, favoring green over red. Since the colored leaves are juvenile, and occur primarily when the plant is growing actively—Mantovani characterized this as a common trait of aroids on the forest floor—it has been suggested that the antifungal properties of anthocyanin are an evolutionary rationale to avoid predation.[93] Since these colorations are at the expense of chlorophyll, which is responsible for photosynthesis, other rationales have also been provided, including a reduction in photosynthesis as a means to reduce evapotranspiration, allowing plants to be more economical in their use of water. However, for the aroids, which often live in dark conditions on the rainforest floor, this rationale seems counterintuitive. While I am discussing plant functional type here, not Burle Marx, if we accept that Burle Marx was an avowed modernist, one might speculate that my description of the characteristics of plants he liked in biological terms might appeal to him, because it fits the "form follows function" precept of modernism. This begs the question: if a plant's leaves, here the aroid's, look a certain way, does that mean that their aesthetic appreciation is then an appreciation of function? Furthermore, in a modernist sense, does this also mean that his appreciation of plants was also a kind of functionalism?

CONCLUSION

Burle Marx said: "You must know the language of nature!" adding: "If you do not know the language you cannot create a poem."[94] Tying the morphological and physiological characteristics defined in biological terms to their use in planting design is obviously vital for their ability to grow. Furthermore, however, developing a language for the viridic that bridges art and science allows for an exciting synthesis that can merge horticulture and garden design. Such a language allows for qualities of plants to have a deep rationale that explains why they exist, at the same time as what they can offer aesthetically.

While it has been an elaborate voyage from the idea of the laboratory to plant functional type, this case study of the Sítio allows for an important bridge to be made between scientific knowledge and aesthetic pursuit. The gap between these two has caused plants to seem either technical or artisanal in the folksy sense of gardening. In the way he pursued plants in the field, and grew them to develop the rich aesthetics for which his designs are known, Burle Marx is an exemplar of the kind of *auteur* one has to be to enjoy planting design—sometimes scientist, sometimes artist—though, as I have argued here, more often than not both at the same time.

In articulating an aesthetics of the viridic, I am recognizing that aesthetic qualities emerge from growth, an organic process experienced by a living being. In doing so, I am tying a plant's qualities to how a plant "is." This can also differentiate the viridic from the tectonic, which might consider the plant as an inert, static object, as Rose did. I pair the term "aesthetic" with "qualities" to dislodge some of the art associations with the term—not because Burle Marx was not an artist, although he clearly was, but so that we can use qualities to unpack the aesthetic of the viridic and, in the process, link plant morphology as growth to the kind of aesthetics in which Burle Marx was interested as an artist. These are different to the morphology of Andersson or Rose because of the kind of qualities he emphasized, like texture and color. However, even as I use the term qualities, I am also recognizing that, as Graham Harman notes, "all human relations to objects strip them of their inner depth, revealing only some of their qualities to view,"[95] "far removed from the object in its withering interior activity, which can never be fully exhausted by any human means."[96] This is particularly true of plants because they are living organisms, like humans, which, Marder argues, exhibit their own kind of thinking and their own designs, often in community with other plants.[97]

The idea of growth was fundamental to Burle Marx's understanding of plants, and is inherently linked to human life. Echoing Andersson talking about his work at Marnas, and how the garden might change when he could no longer climb a ladder to prune, Burle Marx said: "Even in a man's life it is beautiful to be born. ... It is beautiful to grow; it is beautiful to love; it is beautiful to end, to die. If we don't understand that rhythm of life, we won't understand the rhythm of nature."[98]

CHAPTER 6

Marginalia

A GARDENER MUST ALWAYS be open to serendipitous accident, as a bibliophile must also. During a research fellowship at the start of my PhD I was procrastinating in a second-hand bookshop in Fremantle, Australia, browsing the gardening section disinterestedly. I came across an intriguing title, *Some Branch against the Sky*, seemingly a fragment of poetry—not an uncommon thing in garden writing, which tends to be full of gifted amateurs like poets and philosophers: erstwhile speculators on the fusion of nature and culture. The book's subtitle, *The Practice and Principles of Marginal Gardening*, also intrigued me since, rather than a picture of a garden, it was accompanied by a photograph of a seemingly natural forest. As with many garden books in this genre, its author, Geoffrey Dutton, writes in the style of a diary, describing his garden via the seasons in relation to the principle of marginal gardening, where a marginal garden is one "minimally differentiated from its surroundings, and so requiring minimal effort to make and keep up."[1] Dutton's definition pairs design strategy—minimal differentiation from site—with his own personal work onsite—minimal effort. His "marginal" approach

FIGURE 6.2

A glimpse through an opening in Druimchardain, created by G. F. Dutton using only "marginal" effort.

corresponds to the site-specific discourse in recent landscape architecture theory because, most obviously, it is concerned with doing very little to change the site, but also because it is a similar type of "inquiry," a design approach where "very limited time has meant that [Dutton] has become a 'curator' of the land."[2]

With the environment the focus of public culture throughout the 1960s, the quasi-scientific work of Ian McHarg, with its environmental science basis, changed the face of professional landscape-architectural practice, giving it the level of certainty required in public decision-making, and the legitimacy that landscape ecology provided. Preoccupied with the disjunction between the objectivity of science and the subjectivity of design judgment, much professional practice in the 1980s erred on the side of science, treating site as an assemblage of landscape systems rather than a particular place, a trait that has persisted in its descendant, landscape urbanism.[3] As poststructuralist philosophy during postmodernism destabilized such certainties, avant-garde landscape architects sought a *rapprochement* between the two by theorizing design processes that allowed for a more diverse reading of site, a discourse that drew on 1960s and 1970s site-specific art.

While Dutton was an Anglophile, or perhaps a Scottophile, the French term *sensibilité*[4] is sometimes used by French landscape architects to refer to a feeling or vibe for a project that combines the atmosphere of the site and its logic with a language of design expression, seeking a precision in their correspondence. While such an approach might have parallels with a phenomenological reading of architecture, Mosbach and Claramunt's statement that "the development of a project wavers between the intelligible and the emotional"[5] has an element of easy rigor to it that mirrors Dutton's argument that what united his diverse interests was "enquiry," a similar approach to that of Burle Marx at the Sítio.

As I have progressed through the chapters of this book, my focus has moved from working with plants through representation a priori construction—the designer using plants as form to populate the design—to a posteriori, where the gardener/designer engages with the trajectory of plants as found onsite.[6] While Dutton is not a "designer," his approach of working with the site and carefully intervening in it through observation, experimentation, and recursive learning is, I would argue, engaged with design approaches, like site-specificity discourse in landscape architecture, that lend themselves to the viridic.

When I introduce Dutton in this chapter, I emphasize his synergistic approach to "enquiry," and show how he was able to bridge the domains of science and art, which he saw as indivisible, because both have their role to play.[7] Since, as I have been arguing, plant growth and growing conditions are unique at any point in time, and—as we saw at Marnas, so too is the gardener—to engage with plants involves doing so in their current condition, as an experiencing subject. This frame of the experiencing subject mirrors the discourse of site in contemporary landscape architecture, which I then discuss in relation to Dutton. This is pertinent because his mode of operation at Druimchardain parallels it in many ways, since his decision-making in the garden was driven by site experience and "going on patrol" reiteratively: he constantly walked the garden, backward and forward, tweaking it as he went, regularly writing about his experiences and observations in his diaries and poetry.

I describe the site in relation to Dutton's description of it, which shows how impossible it is to delineate the site's description from the experience of it. This correlates to his approach of marginal gardening, which I describe as design strategy, because it is characteristic of the way designers think about design not simply as an artifact but as a logic. With the subject at the center of the description of and action on the garden, time assumes a role, and representation changes. For Dutton, poetry was a key negotiator between the empirical site, as a place with elements describable in geological, meteorological, and horticultural dimensions, and these same things as ephemeral phenomena that he engaged with as a subject. Therefore I use the seasonal structure of his book of poetry about the garden, *Harvesting the Edge*, to unpack the garden and his acts in landscape-architectural terms, where certain actions have formal consequences linked to the modality of the garden in those seasons, using poems themselves as evidence. When introducing this section I explore poetry as a representational mode and Dutton's poems as algorithms, with consistent variables reflecting on the site, he himself acting as subject and revealing self-consciousness of the act of writing in his prose. Concluding the chapter, I suggest that a site-specific practice in response to plant growth, nested in its environment, that utilizes alternative modes of post-factum documentation is appropriate to the viridic. The designer of the Parc de La Villette, architect Bernard Tschumi, has used the phrase "scribbling in the margins" to describe a normative process of urban design where the architect "take[s] what exists, fill[s] in the gaps, complete[s] the text, scribble[s] in the margins,"[8] a description which Tschumi is also said to have used pejoratively of landscape architects.[9] Dutton's use of poetry in his garden of margins turns this insult into a precise tool for negotiating site and working with what is found.

GARDEN FOR A POLYMATH

Referred to as G. F. Dutton by the publisher of his poetry, to distinguish him from the Australian poet of the same name, Geoffrey Dutton was born in England in 1924. He was an internationally recognized researcher in molecular biology, and professor of biochemistry at Dundee University, where he stayed during the week, working on his garden, Druimchardain near Bridge of Cally in Perthshire, on weekends.

Dutton's research was into chemistry's relation to medicine, specifically steroid metabolism and glucuronides conjugates, "an important metabolic modification of endogenous and exogenous compounds." Dutton was "a pioneer in our understanding of chemical defence [and] how these toxic chemicals could be rendered harmless … in the dawn of biochemical pharmacology," his doctoral research "the first unequivocal demonstration of the biochemical mechanism for any reaction of drug metabolism reaction."[10] He published two important volumes, *Glucuronic Acid, Free and Combined* in 1966[11] and *Glucuronidation of Drugs and Other Compounds* in 1980,[12] both still in use today.

Dutton was a Renaissance man of multiple interests apart from his science, including mountaineering,[13] "free" swimming through underwater landscape,[14] and poetry.[15] The garden was the subject of a book of

FIGURE 6.3
One of Dutton's photographs of underwater forests during one of his "free swimming" expeditions in Scotland (Courtesy of G. F. Dutton).

poetry, *Harvesting the Edge: Some Personal Explorations from a Marginal Garden*; he also wrote for a gardening readership in the *Journal of the Royal Horticultural Society*, and in *Some Branch against the Sky: The Practice and Principles of Marginal Gardening*.¹⁶ In his obituary of Dutton, his protégé biochemist Brian Burchell notes that "there [was] a link between all these excellent achievements. Exploration of rock, ice, rivers or lakes, horticulture or molecular biology requires the same self-imposed discipline and obsessive behaviour, all of them being intellectually demanding and equally rewarding."¹⁷ This crossing-over of interests was evident in his after-dinner chats as a speaker "in the style of McGonagall or Pope," where he "imaginative[ly] use[d the language of] biochemistry to describe personal events, such as retirement: "The deadly peptide reminisin activates a cascade of events releasing high levels of pontific acid and other peptides such as haverin and bletherin and the lachrymatory maudlin."[18]

In his obituary, Burchell makes a link between Dutton's science and his garden when he describes Dutton's interest in "enzyme ecology," which was "encouraged by his studies in wider ecology" during weekends in the garden which, recalling Burle Marx's use of the Sítio, "were for ecological experiments in biology, horticulture and forestry in a few mountain acres."[19] Asked about what he was doing in retirement, Dutton said that his work in his garden "[is] related to the scientific work because it is ecology on a vegetational scale where my work in the lab was really molecular ecology—based around the fact that the tissues of the body have their own particular ecosystems. It's an amazing parallel... it's all part of one."[20] The term "ecology" is defined by the *Oxford English Dictionary* as "The branch of biology that deals with the relations of organisms to one another and to their physical surroundings." While ecology has become a generalized model for different systems of relationship in contemporary culture (the process discourse, for example), it can really be used only for specific relationships between organisms and places. While Dutton uses the term in a general way when he talks about enzyme ecology, his interest in Druimchardain was highly specific, observed through a close, longstanding and ongoing relationship with the various constituents of this particular place, on the basis of which he made his modifications to it.

As I start my journey, the context of Druimchardain is breathtaking: from Aberdeen we drive through long open valleys where the road is a trace perched on the side of pasture land, a river below and the hills green with specklings of gorse, underlain by a texture of rock.

Since it is covered in vegetation and clustered around a creek, literally on the creek bank, Druimchardain seems small but dense, with an "overall feel [of] not quite knowing whether one is in a garden or not, [where only] some clipping of shrubs or mowing of paths illustrates intention and design."[21] With only an old garage on the road, surrounded by trees, it is hard to make out the "start" of the garden, and no easier when one enters, because "the crumpled topography complicates mapping and

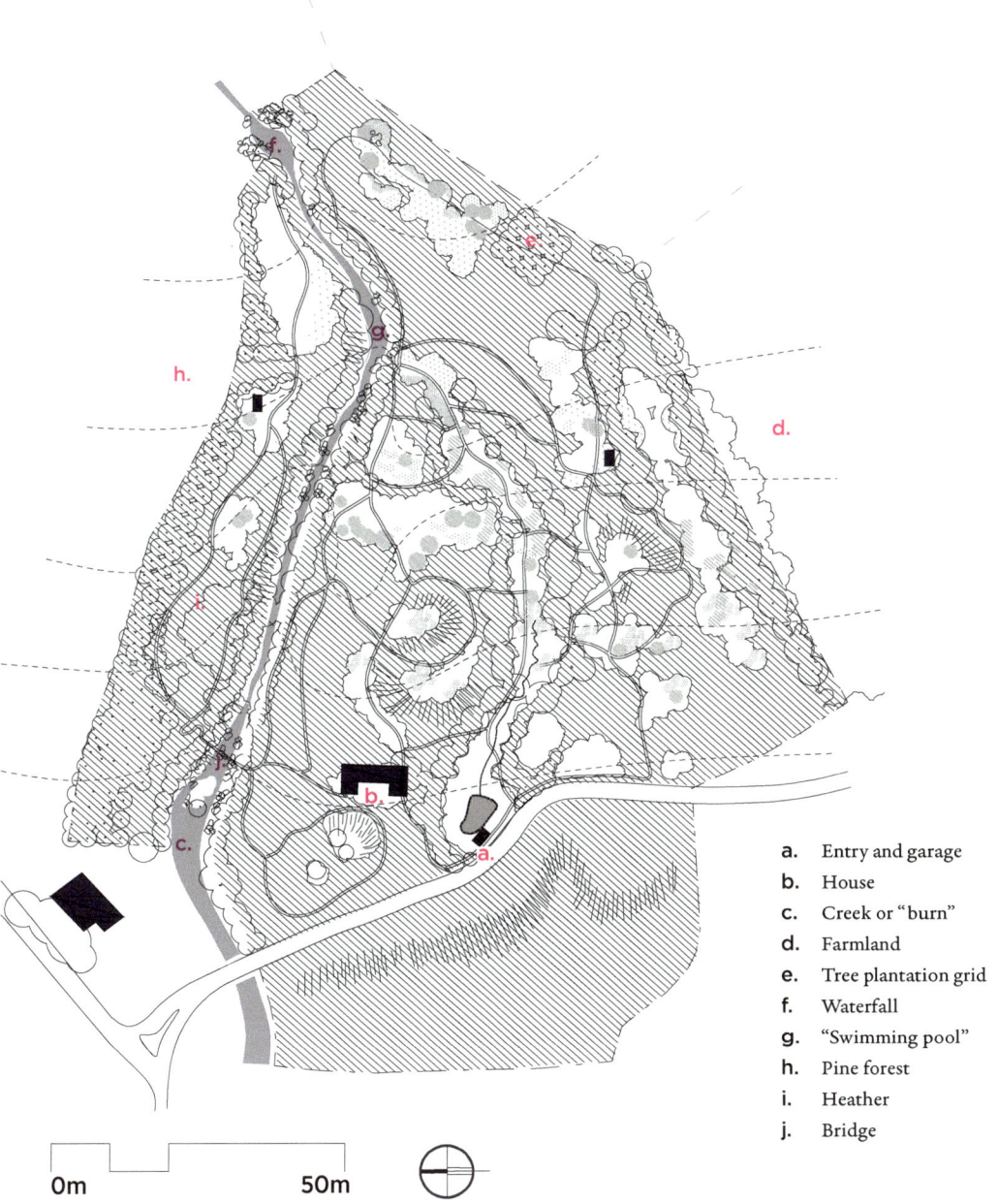

FIGURE 6.4

Plan of the marginal garden, interpolated from Dutton's plan, site visits, and aerial photography.

a. Entry and garage
b. House
c. Creek or "burn"
d. Farmland
e. Tree plantation grid
f. Waterfall
g. "Swimming pool"
h. Pine forest
i. Heather
j. Bridge

FIGURE 6.5
It is difficult to divorce the sublime landscape of Scotland seen as one approaches Druimchardain from a reading of the garden as its margin.

FIGURE 6.6

The nondescript entrance to Druimchardain, lost in vegetation, provides no hint either of Dutton's complex thinking or that the site is in fact a garden at all.

measurement, but makes the more 'gardened' area of 5 or so acres (2 hectares), with probably another acre lost among the folds, appear larger to walk than it is."[22]

Since it is a strip—a margin—Dutton describes the garden as three long paths, all quite close to each other but each hidden inside a ripple of the folded geography. For convenience, it is easier to think about it as a creek and an agricultural boundary, with the two strips between. From the garage, one can split left toward the ridge above the creek, where the house is located, or to the right, into the first strip with a bog at its base. The house has the characteristic look of a holiday house expanded to become a home, and the rock wall, steps, and path in front make it the most visibly designed or configured "garden" space on the property.

The creek below is almost entirely natural, or seemingly so, and surprisingly sublime, with lush vegetation and ferns, large boulders and trees hanging over it. Since the opposite bank is also part of Druimchardain, Dutton arranged with a group of Dundee University medical

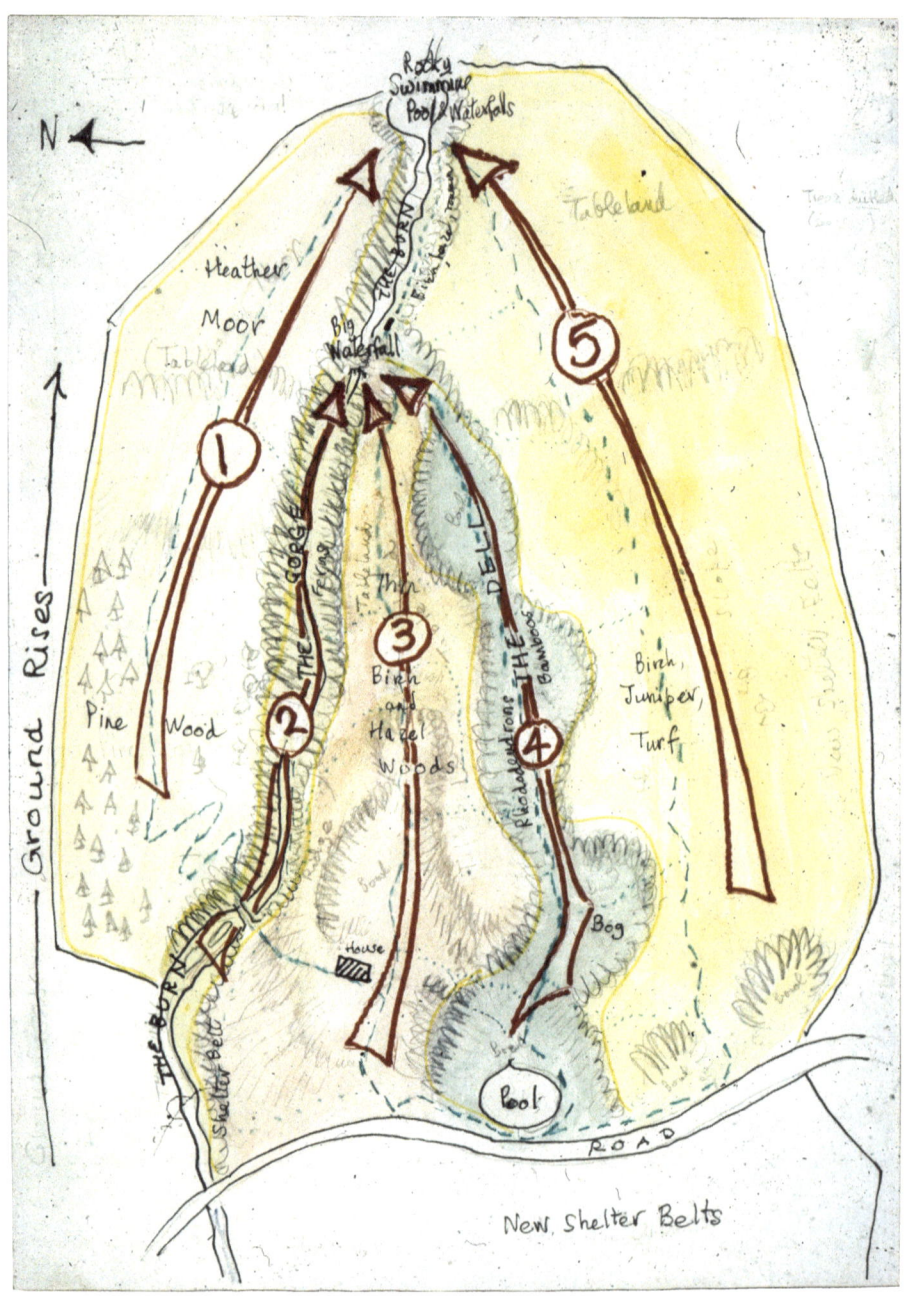

FIGURE 6.7 (above)

Dutton's explanatory map of the garden, with its three long paths that are also calibrated to soil type and pH (Courtesy of G. F. Dutton).

FIGURE 6.8 (opposite)

A photograph, taken by Dutton during the 1980s, of the house at Druimchardain where his family lived while he was at the University of Dundee during the week, working on the garden at weekends (Courtesy of G. F. Dutton).

FIGURE 6.9
The bridge across the river, or "burn," built by a local Scout troop, the most significant infrastructure on the site.

students to build a simple and elegant bridge across it, the only piece of visible infrastructure in the garden, and somewhat out of place in its formal forthrightness. Apparently Dutton liked to scramble, as the mountaineer he was, in among the boulders of the creek, investigating nooks, perhaps inserting plants here and there, but otherwise leaving it as it was. When I saw the creek and its wildness, with something epic about it, I had no doubt that it was the initial reason for purchasing the property, and while I agreed with the decision to leave it alone, its grandeur is tantalizingly attractive. As one searches through the growth and subtlety of the other humbler gardened parts, psychologically one is always pulled back to the creek.

While it would be easy to characterize Dutton as simply a gardener or plantsman, he brought a certain landscape-architectural thinking to the project of making the garden. He identified and worked with the existing features in a grounded geographic but picturesque way, using clearings that he discussed in terms of spatial ideas about "rooms." On this framework his interest as a plantsman was used to great effect, almost as interior decoration, inflecting the particular topographic and spatial situation: a balance between optimization and intervention. In view of Dutton's marginal gardening strategy, it is not surprising that each of the garden spaces is now hard to recognize since his death, and I found myself looking for clues in clearings, signs that he had done something where the garden seemed to be simply a wilderness. These signs, then, would have to endure, resist the effects of growing over, of species reduction, as the balance between the ornamental and the invasive deteriorated without intervention to favor the former.

In essence, I was looking for "landscaping": inorganic materials like stones that were nonrandom or naturalistic. Since Dutton had to carry everything up the hill, it is not surprising that not much landscaping is visible, and what was visible is generally overgrown by vegetation. Dutton's daughter Kirsty explained that while he did move rocks to create stepping stones and the like, he had an inherent compositional system that favored the almost seemingly random, about which he was nonetheless very particular: "no, not like that, like THAT." Thus there were occasional rockpiles that were steps, and groupings of stones in turf that were not quite stepping stones.

The three "axes" that Dutton used to explain the garden also represented the ways in which he moved materials around the garden to support his work. The first of these was from the garage on the road to the house, located on a ridge above the river, which pushed through vegetation. The second came from near the garage, leading from a naturally occurring bog that he had further developed to meet the first at a high point above the creek, near the "waterfall." Adjacent to the fence on the field edge furthest from the river, incorporating a later purchase of land, another path/axis runs close to the fence up to the top of the site, into a tree plantation that Dutton installed later, but which never quite matured; nonetheless it is a welcome moment of form among the amorphousness of the overgrown garden. On the other side of the creek,

FIGURE 6.10

An opening in the garden that Dutton used to make "rooms," adorning them, almost like interior decoration, with flowering plants (Courtesy of G. F. Dutton).

FIGURE 6.11

One of Dutton's "rooms" now, with only strimming-brush cutting to keep it open and only a few of the ornamental plants remaining.

FIGURE 6.12
A grouping of rocks, some of the little "landscaping" visible at Druimchardain, about which Dutton was nonetheless particular (Courtesy of G. F. Dutton).

FIGURE 6.13
The bog when it was "gardened" by Dutton, with two of his children looking at a hogweed. Both of them walked through the garden with me 30 years later (Courtesy of G. F. Dutton).

FIGURE 6.14
The bog, now unrecognizable, but the hogweed is still there. Dutton's adult son, now a doctor, warned me to be careful brushing against it, because it might interfere with my psoriasis treatment.

another path traverses a loose rock face adjacent to a pine forest to lead back from a crossing of the creek near the top of the site, which has a "swimming pool," down a hillside of heather, to meet the bridge and link back to the house.

While the cartoonish map of the garden—the author of which is unknown—used in *Some Branch against the Sky* emphasizes these longitudinal axes, in practice in Dutton's perambulations, as Kirsty remembers them, he in fact crossed over repeatedly from one axis to another, so that one rarely gets a strong sense of each, except that the small stony ridges that separate them are very evident on the ground. Organizing these paths longitudinally, on the one hand, provides maximum circulation

FIGURE 6.15

The waterfall on the burn, at the top of the site.

FIGURE 6.16

A plantation of trees at the top of the site, adjacent to the neighbor's farm, which never quite matured but is still a welcome moment of geometry in the overgrowth.

FIGURE 6.17

The children climb a hillside of heather on the opposite side of the creek from the house and main garden (Courtesy of G. F. Dutton).

on the narrow site, making it feel bigger than it is, but also frustrates some of the logical desire to move to the creek, whose tumbling sound is always present. The fact that Dutton did not base his design around the creek seems perverse until one remembers that he was an adventurer, an explorer of sea and mountains, and so logically chose to keep exploration as the primary circulatory mode for this wild feature.

Considering the steepness of the terrain, and the distance from the road that increases as one climbs, it is not surprising that, pragmatically, Dutton's marginal approach resembles a military operation. Both to store sets of required tools close to their location, as well as to shelter from the rain, Dutton created a series of small buildings throughout the garden. These resemble miniature sheds and operate rather like mountaineering base camps, from which tools rather than provisions could be distributed. The military theorist Carl von Clausewitz, in his book *On War*, discussed the difference between strategy and tactics: the former comprised top-down plans to meet military objectives, while the latter were used to deal with specific situations on the ground.[23] The act of provisioning, then, is strategic, insofar as it requires forethought of what should be where and when, for what purpose, but the use of such provisions is tactical. Since marginal gardening as a strategy was entirely tactical, these sheds and their deployment of resources did not follow an overall objective but were located and organized at a point where they could be used in a range of nearby locations, for reasons that would emerge through the gardening process. While in his writing Dutton described these huts as places in which to store tools, his daughter Kirsty and the family remember them as being "more for fun, each one with a different character, and built from different materials, at various stages of the garden's development. These were more follies… a fun place to shelter from the rain."[24]

In the search for evidence of Dutton's hand, one instead needs to surrender such recognition to beautiful moments that might seem to be natural, or exist autonomously, but must have been groomed to be visible by the marginal gardening strategy. While I had expected the clearings to provide the majority of these moments, in fact it was the transition between clearings, made up of agglomerations of rock and trees or shrubs,

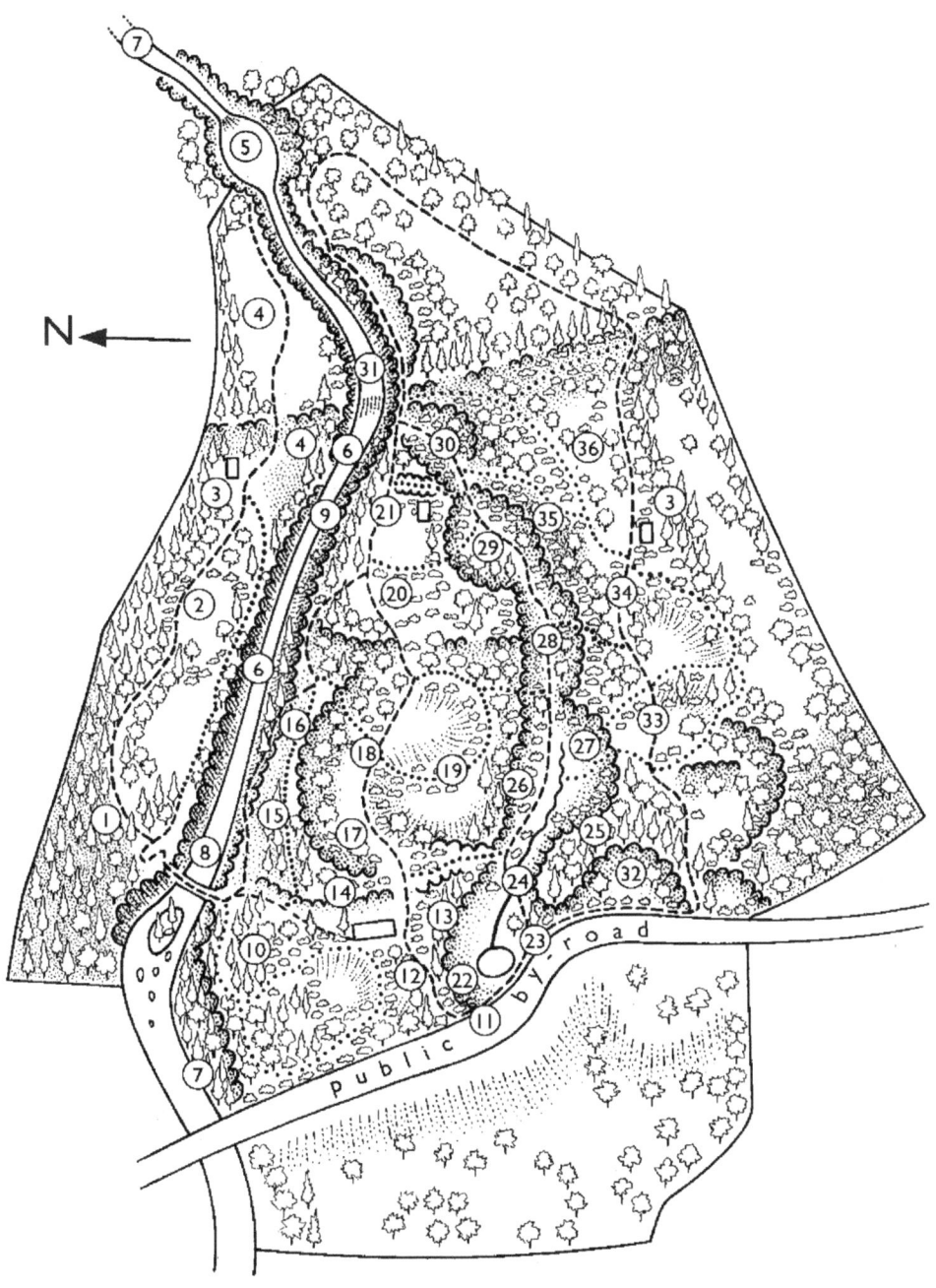

FIGURE 6.18

Map of Druimchardain from *Some Branch against the Sky*, used by Dutton, though its author is unknown (Courtesy of G. F. Dutton).

their long wavy limbs covered in the moss spanning them and their rock bases, merging them into one non-formal mass. In contrast, the clearings seemed empty, openings around something that was no longer there: a far cry from Dutton's descriptions and his photographs.

Now that their father has died, the upkeep of the garden by his daughter and sons seems somewhat *ad hoc*, which in principle suits marginal gardening but is in reality the path of least resistance now that no one lives on the site to give the garden constant attention. Dutton's widow, who lived there for most of the time, talked without bitterness about how much the garden was "his," yet she and the children worked on it constantly but were rarely recognized or creatively welcomed into developing it, though Kirsty felt differently: "We didn't feel cut out or un-recognised. Dad was definitely the creator of the garden but we all felt involved and appreciated for our input into upkeep, which was not considered a chore by us, just a way of life when you live in such a place."[25]

Dutton's daughter Kirsty and his sons Alasdair and Rory now (primarily) undertake the maintenance of the garden, each with different tools and approaches. Kirsty focuses on keeping grass down and passages open using a "strimmer" or weed-eater with a cable, while Alasdair focuses on opening and access using a pruning saw. When I asked Dutton's widow and children about whether they used their father's marginal strategy to guide their actions, they professed not to have been "involved in, or aware of his plans until we became involved in helping bring them to fruition."[26]

It seems clear when one visits the garden that it is going backward, losing both definition and diversity, though this is to bring a human judgment to bear on an ecological system that is performing perfectly well. When I ask Kirsty about what she wants to do there now that the place is theirs, she says that maintaining her father's authorship is the top priority,

FIGURE 6.19
One of Dutton's shelters that he used to store tools and materials along his routes, like a mountaineering base camp, and to shelter from the weather.

FIGURE 6.20
Rather than the spaces or rooms, the passages between now show most clearly Dutton's marginal approach, mostly because they can easily be maintained by his children since his death.

though she also likes the wildness of it, while acknowledging that her father would not have appreciated this. I point out that the qualities it had and has are the result of judgments about direction, action, rules and criteria, and that maybe she needs to take a position on the garden herself. Kirsty notes, however, that "it is important to acknowledge that my dad himself said, 'This garden will, I think, "ruin well".' He just couldn't let the ruining begin while he was still around, despite being much less able," further noting that the publisher and instigator of *Harvesting the Edge* had recently contacted them in a letter in which he commented: "the garden must be heading back to nature, as Geoff was very clear that it would. That was the nature of the garden, as it were."[27]

The closest contemporary landscape architecture theory and practice gets to a nonrepresentational engagement with the dynamic qualities of landscape is not through the development of better simulations but through design processes for real engagement with site qualities, a discourse I would call "site specificity."[28] Dutton's approach of "marginality" is a site-specific approach, but it differs from site specificity in landscape architecture because Dutton's is really a philosophy of practice, a criterion for engagement with what is literally in front of one as one makes a decision, rather than a change of inputs into the front end of the conventional design process in an office. It is interesting and useful to compare Dutton's idea of marginality with site-specificity discourse, because it highlights how his approach has landscape-architectural parallels.

Like Dutton, with his multidisciplinary approach to inquiry, the French landscape architects Catherine Mosbach and Marc Claramunt argue that "the compartmentalization of the process of [the]scientific ..., on the one hand, and [the]artistic ... on the other" "deprive each other of reciprocal connections," which Mosbach and Claramunt refer to as too often "exclusive systems," of phenomenon and memory respectively.[29] This position mirrors that of Dutton, and his claim that the separation between creative and scientific work was "artificial" recalls what Christophe Girot calls the "age-old opposition of nature and culture" in French landscape architecture since Le Nôtre.

Key to the contemporary interest in site is a recognition that place is a "more complex tangle of interrelated phenomena," which Girot has described in "Four Trace Concepts of Landscape Architecture," representing a design method which merges intuitive site response with rigorous scientific and historical research, revealing a continuity from site to design proposal that is site-specific.[30] These four concepts are Landing, Grounding, Finding, and Founding. Landing refers to the "first act of site acknowledgement... mark[ing] the beginning of the odyssey of the project," and "conveys the idea of touching ground and reaching for the confines of an unknown world."[31] During Landing, "everything is apprehended with wonderment and curiosity, with subjective and interpretive eyes."[32] While Landing happens only once, "Grounding is more about reading and understanding a site through repeated visits and studies."[33] For Girot this is a more rigorous and laborious stage, where initial intuitions are tested and attempts are made to understand the invisible logics of the site. It is difficult to distinguish "Finding" from "Grounding" in its emphasis on searching, though it alludes to a hunch, "the *je ne sais quoi* ingredient that conveys a distinct quality of place," but is an active engagement with site.[34] The "alchemical component in the design process," Finding "discloses the evidence to support one's initial intuitions about a place."[35] The final step, "Founding," is "the most durable and significant of the trace acts," where "the three prior acts are synthesized into a new and transformed construction of the site," though Girot notes that "Founding is always a reaction to something that is already there."[36] This idea about Founding is clearly linked to Dutton's strategy of marginality, though his impetus is as much pragmatic as philosophical.

At the beginning of *Some Branch against the Sky*, Dutton establishes his interest in site specificity with a chapter describing the site entitled "A Walk Around," the first line of which is "The design of any wild marginal garden is dictated by site, and none more truly than my own."[37] Considering that the *OED* defines "inquiry" as "the act of asking for information," when Dutton unites his scientific work with his garden work via inquiry he is treating the proposition, his work in the garden at a point in time, as an intermediate stage in an ongoing series of experiments. Like the foundation for a building, Girot's "Founding" is the platform for the next stage of evolution, continuous with what is already there, a new part of its existing story rather than a separate autonomous project; as Dutton notes: "much of the pleasure has come from using these few resources [of the site] in the most effective way, and from finding that way in the first place."[38]

As a poet might, Dutton articulated this approach on a number of different levels around the analogy of "margin," which is "the edge or border of something" (*OED*).[39] In terms of land use and ownership, Druimchardain has two margins: on one side the margin of agricultural land that was long ago cleared for sheep grazing; on the other a largely natural creek. Indeed, this marginality is what permitted the purchase of the property from the neighboring farmer, who did not even regard it as a place, since its topography and vegetation precluded use, agreeing to excise this useless "margin" from his adjacent field.

Located at "the limit of cultivation…the land itself is classifiable as marginal"—in terms of productive agriculture, since it is composed of "fluvoglacial boulders and silt heaped about shattered bedrock," but also in terms of altitude limiting plant growth, on the margin between climate zones.[40] Dutton talked about the folds of the geology on the site, which could also be referred to as a margin. The garden was therefore also of "marginal" economic value, corresponding to another definition from economics of marginal as "close to the limit of profitability, especially through difficulty of exploitation" (*OED*).

The gardening that Dutton was undertaking was also marginal insofar as it "relates to or results from small changes" (*OED*), the garden "minimally [perhaps marginally?] differentiated from its environment."[41] This was because of the difficult nature of the land, which limited the possibilities of what could be done economically, as well as the existing "attractiveness" of the site. Dutton worked with what he had in small and incremental ways: "gardening therefore had to be unobtrusive: a guiding of the latent design, a prolonged consultation with the Genius of the Place [which] intensive horticulture would ruin,"[42] where, despite the detailed historical lineage of the concept, *genius loci* could broadly be read as an earlier incarnation of the notion of site specificity.[43] At the same time, however, Dutton still thought it could be improved, since "[I]n the jargon of ecology it was moribund and called for a healing hand. Still, restoration would invite, as always, 'meddling' (to employ a Jekyllian rebuke)."[44]

Dutton also saw himself as a "marginal gardener": "I manage the place alone, and for 25 years did so only at free weekends and occasional evenings." However, as both he and his garden aged, reminiscent of Andersson's hypothetical difficulty of climbing the ladder at Marnas to prune his henyard as he too got older, Dutton wrote: "Now that I have more time to dig and hack, I grow less physically able. I remain marginal, a curator; unable to interfere too disastrously."[45]

Dutton's definition of the marginal gardener is based on his own labor, so it is not surprising that as a scientist he used energy as model and criterion for considering action in relation to its result, focused on accepting the site as already operational or active thermodynamically, and proposed that any change should be "minimally costed in gardener's energy."[46] Such meddling needs to be economical because, as he explains, "the natural forces operating here are so violent, the vegetation exploiting them so precisely selected, and the biological equilibrium therefore so finely poised, that a gardener is rapidly taught humility."[47] He takes a calm and pragmatic view of the form of the garden as a provisional state of energy at a particular point in time; thus "a marginal garden can be made anywhere and to any degree of formality, consistent with minimal input of energy."[48]

In this careful dynamic of doing and not doing, of balancing horticultural or space-shaping desires, "marginality is highly instructive," "the gardener taught humility … as time and again, presumptions blasted apart, he must escape to shelter to digest the lesson." Just as Burle Marx said that he learned everything he knew at the Sítio, for Dutton, "experiences in this place should therefore interest all who like to know more about plants," since he was able to test the limits of species in different locations and under different regimes, such as drought or frost.

SITE POETRY

When one is talking to designers, it is easy to forget that drawings are just one type of representation, with their own propensity, more often than not, for proposition as much as analysis. However, for the gardener, working across seasons and through the daily drudge of gardening work, prose, often in the form of a diary—or, in Dutton's case, a poem—is more often used as a representation of the relationship between garden and gardener. For Dutton, verse was a way of precisely traversing this relationship. He talked about the "external" experiences of what would now be called "extreme sports" in similar terms to the way he talked about his science, comprising "fairly vigorous bundles of sensory data...disciplining [his] response...so that [he] stayed sufficiently alive to bring in more," while his poetry was concerned with "the internal environment."[49]

Poetry was a representational medium for Dutton, an interface which, "when tuned...to the whole explored environment—inner and outer—[brought] insights which supplant prose logic, an artifact provocative enough to grasp the hand that holds it."[50] This dynamic is skewed more to the internal for Mosbach and Claramunt, the project and the writing about it being facets of the same thing, projecting: "A project, a text or a work have more value thanks to the internal conditions of its coming into being than the reproduction of a real situation."[51] Discussing Dutton's "curious mixture of poetry and science," an interviewer asked him: "Do you keep the mental landscapes distinct and compartmentalised?," to which he replied: "I'm interested in exploring things and I can see no great difference between exploring one area and another, whether it's lab research...or messing around with plants and forests....It seems to me they are different aspects of the same thing, which is enquiry."[52] Following on, the interviewer asks: "Do you think about science in poetic terms and vice versa?," and Dutton replies: "No. These are artificial terms and labels. If you are trying to understand physical happenings of geology or physiology you tend to follow certain rules. If you are trying to express yourself in language, that's much the same....The main thing is to keep your eyes and your mind open."[53]

Dutton's approach to poetry could also be described as "marginal." Ward admires the way he is "able to maintain the maximum energy in minimal structures of word and image for reasons which are connected with the fact that they belong so securely to one place, its language and its landscape."[54] The critic Alan Wall described Dutton's poetry as "clean as a whistle," referring to this minimal—or, rather, marginal—quality.[55]

While he was a private poet, Dutton shyly showed his poetry to a visiting American poet in residence at Dundee University, Anne Stevenson, who encouraged him to publish it. Stevenson went on to write extensively about Dutton, admiring his poetry, "which reverences existence in all its manifestations."[56] Stevenson also notes that "on a first reading, Dutton's work appears cold, remote from human feelings, concerned as it so often is with the mountains and waterfalls and rocks and seas of Scotland"; however, "actually, people are very much at the centre of it. He is writing about the human predicament. Since it is a predicament that involves people in the world, it is this relationship that Dutton explores."[57] This description of the writer as an experiencer of landscape recalls the models of site specificity that Claramunt and Mosbach outline, as well as Girot's model, where there is a dynamic and not necessarily unscientific relationship between human and natural subjects.

Reviewing a collection of poems related to science, Stevenson notes the fears of the poets Blake and Keats about the rise of the "Newtonian universe" and the destruction of the poet's

> cherished preserve of mystery, romance and the life of the spirit. Perhaps what they feared most of all—and what poets fear today—was that science, with its exact instruments, its logic, its ruthless measurements and indifference to personality would eventually marginalise them. A world in which science replaced poetry as a vital force would enslave the language and put it to work for materialism.[58]

Instead she commends the editors of the volume for "remind[ing] us that Wordsworth (differing from Blake and Keats) did anticipate a time in which the poet might be called upon to carry 'sensation into the midst of the objects of Science itself.'"[59] With the person positioned at the center of phenomena, the disjunction between empirical analysis and creative proposition is removed, and this makes Dutton's poetry the logical key to understanding his garden. Unlike drawing, where the proposition stands alone, separate from its future incarnation, Dutton's marginal strategy parallels the growth of both himself and his garden, articulated through the documentation and reflection of what he did.

Marian Macken calls this type of representation "post-factum documentation" and discusses the propositional nature of architectural representation, which "is predominantly concerned with architectural space yet to be materialised," instead proposing another type of drawing "post-factum" documentation that comes after, literally, the existence of the building.[60] Macken notes that since "post-factum documentation is seen as occurring once a project is finished, it is excluded from the design process." Instead she suggests that "by examining the place of post-factum documentation in more depth, it is seen not as neutral representation, but rather as interpretive and, therefore, exploratory and generative." Macken's definition indicates how one could think of Dutton's use of poetry, since it captures experiences and leanings that inform his developing practice of marginal gardening, making the post-factum documentation "integral to the design process...acknowledging the reflective and recursive nature of this process."[61]

If we treat the poem as a type of design representation, with logic and rigor, then we can unpack Dutton's practice from his poems, and see how that practice engages with site. The poem from which his book on marginal gardening gets its title, *Some Branch against the Sky*, is instructive in showing the dynamic relationship between author and garden, offering a kind of algorithm that I will then use to study the other poems:

   Why,

   ... just to choose
    a corner of the wilderness
    is to enclose

    it with intent
    Is to create
    Garden, gardener

    a life spent
    cropping the rubble, a desire
    to regulate

what goes by,
catch at a scent, ensure
some branch against the sky,

is to incur
from the first day
what creation cost, the haste

to cut and tear,
rake things over.
At the least we need

to look about, decide
what wild flower,
that may have led you there,

is now a weed.

To the poem he appends a note: "No small responsibility, a garden; however marginal."[62]

From the start of the poem, Dutton states his position on the culture/nature divide, which has caused havoc for landscape architecture: whether through creating a separation where none exists, or through fixating on the debilitating debate required to qualify the relationship between nature and culture. By placing "choose" next to "wilderness," Dutton is clearly locating himself in the paradigm where the natural world is rendered cultural through the act of site selection, which he describes as "enclosure," recognizing that the act of choosing a place is artificially to separate a moment from a larger contiguous ecological situation. Here he is recognizing his indisputable agency in the place, confirming that both garden and gardener, himself, are created in this process. Like Andersson's, Dutton's observation alludes to a recursive dialectic of simultaneous and adjacent change in both garden and gardener.

Dutton's marginal strategy is one where he inflects what exists, which has been called curatorial, but his process is often indirect. I have used the term "working at a remove," which Roel van Gerwen has called "steering processes,"[63] to describe this way of working. Whereas design specifies what something is, when we are working at a remove we are focused instead on what something does. Dutton calls this "regulation" of the system; he uses rubble to create space for things to grow or not grow. Here the poem is alluding to his way of working, carefully calibrated to site and to phenomenal experience, guided by a "scent." Critically for the viridic, taking such ephemeral cues from site is possible only when one works in real time in the space itself. Apart from the autonomous existence of site phenomena, such phenomena can direct one to formal or aesthetic aspects of the existing site, such that a smell could be a cue to look up and see a branch that might influence an onsite design decision.

Dutton's thermodynamic view of marginal gardening is also evident in the poem when he speaks of the "cost of creation," meaning the difference between short-term actions and the energy used to undertake them in "haste," like "cutting," "tearing," and raking," and their long-term effects, or lack thereof in the face of the inevitable trajectory of the garden that can be modified—or, as I prefer to say, "aimed"—but not entirely circumvented. Coming full circle back to the start of the poem, where he talked about the interdependent creation of garden and gardener, he returns to the development of judgment over time, acknowledging that one of the very ephemeral factors that might have triggered acts in the garden, a flower in bloom, might, after the passage of time, be deemed a weed. This is the process of learning from things that have arisen through regulation, then changing future decisions that cannot happen in representation: a key feature of the viridic, which we also saw in Burle Marx's work at the Sítio, and Andersson's at Marnas.

Since both people and plants grow and change, the passage of time of the environment is something that the gardener shares with the plants she tends; both are exposed to the same vagaries of climate which, to a considerable extent, determine their activities. If landscape-architectural readings of landscape designs tend to be interested in notions like "space," much gardening literature uses seasonality as a similar structuring principle. Poetry is a serious mode of post-factum design representation, calibrated to the real world as found, where time and change are inherent parts of that world. Correspondingly, the seasonality of Dutton's poems in *Harvesting the Edge* paints a very dynamic picture of the experiential space of the viridic.

WINTER

The description of the garden in *Harvesting the Edge* is inseparable from the seasons that affect it, beginning with "winter's first crystal," winter "logical to begin," since it "halfway interrupts the programme of growth," whereas to end with it would "slam the door shut."[64] Winter is interesting to Dutton because it is during this time that plants are most clearly architectonic, recalling James Rose's taxonomy from chapter 3. For Dutton, early winter "opens the garden to searching introspection" where "tree-form and proportion of evergreen stand bare, unassisted by autumn colour or spring promise; and before snow has arrived to bury or bend everything to its own purposes."[65]

Kirsty describes how, during heavy snow, Dutton would wrench up buried limbs from beneath a surface of snow to stop them being broken by the weight of it: an act involving an unusual intimacy with the plants, like rescuing whales from a beach. When the shape of the garden was visible, he used this legibility to make decisions about space and visibility, and "resolv[ing] what trees would be better away."

During winter, Dutton said, he "tread[ed] snow somewhere in this garden for eighty-seven days in a year, sometimes over a hundred."[66] From his patrols of the garden during winter comes Dutton's most quoted poem, used by Anne Stevenson in her obituary:

> it is only the simple sunlight
> on a fence post, out of snow,
>
> and I come to set it upright
> at the cost of a single blow.
>
> then I leave them to the sunlight.
> one straight post,
> trodden snow.

The shared meter of garden and gardener are clear in this poem, with its description of parity between him and his environment, both affected by and affecting phenomena. In material terms the garden is qualitatively different, as in winter it is made of snow that registers the

FIGURE 6.21

Dutton appreciated the way winter brought out the architectonic qualities of plants, much like those analyzed by James Rose (Courtesy of G. F. Dutton).

sun differently: the glorious contradiction between a sun that warms and melts and the snow of winter that should resist but actually complements it. Just as the snow will pass, so too will most of Dutton's activity, the signs of his patrolling treads in the snow that will disappear as it melts. But at the same time, the post is now corrected, its straightness a statement: I was here.

In architectural theory, where the phenomenal is important but foiled by the solidity of building, phenomenology would be the discourse used to describe situations like this. However, as Graham Harman notes, this discourse generalizes the particularity to the physical out of existence, not allowing it to inflect the definitions used to describe it.[67] In object-oriented ontology, on the other hand,[68] the object remains opaque and persistent in some secrecy after the human has interacted with it: the post now straight but left behind by Dutton, only partially known since no one is left to see it. In the timespan of the garden, the gardener and his subject interact but move past each other, each on their own path, their vectors only slightly redirected.

Another sign of this calibration, with the weight of the difficulty of working in the snow, is Dutton's labor in setting the post right, "at the cost of a single blow." As mentioned, the notion of "cost" of labor in Dutton's work is described in *Some Branch against the Sky* in thermodynamic terms: another dimension to marginal gardening, which is about maximum effect from minimal labor, as Dutch artist and teacher Louis G. Le Roy would agree: "for anyone who thinks and works ecologically, the most important aspect is the management of energy."[69]

Since energy is never destroyed, "thermodynamics" essentially refers to the way it is transferred, as described by the First Law of Thermodynamics, via the energy's changes of state: from water to steam, for example. The Second Law of Thermodynamics describes how "entropy," often called disorder, increases as this change of state occurs, until the system reaches equilibrium, when it becomes static or unchanging.[70] While this was a problem for classical thermodynamics, for Dutton it is a welcome, unifying factor that calibrates the actions of man to the environment, such that he can speak of the "cost of a single blow" and the phenomena of the environment in the same poem.

Thought of in this way, as Erwin Schrödinger writes, "entropy is itself a measure of order,"[71] but also, in Dutton's hands, a logic or ordering. At Druimchardain, therefore, Dutton is forming entropy, a role that Luis Fernández-Galiano ascribes to architecture, which "can be understood as a material organization that regulates and brings order to energy flows."[72]

The order in one system arises from the loss of order, or a leak, from another system across a state-change boundary. In the poem Dutton's path to the post and the light on the snow are part of the same energy cycle, where heat acts to regulate both what is possible for Dutton and the qualities of light on the snow. Speaking in terms of thermodynamics and entropy, the most that can be described in an ordered way is not the thing itself but its form in a moment of change, as its energy moves through time and space—something which Sanford Kwinter discussed in relation to Boccioni and the futurists, as I said in the Introduction.[73]

Prigogine and Kondepudi use the notion of local equilibrium as a way of literally measuring entropy in position and time, treating a moment as an autonomous system before it again changes state, at which point it becomes another system with different properties.[74] If we take Harman's model of objects as unknowable, and place it alongside thermodynamics, we see that objects are always changing state, inflecting and being inflected by their environment. Dutton's activity in making small changes to the energy flow of the site is part of a process that leaves few direct traces, but has a flow-through of effects.

SPRING

While spring is regarded as a time of growth, at Druimchardain it is marked by winds which limit Dutton's activity in the garden, since "nothing is so tiring as continual wind. There is nowhere to rest."[75] Wind heralds the end of winter and the start of spring: "for example, a southwesterly hastens it," whereas "an east wind calls back winter overnight."[76] A plant that can survive and prosper in such winds must "balance contentedly in equilibrium between received stresses and the strategies—external and internal—it has evolved to overcome them." Dutton is interested in external adaptations, such as "a leaf... cunningly arranged

FIGURE 6.22

A space in spring, protected from damaging winds and frosts by baffles of vegetation at the edges (Courtesy of G. F. Dutton).

to receive optimal sunlight," as well as internal, as a molecular biologist and a proponent of "enzyme ecology" would be: the "molecular photochemical system" that the plant possesses, "built, stocked and tuned to give maximal efficiency to whatever light its position exposes it to." Both these are linked to the governing system of thermodynamics, since "these subtle changes far below the visible [are] tied into the energy budget of the whole plant by alterations in other working modules."[77]

Dutton uses the architecture of plants to moderate the wind by creating "baffles...with informal 'hedges' or grouped bushes in a 'Japanese' way that 'check wind'" as well as "help to make compartments, and reduce frost build-up by assisting drainage of cold air."[78] While it operates microclimatically, "the touching up of walls, doorways, even vaulting, of the garden compartments is almost compulsive." Like Andersson, with his hedges and his thought experiment about the hens becoming a hawthorn grove when he can no longer climb a ladder, Dutton's tools ("ladder, saw, secateurs and shears") govern what can be achieved, though he cautions that, as in wood engraving, "what you take out can't be put back."[79] However, even though we cannot put back removed plant form (as we saw in the case of the Marnas garden), the plant will nonetheless respond with growth, taking a trajectory established by the tools in response to its existing shape. By way of illustration, Dutton provides a poem, ambiguously situated between critique of pruning practices in the suburban garden and a description of his own pruning practice:

> ... look at the wild birch,
> and then what you have done.
> with your sly touch,
> your knife's edge,
> to make it fit
> under your sun, sit
>
> in your hedge,
> inhabit
> your street. to make it sweat
> through that clean cut
> all last night such hate, white
> from the root.

Dutton's predilections in terms of garden aesthetics are clear in this poem, even though he states elsewhere that the marginal garden has no set form, since it is governed by the dynamic relationship between human labor and environmental response. By "looking at the wild birch and then what you have done" he is seeking to calibrate gardening practice to the nature of the wild plant. In itself this does not contradict the energy dynamic of the marginal garden, but it does demonstrate its nuanced or styled naturalism, which makes it difficult to see what has been done onsite.

The "knife's edge" refers to a literal part of the tool used to manipulate the plant, but, considered with the pruner's "sly touch," implies an act of judgment. The gardener's touch is sly because he has an agenda whereby one has to be careful, one's decisions a "knife's edge" between an appropriate level of modification to keep the natural plant's form while also making it "fit under [one's] sun"; the tool's use an instance of interspecies judgment.

At this point the poem flags up an ethical shift of focus, making its straw man gardener aware of his specific agenda, the fact that, despite photosynthesizing the same light as humans might burn under, the sun is "yours," the gardener's. Highlighting the fact that the plant is in the gardener's space, after these acts of modification have been undertaken, Dutton asks the pruner to somehow get into the space of the plant, to "sit in your hedge": to see what one has done, but also to understand something of what it is to be a plant. In cutting the plant, the gardener has made it "sweat": made it adjust its physiology to suit his own desires, and then drawn upon human emotions to describe its anger at what has been done: "hate, white from the root." While Michael Marder's turn toward the plant tries to treat it as sentient, Dutton's characterization anthropomorphizes it, giving it human emotions like hate. Marder attempts to speculate on a plant intelligence whereby its emotions, if one could call them that, are communicated via growth and hormonal response, and certain trajectories in relation to the environment.[80] Sharing a space of the same energy and physiology that plants occupy, Dutton's anthropomorphism reminds us of our parallels with them.

SUMMER

In summer, "the sense of urgency has left garden and gardener" as "summer unfolds, spread[ing] into an upholstery of foliage. Leaves lie back, drink the lazy sun; flowers relax."[81] Even as Dutton was interested in and attentive to different plants and their qualities, he always had an eye on the garden as a whole and its series of spaces, which were threatened by the intensity of growth during summer: "All this expanding paradise ... tends to engulf the structure of the place; its compartments become stuffed with flowers and confused by foliage. Yet we are so topographically complex we must keep the overall plan visible; otherwise, rather than surprise, it bewilders—delightful in detail but overwhelming in the mass. An unorganised profusion."[82] Like James Rose, in summer Dutton works on "horizontals" and "verticals" to "restore calm."[83]

The "summer horizontal" is comprised of "largely flat" grassy planes which, Dutton says, provide some relief and respite from the garden's topographical complexity. Their strict planarity and close cropping—by Dutton's mowing, and now Kirsty's "strimming" using a weed-eater—allows for the "vertical" forms of the shrubs that constitute their edge to be more pronounced. Dutton said he could "hardly overstress the importance of this closely-mown green horizontal of lawns and paths."[84]

It was important for them to be flat and short, because "even two inches' growth blurs the picture." In Dutton's taxonomy of horizontals and verticals, the horizontal is a graduated arc from a closely shaved base (which he calls "the horizontal stabiliser of the plan") to a fuzzy curve where it blends into the vertical. This graduation of lawn into forest is similar to the one used by Olmsted to blend these two types of space in his parks.

To minimize labor, Dutton encouraged mosses and other short species that did not require maintenance but otherwise resembled a trimmed lawn. At each of his huts—which I have been calling "base camps"—he kept a "Scandinavian hand mower" for the paths, and he described keeping them short at the center, then allowing them to grow longer where they blended naturally into vegetation, their height varied by "tilting the mower to one wheel, which appears to broaden the path and enlarge the lawn."[85] Dutton "shuns motorised assistance where possible"—not only because such equipment is heavy to carry up the slope, but also because its "noise and fumes and maintenance obstruct one's partnership with the living garden."

In practice gardeners tweak their gardens all the time, reacting to changes as they emerge, using tools and techniques to directly affect the landscape. However, for landscape architects the use of a tool is either ignored, or specified for others in a document rather than undertaken directly. Dutton's focus on logistics and the experience of undertaking maintenance acts is calibrated to this spatial ambition in much the same way as that of the French gardener and *paysagiste* Gilles Clément, who

FIGURE 6.23

Dutton emphasized "verticals" and "horizontals" in summer to control chaotic growth (Courtesy of G. F. Dutton).

FIGURE 6.24

Mown paths in summer, their edges shaped by tipping the mower up on one wheel (Courtesy of G. F. Dutton).

also used mowing to create hybrid vegetation types in his "garden in movement" projects, such as at Parc Citroën (1986) and the Parc Henri Matisse (1992).[86] The garden in movement "refers to the physical movement of plant species on the land, which the gardener interprets in his own way," interpretations that comprise maintenance or gardening acts.[87] As in the purported Zen koan "before enlightenment: chop wood and carry water; after enlightenment: chop wood and carry water,"[88] both Dutton and Clément merge their aims with the kinesthetic banality of their acts. Dutton, for instance, achieves his spatial effect of gradation from the horizontal to the vertical by tilting the mower, which we can visualize in our imagination as his body twisting, and the wheels leaving the ground like a racing car taking a corner.

While Dutton is intimate with many plants in the garden, if volume of description is anything to go by, lawn, or the horizontal, is not a plant for him in the way that a rose is: a vertical. Therefore, on the whole he prefers not to cut the vertical, preferring correct selection and placement to achieve his effect, noting of the rose that it "romps freely … as it should … for a clipped wild rose is like a pinioned bird."[89] Another plant with an important vertical role is the "un-clippable" giant hogweed, with its two-meter-tall flower spike and large leaves, that Dutton trains to "rise in important places and toast the summer."[90]

Compared to the "imperial gestures of gardening"—which, we might suspect, is a reference to the English landscape garden, closer to landscape architecture—"just to rule over these ephemerals [of summer] can sometimes please better than more imperial gestures of gardening. You live like them, king for a day.

> … of course it is
> gratifying to see
> those great cedars I planted,
> evergreen
> acres of them, such a fine
> memorial, but in some ways
>
> I should like to die
> clean.

>   annuals make
>
>   the best subjects."

When Dutton talks about change in the garden and the landscape, the grand old tree is a symbol of growth, the passage of time, because it is so old. However, I would argue that what is really interesting about plants in the landscape is not time, which is simply a universal system of measurement, but rather change, which is the physical result of time's passing, not an abstract measurement of it. In his poem, Dutton reflects on this dialectic between time and change in relation to himself and the other organisms, plants, in his garden. The "great cedars" he planted, which are now huge, while still paralleling his own growing into old age, seem like a memorial. In their magnificence, looking at them is like looking in a mirror, more a representation of all that has gone before than what is happening now, their growth and change, like that of people, almost imperceptible in the moment but visible in old photos, which one looks at and thinks, comparing them to one's own internal vividness: "Is that me?" The cedars are a memorial because their scale is a reminder of their proximity to senescence, to death. In other writing on the garden, Dutton notes, about photographing the conifers, that "the photographic record of their growth, along with that of your family, is fascinating."[91]

In this poem, however, Dutton prefers "annuals," which "make the best subjects." There is some ambiguity here: does he mean that the annuals are subjects in the sense of a focus of study or observation, or subjects in the sense that Dutton is their ruler: a model that resembles Ferrari's (discussed above), where the gardener is the totalitarian ruler whose fickle aesthetic tastes determine whether a subject, a plant, lives or dies in the ruler's domain.

If we bear in mind Dutton's emphasis on the seasons in his book, it is not surprising that he likes the annual, because its whole life cycle is played out in four seasons. Although every plant is growing, as a representation of growth the annual cycle perceptibly, and within short-term human memory, encapsulates the entire life process, gives it a perceptible dimension. The annual in Dutton's garden is like the speeded-up tree.

Since the gardener practices design in the same "meter" as the garden, perhaps Dutton wants to revel in the "present" of growth like the annual, rather than the trees, a mirror of future age and decay.

AUTUMN

Whereas summer is about green foliage, in autumn "colour comes back, as tired August greens sharpen to yellows and orange, washed lucent by rain."[92] It is also a time when "flowers become superfluous."[93]

Inasmuch as autumn signals a change of color, from flower to foliage, for Dutton it is also a time when there is a change of material focus in the language of the garden: alchemical, from color, initially of flowers, but then to form, and, in a way, from space. Whereas in summer pruning edits leaf mass to define a space, leaves providing an opacity from one space to another, in autumn the transparency through trees allows for another emphasis on structure, always a concern for Dutton. In a digital design analogy, it is like going from a rendered to a wire-frame mode, where all the constituent parts, rather than just their effects, can be seen at the same time.

In autumn Dutton undertakes what he calls "brashing," which is the thinning of branches: he cuts them off above head height, which "wonderfully clears both wood and mind; new perspectives open once that clutter is removed."[94] Here again we see Dutton drawing parallels between himself and the landscape: an analogy between the physical state of the landscape and his mental state. This parity demonstrates the deeply rewarding engagement that people have with the plants in their gardens, which might sound romantic but is in fact quite pragmatic, because it involves small, simple actions in the space and time interval of growth.

> He wrote about
> felling trees
> and planting them.
>
> as when he cut down
> a fifty foot larch
> he put there at nine inches

FIGURE 6.25

In autumn, "colour comes back to the garden" (Courtesy of G. F. Dutton).

and planted a pine

at four and a half. that

is not to create.

it is what he was writing about

a weeping of forests

from one genesis.⁹⁵

When Dutton says that felling trees "is not to create" but "what he was writing about," he is demonstrating self-consciousness about his act of representation in writing about the garden, which is an inherent part of the way he gardens. Here Dutton reminds me of Ian Burn, who produced "Value Added Landscapes," artworks that incorporated amateur landscape paintings he found in thrift stores on his travels, on top of which he transposed a layer of text, written by himself, that sought to express what the painting was saying, as well as commenting on writing about landscape.⁹⁶ As with Dutton, these are reflections, and a recognition that landscape exists in the telling.

As in the summer, when Dutton wrote about the cedars as a mirror, here he is writing about growth and consequence. Planting for both the landscape architect and the gardener is an act of gambling, an estimation of future size. The gardener, though, must live with the consequences of their decisions, while for the landscape architect they are generally someone else's problem. The perspective of seeing things grow that I am celebrating in this book, then, can be as much a curse as a blessing, since it also makes the gardener patently aware of their mistakes; Dutton's conifer forests are an example of this. In the color brochure he produced to accompany *Some Branch against the Sky*, entitled "The Year's Colour in a Marginal Garden,"⁹⁷ Dutton has a photo of a small Douglas fir, taken thirty-five years earlier, with the caption: "One remembers carrying armfuls of future giants." Elsewhere he regrets planting so many conifers, and indeed when one visits the site now, large parts of it are monocultures of trunks, their removal too serious an exercise, and difficult logistically on this topographically challenging site.

With the site overplanted and so dense with vegetation, as I found it too, for Dutton, any removal "seems an improvement...any rawness balanced by floods of light and the comfort that young growth smooths things over."[98] Thus, while removal is "not to create," as he says in the poem, in his final analysis such removals catalyze ecological effects with desirable spatial outcomes. This is an interesting dimension to working as a gardener with ecological effects: often it is not the process of tending which gets results, but the influencing of conditions to trigger plants' own processes. Often, subtracting or doing nothing has the greatest effects.

CONCLUSION

Landscape architects tend to have little serious interest in gardens, for precisely the reason why I focus on Druimchardain in this chapter: they have little, if any, evidence of design in a formal sense. If one relies almost entirely on plant growth, few artifacts exist to be grabbed hold of, captured in any enduring way, to say "Here! I did it!" They are slippery: their entire presence is dependent on what happened, and how recently. Yet when we read Dutton's writing about his garden, it evidently has a strategic and design sense that is clearly landscape-architectural. That is why it was strangely disappointing, when I visited the garden, to find little record of this, as the practices of maintenance have changed since he passed away, and his children, who work on it, do not share his vision: instead of focusing on his approach as a guide, they focus, naturally, on parts that remind them of him.

I emphasize the role and problems of representation so much in this book because I feel that they tie landscape design to a static paradigm which does not suit the nature of the material that makes it interesting in the first place: growth. Instead, as we have moved through the case studies, I have been arguing for a separation of design from representation and its redefinition as a type of judgment linked to concerns that are reflected in design, such as form, space, material quality, and—importantly—a certain strategic speculation. Dutton's garden demonstrates the danger of doing this, because it can seem as if all is lost: because its quality was dependent on a single moment of perfection, long past. However, I argue that if the ball was thrown at the moment when drawing was left behind, and was then in the air, decontextualized, Dutton's poetry as a post-factum documentation, as a capturing of what was done and its effects, provides a model for the way representation can be brought back into a design-oriented discussion of the garden.

In Dutton's poems we see how embedded the gardener is in their own subjectivity in the garden, engaging intersubjectively with plants. Working in the intervals of the garden, the gardener is calibrated to the plant's growth; the qualities of such growth are anthropomorphized to become a description of the gardener's emotion; the subject/object barrier is dissolved. This proximity and intimacy do not sit easily with the professional, dispassionate, and rational methods of the landscape architect. A relationship like this is claustrophobic, precarious, contingent, with too much at stake.

The joy and the horror of the garden are two sides of the viridic, and can be seen clearly at Druimchardain: growing and overgrown. They are the same thing, really, because the trajectory of growth is independent of human desires until we intervene in it. If we don't intervene, it just keeps going. When a landscape architect is judged, years later, on how their planting has worked over time, when all they did was specify a species and a location, that is hard on them. In a sense the gardener has it easier, since they can direct it as they go. But, as I have been arguing in describing the viridic, there is no need to choose: we can do both, and this is why the next and final case study, Insel Hombroich, is so relevant.

CHAPTER 7

WAIT and SEE

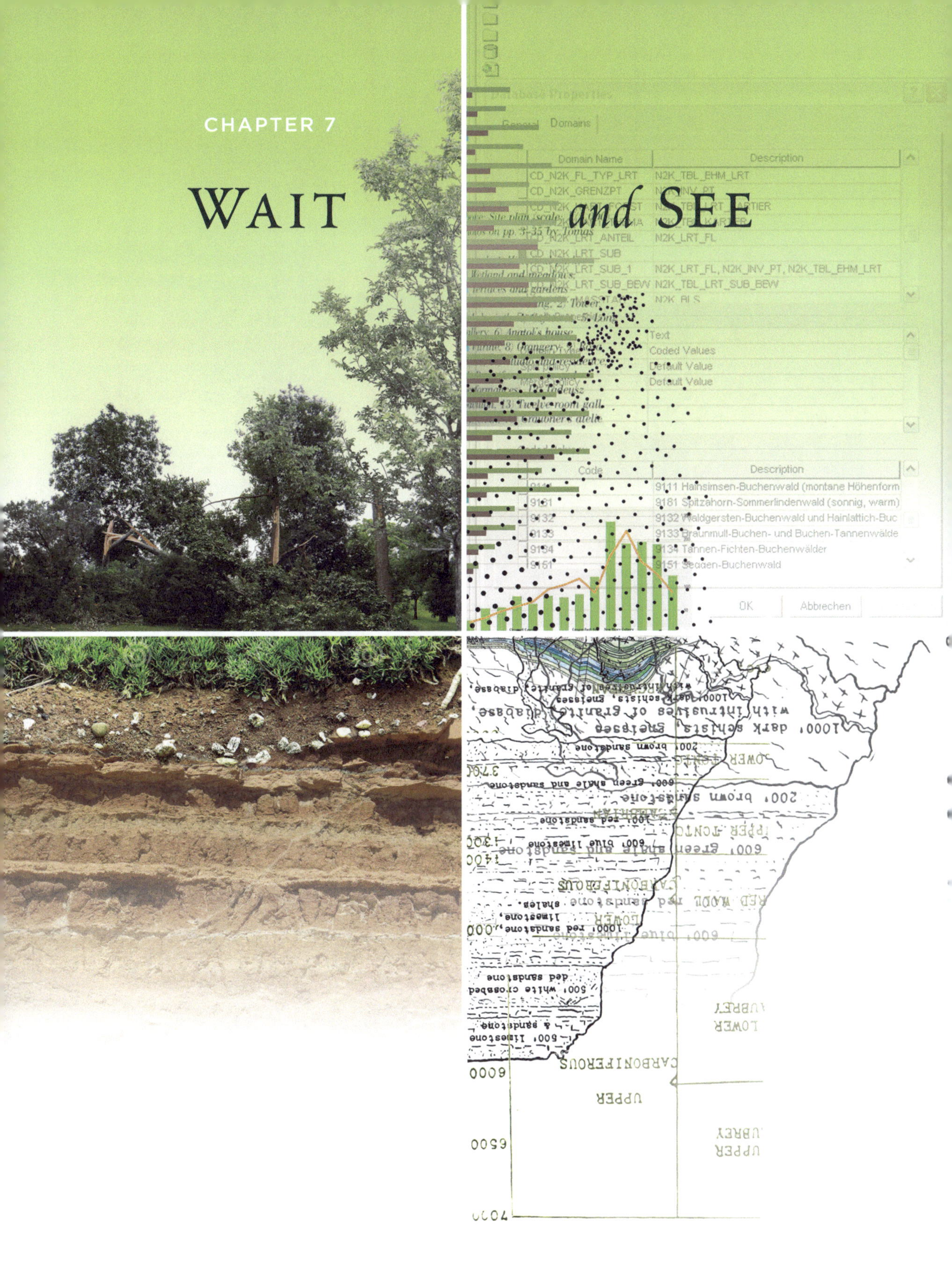

Dislocated from representational design practice, developing over many years, the pursuit of a designed landscape becomes a question of management. Where all the materials of a landscape are ephemeral to differing degrees (perennial plants very much so, trees less so, and the soil less so again), personal philosophies, approaches, or fads and fashions of the time determine how a landscape changes. Often, where a plan produced by the designer does exist it is relegated to a drawer in an archival filing cabinet, while the progression of the landscape is marked by different but linked recursive activities, ranging from daily sweeping of paths and rubbish collection to periodic mowing or annual pruning, for example. Exceptions to this are occasional capital works aimed at replacement and upgrading of failing elements, or dealing with unforeseeable disasters. Often the hierarchies of organization replicate at each scale and with the passage of time, as the concerns of diverse workers involved in a project are reflected in the way they regard that project, and what they do there.

FIGURE 7.2
Erwin Heerich's Hohe Galerie at Insel Hombroich (1988), with the mature plantings of landscape architect Bernhard Korte.

While I was talking with a German friend about my research on gardening and my interest in how landscapes are shaped by horticultural technique, she suggested that I should visit the Stiftung Insel Hombroich near Düsseldorf, where she had seen activities like tree-trimming used creatively.[1] While I had enjoyed the project thoroughly when I visited the site for the first time, I had focused on elements like pollarded trees, not fully appreciating that the whole site was a creative management project. In my research for this book I interviewed a range of protagonists on the project onsite; these visible signs of maintenance then retreated in significance and I was instead reminded of my experience as a gardener working for three years in a park in Sydney, where a myriad of small and seemingly banal activities, like rubbish collection, came together to regulate the site. In their performing and repetition, such activities engender a familiarity that becomes knowledge, then a forward trajectory for action, as the rhythm of these acts and the rhythm of the site converge. I was also reminded that one project can have very different readings depending on one's role on it.

The combination of these factors—personal philosophies, fashions, practices or techniques, and institutions—inflect any ongoing sense of what a project is "like," and this is nowhere more true than at Insel Hombroich, where I talked to three different "actors" involved in it in different ways. Talking to each seemed like a constant asking and answering of the question "What is this place?," a question that in itself demonstrates how different and open for debate is a landscape that has its own momentum, entirely autonomous of the people involved in making and managing it, despite the fact that they can redirect it in fundamental ways.

It is this autonomous momentum—starting from a foundation of design, perhaps, but then becoming so much more—that completes my case studies of the viridic because it shows how, without a mechanism for continuing a design involvement in a project, that project can be transformed but also remain the same in fundamental, infrastructural ways. It shows that the views of an initial designer become less and less relevant as time has its way with what they created, but that their initial acts set up trajectories that play out over time. That a designer might not like what a project has become once they stop being involved says more about the designer than the project, because their desires are personal mental constructs, while a landscape is an evolving thing. For a viridic approach to landscape architecture, understanding the nature of maintenance as practice guided by a philosophy is of crucial importance to perpetuating both this design trajectory and the inherent "will" of the landscape, the *élan vital* of that trajectory. This idea of the will of a landscape suits the Hombroich because it corresponds to the creative agenda for the project, as a place that showcases both the creativity of people and the creativity of nature.

I cite conversations with Bernhard Korte, the initial designer of the project, Burkhard Damm, managing director of the Stiftung Insel Hombroich, and Klaus Fischedick, the head gardener,[2] to provide the evidence for this chapter, looking at how the position of each in the life of a project affects the way they talk about it. In her book *The Human Condition*, Hannah Arendt discusses how the *vita activa*, or "active life," of the classical Greek city comprised *labor*, *work*, and *action*, of which speech, as part of action, was the most important because, though it left no material trace, made up as it is of sound waves in the air,[3] its effects could play out over long periods of time.[4] In concluding, I argue that in a viridic practice detached from representation, embedded in living, an idea or philosophy, can set in motion consequences for management that can significantly affect a place in design terms—and not always, as landscape architects tend to assume, in undesirable ways.

A GALLERY FOR ART AND NATURE

The Stiftung Insel Hombroich is an art foundation that has developed from the estate of Karl Heinrich Müller and his private art collection, located on and around the historic Insel Hombroich, and on the site of a former rocket station near Düsseldorf. Müller purchased Insel Hombroich on the river Erft in 1982; it comprised the Rosa Haus (Pink House), built in 1816, together with another building from 1906, and an overgrown nineteenth-century English garden, as well as adjacent farmland. In 1994 Müller purchased the missile silos and bunkers of a rocket station two kilometers northwest of Insel Hombroich, which was also

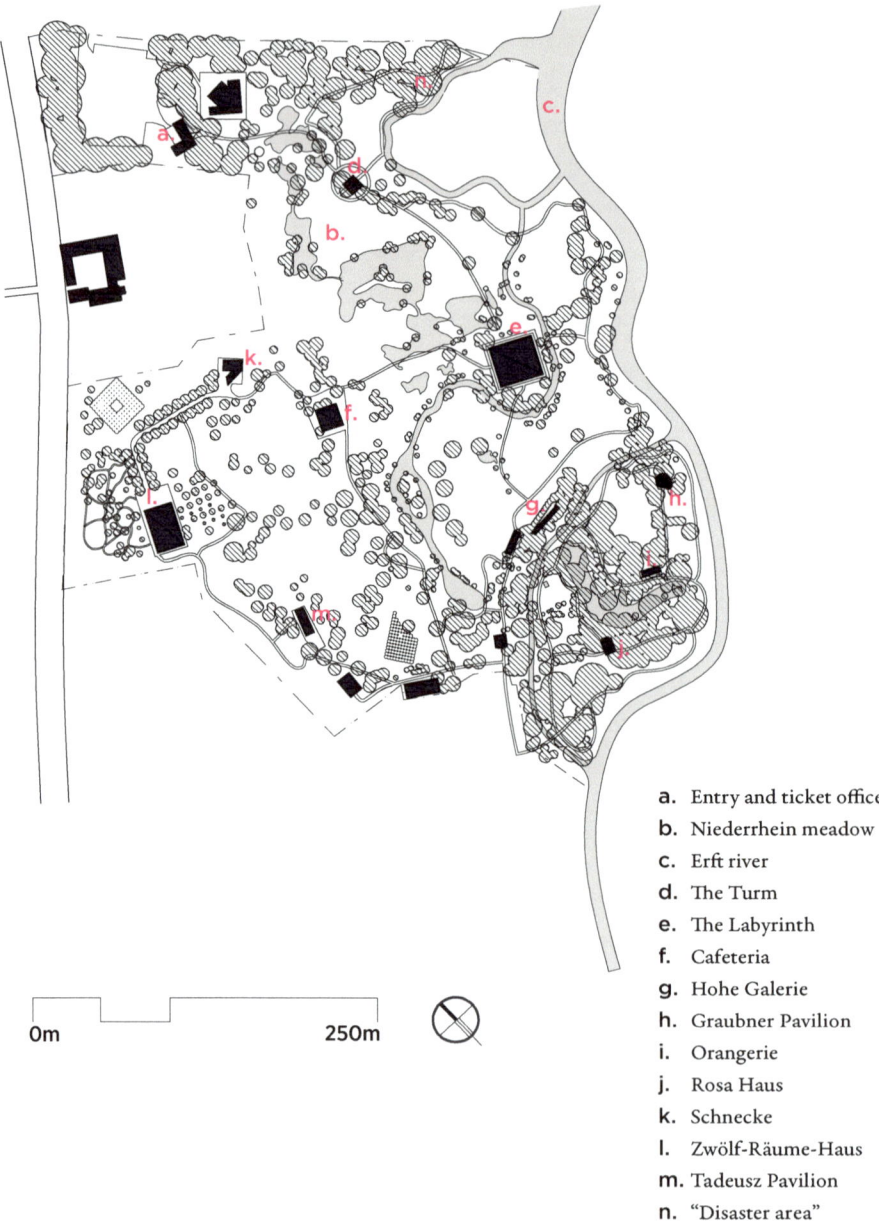

FIGURE 7.3

Site plan of Museum Insel Hombroich.

FIGURE 7.4

The Rosa Haus (Pink House) from 1816 in its
English landscape garden on the Insel Hombroich,
on the Erft river.

added to the museum complex. In this chapter I will focus on the original part, Insel Hombroich, which was restored in 1984 by German landscape architect Bernhard Korte, who also converted the agricultural land to a typical Niederrhein (Lower Rhine) water meadow, restoring older meandering watercourses on the plain. Throughout both the island and the rocket station the artist Erwin Heerich designed a series of pavilions that distribute the collection over the site, each using the same brick material with varying geometric forms that resemble his own art, "walk-in sculptures," where "he was able to apply his view of sculpture to architecture."[5] Curator Gotthard Graubner "developed an artistic approach to exhibiting objects based on the mutual encounter between individual works of art,"[6] so that, without any information about artists or the names

of works in the pavilions, the visitor has a "sensual experience," where "intellectual evaluation gives way to emotional acquisition."[7] Describing the relationship between his pavilions and the landscape at Hombroich, Heerich says: "Art and nature are the same in their presentation above all in coming to terms with things: going back to fundamental experiences, questioning approaches and finally, defining action."[8]

The museum is located on a local road between the towns of Holzheim and Kapellen, near the regional center of Neuss, which lies to the west of Düsseldorf. From a car park in a forest setting, one of Heerich's pavilions forms a wall-building, with a door through which the site is entered. Moving through it provides a vantage point that head gardener Klaus Fischedick described as critical where one can see the whole of the artificial meadow that Korte created, like a picture: an infrastructural "base plane" from which all of Heerich's pavilions are visible. Walking across this meadow, which one experiences as a series of grassy open islands among tree-lined tributaries of the Erft, one arrives at the first pavilion, the Turm, through which the path runs: the center of a literal circle, with paths converging on it from quadrants. While it still allows only a single ongoing route, this pavilion establishes the idea that there is a choice for the visitor—a choice really delivered at the next pavilion, the Labyrinth, which is enclosed by vegetation and has a disorienting interior organization without a prioritized front or back, so that on leaving it one must really begin choosing one's route.

Since the landscape at Insel Hombroich is ambiguous, and many paths are possible, from the point of leaving the Labyrinth the description of the project is contingent on the way it was visited: "it is a place for taking responsibility for and finding oneself, a place of subjective

FIGURE 7.5
A NATO rocket station was added to the Stiftung Insel Hombroich in the 1990s.

FIGURE 7.6
The characteristic "Niederrhein" water meadow, adjacent to the Insel Hombroich, restored by landscape architect Bernard Korte.

FIGURE 7.7

The first of Heerich's pavilions after entering Insel Hombroich, Turm, with the path running through it.

FIGURE 7.8
The Labyrinth is surrounded by a hedge and has no clear hierarchy; the transition from landscape to art is seamless.

insight."[9] From the main path at the north, the routes from the Labyrinth go toward the west to the cafeteria, toward the south to the Hohe Galerie, and toward the east to the Erft, the route I took during my first visit. From here one looks across the river to farmland opposite; the path is punctuated by the occasional pollarded tree at corners, then as one rounds its bend, there is the Hohe Galerie, a bridge-like pavilion acting as the threshold to the historic Insel Hombroich. The Hohe Galerie is perhaps the most bizarre area: the open-air studio of artist Anatol Herzfeld which continues to produce what looked to me like rather ugly, folksy timber art. Apparently, this studio represents a long-term commitment to the artist by the original owner of Insel Hombroich.

Once on the island, one can stay with the river, an option throughout, passing the abstract circular volume of the Graubner Pavilion looking out onto an amorphous box hedge; or continue straight from the Hohe

FIGURE 7.9
An old hedge from the original Insel garden outside the Graubner Pavilion that has been allowed to become amorphous.

FIGURE 7.10
Khmer heads look out at the garden from the Orangerie.

Galerie onto the island, around the old picturesque lake of the original English garden surrounded by ancient trees, including swamp cypress, *Taxodium distichum*, which have developed their characteristic pneumatophores or "knees." Most striking for me is the linear Orangerie pavilion, which contains nothing but seven Khmer heads on plinths, looking silently through a large window out at the garden. Walking around the lake, one finds ruins of the old garden, and the historic Rosa Haus, now a library, archive, and artist's studio. This sequence from the entrance, across the meadow and culminating with the historic English garden, is one continuous, high-quality treatment that resulted from Korte's work on the project in the first stage.

If one takes the route west from the Labyrinth toward the cafeteria, one is in effect leaving the meadow and moving up a hill back toward the road. The cafeteria provides food which seems also to be an art project and cannot quite be described as tasty, though it is free, or at least included in the entry price. With its angled glass façade facing toward the meadow, the cafeteria is more like a winter house, and is surrounded by trees that weep toward the ground, enclosing tables underneath, forming green pods. Like the pollards on the meadow, these pods indicate an interest in manipulating vegetation for formal and spatial effect that is characteristic of Korte's approach, and is demonstrated further on this side of the project.

As one moves up the hill, away from the meadow, grids and groups of trees interact with outdoor sculpture, downplaying some of the significance of pavilions such as the Schnecke and the Zwölf-Räume-Haus (Twelve-Room-House) at the top, the latter combining pre-Columbian material with European modernism. Next to the Zwölf-Räume-Haus is a perennial and productive garden along the lines of Piet Oudolf. Leaving

FIGURE 7.11

Cafeteria at the edge of the meadow, and the terraces.

FIGURE 7.12

The start of the terraces, developed later, where Korte took a more formal, less natural approach.

the Zwölf-Räume-Haus, one takes a path uncomfortably pressed against the boundary, circling an adjacent field, then arriving at the Tadeusz Pavilion, which looks out over the landscape and is like a building and a bank combined. Leaving the pavilion, one takes a path back down to the island and the functional garden depot where vehicles and tools are kept. One then walks down this path past another grid of trees planted by Korte that is more successful because it articulates a threshold between two separate spaces, rather than treating the group of trees like objects, as is done closer to the Zwölf-Räume-Haus.

Architectural historians like to valorize designers of surviving masterworks as much as the designers themselves like to. While this is relatively easy with architecture, where a work is static and can be reasonably expected to endure, the same is not true of landscape, since, as I have been arguing, change is the essence of the viridic. Nonetheless authorship remains important for landscapes, including Insel Hombroich, but landscape acquires an added dimension. Rather than simply protecting the artifact from change, as one might preserve a piece of architecture, future managers of a designed landscape must effectively guide it in line with a state that the designer envisaged, but they never saw themselves. How multiple players undertake that process over time, and how a project gains a life or "trajectory" of its own, is important to working with the changing, growing nature of the viridic, where management must be a creative tool. By talking to a range of people about the same project, one gains a sense of what the interests of people with different roles do to the project over time, and how they conceive of it. Working from the designer, to the manager, to the gardener in discussing Insel Hombroich, I began to appreciate how proximity to the project—that is to say, literally, how directly one works with it, and the time or duration of involvement—affects a sense of what "design" is in that context. Such a conception of design is vital to ensure that any definition of the viridic is not simply gardening. However, as I learned from Hombroich, perhaps even more importantly, a long duration of working with a project also engenders in managers a sense of the landscape's own "life": its personality, or its propensity, what it wants to do, which is the thing that managers must ultimately deal with.

THE DESIGNER: BERNHARD KORTE, AN AESTHETIC PRACTICE

It seems significant that Bernhard Korte suggests I meet him in the Neuss Botanic Garden for our interview to talk about his work at Insel Hombroich, rather than at the Hombroich itself, his office, or a café, for example. While a park might seem like neutral ground for two landscape architects to talk, during the interview I come to realize that the location reflects Korte's own interest in landscape—gardening—but, more importantly, it illustrates his belief that gardening is first and foremost an aesthetic art whose medium has particular qualities that arise from the fact that it is comprised of living things. Bernhard is a dapper aesthete in his sixties who talks about the Hombroich in a fey manner while we sit on a bench beside a small pond, surrounded by trees and a well-developed understory including *Agapanthus praecox*, a generic garden plant indigenous to South Africa, which I now call home.

I wanted to get a sense of how Korte's work was situated in the cultural milieu of the time when the Museum Insel Hombroich was created, and how its design was informed by other ideas, but this was difficult because Korte consciously disavowed any "academic" or "philosophical" background, claiming that landscape architects had been asking him about the philosophies that shaped the project since its conception, and that he has remained silent in the face of such questions. Nonetheless, one can still see the outline of his philosophy in his rejection of the philosophies of his contemporaries, and also in his focus on the immediate experience of landscape, which might be called phenomenological, but to him is the "aesthetic." Korte's background, his practice as a garden designer, and his lack of interest in or training as a landscape architect inform such an outline.

Korte studied horticulture at Leibniz Universität Hannover, completing a doctorate related to the economics of nursery operations, but he did not study design. After teaching for two years, he left the university and opened a commercial antiques gallery in Düsseldorf, which he credits with developing his aesthetic interests, mentioning in particular Art Deco and Art Nouveau. After some clients had questioned what his

FIGURE 7.13

Bernhard Korte, the orginal landscape architect for Insel Hombroich, in 2015, interviewed in Neuss Botanic Garden.

doctorate was in, he was invited to design their gardens. Karl-Heinrich Müller, who had recently purchased Insel Hombroich, was one of Korte's customers, and collected Art Deco lamps for the Rosa Haus. Korte thought the island "so beautiful and full of promise," and was happy to work there as a gardener rather than as a landscape architect, for which he was proudly unqualified.

Müller had a vision for the project which brought together all the different creative disciplines—sculpture, landscape, music, architecture—into an "all-embracing life model for the future"—an "architecture of life," as he called it.[10] This emphasis on life as a creative force treated life and art as synonymous, since art is "an independent creature: it is alive, and so belongs to no one."[11] This synergistic view of nature is reflected in the motto of the project: "Kunst parallel zur Natur (Art parallel with Nature)," based on the words of Cézanne.[12] Nevertheless, Korte recalls that each person who worked on the project in the 1980s (primarily the curator Gotthard Graubner, the sculptor Erwin Heerich, and Korte himself) had their own interests and autonomy in approach and work. While Korte's own non-philosophy (since he was avowedly anti-academic, he did not call his approach philosophy) resembled Müller's, it is interesting to look at the language he uses, albeit in translation, to describe the aesthetic, his key term in describing his work and ideas.

There is an ideological tension in the project between the ecological and the aesthetic, because Korte felt prevailed upon to focus ecologically since the local authorities imposed strict conditions on the project in terms of environmental and cultural heritage before they would grant permission to construct the museum complex. This involved restoration—or, rather, reinstatement—of the previous Niederrhein landscape, preservation of the agricultural landscape, and the screening of the gallery buildings.[13]

The German section of the Niederrhein once consisted of peat bogs and ephemeral watercourses; however, these have been largely replaced by agriculture, and subsequently destroyed further through open-cut lignite (brown coal) mining. In reinstating the wetland landscape, Korte examined old aerial photographs from the 1950s taken by coal-mining companies and discovered the faint outlines of a former river and small lakes, which he used to give shape to the water meadow restoration, reinstated with grasses and irises, among other species. While the authorities treated this reinstatement as an ecological project, Korte's aesthetic interest was in the qualities that the landscape might have, the result of ecological acts valued in aesthetic rather than ecological terms. While Korte talked about this tension ideologically, in essence I argued that such a tension does not in fact exist because to do anything at all in a garden is, by necessity, to work ecologically.[14] However, he disagreed, instead insisting that nature worked aesthetically.

When Korte describes the resulting re-created meadow as "an ideal landscape with rivers and ponds," he is recognizing that it is not necessarily ideal as in "right" but as an "idea" of a natural landscape, since the

14 hectares of designated conservation area acquired in 1984 was farmland, with no trees or shrubs. Korte admires, but did not replicate, the English picturesque garden. Although the resulting meadow is more like a landscape painting than an "ideal" nonhuman natural landscape, Korte sees it, rather, as "a colourful, sensuous meadow…[a] real, living community made up of plants, animals and human people—in a region that had been greatly changed and partly destroyed by open-cast lignite mining."[15] The conjunction of a sensual view of the aesthetic and a community of organisms mirrors Müller's view. When I ask Korte about the aesthetic dimension, he refers to it in relation to "beings": insects, people, etc.

Korte's writing about the Hombroich elucidates this aesthetic of beings, the core of which is the human experience of "the sensual circle of plants [since] plant life follows an order that has largely been lost to us human beings today." For Korte, gardening is a way into this order, finding "its best meaning in symbols and signs for free interpretation." Thus humans can find an aesthetic in "the power of nature in year old ash tree shoots, the alien quality of a parthenocarpal pear, the purely male offspring of a hermaphrodite or the transitional stages that often find no place in the garden, for example seed umbel, tree ruins or fallen foliage."[16] Gardening is a tool that unlocks the content of these natural processes, as well as revealing their inherent aesthetic nature.

That Korte should oppose this to the ecological frames a different version of the aesthetic that is reminiscent of Ferrari and his description of the garden as a community of beings, as a living work of art,[17] since "[at the Hombroich] nature is not exploited and exhausted by man, but tended by him, with care addressed to things that grow and flourish."[18] However, although it is made of living things, Korte "took decisions meter by meter…[where] every bit has been composed, even if I just allowed spontaneous plants to arrive: I didn't allow it if it didn't fit my idea,"[19] reminiscent of Ferrari's suggestion that the garden was fundamentally totalitarian. Since he was focusing on the qualities that arose from the interactions between the different "beings," even though he selected all the plants, he never focused on the collection in a botanic sense, since identification was an intellectual idea that got in the way of the sensual perception of these qualities: a criticism he makes of the current gardener,

Fischedick, whom we will meet later in this chapter.[20] When we discuss the work of Piet Oudolf, whom Korte admires, I mention that Oudolf uses an ecological rationale for choosing species that occur at certain strata in similar natural niches. Korte is clear: "No, Oudolf is interested in aesthetics primarily"; and when I discuss the ecological theory, he says: "Well, it is easier to say such things."

Korte's aesthetic non-philosophy-on-the-ground governed design decisions at the Hombroich, our discussion including stories about how things were serendipitously found and incorporated into the garden—impossible in a purely representational practice of drawing and handing on to a contractor. Korte utilized pollarded *Salix* spp., transplanted from farms in a similar water landscape in Belgium, to provide an instant landscape. Purchasing 128 of these ancient trunks with knuckles from a farmer, he describes how he was told at the border that the trees would have to be burnt for quarantine reasons. Playing along with this, since it was winter and they had no leaves, he said that they were dead and were being used for firewood. When he chose to install them at the Hombroich, Korte again repeated his sophistic mode of operation, using the language of the authorities, in this case arguing that such trees formed part of the historic landscape; in actual fact, however, he had totally different aesthetic desires: to achieve instant form in a largely denuded landscape. Like Heerich's buildings, for Korte the willows were sculpture, giving relief to the flat field of the meadow. Similarly, the use of weeping *Fraxinus* as enclosures to sit under near the cafeteria was justified as a cultural decision, since they are also used like this in the region, but in fact had a sculptural appeal for Korte. Even the screening of the buildings came from windbreaks used in the Niederrhein, from the cultural landscape, though Korte did not want to screen them because he admired Heerich's pavilions, their quality as objects on the water-meadow plain.

As a gardener rather than a landscape architect, the only plans Korte produced for the project were to satisfy the authorities. All other decisions arose organically through spending four years onsite with a gang of four young German laborers who had returned from Brazil and smoked marijuana constantly.[21] He looks back on this way of working with some wistful nostalgia, saying that this time onsite was the height of his career.

FIGURE 7.14

One of the 128 pollarded willows in the meadow leading to the river Erft. Korte imported them from Belgium in winter, telling the border authorities that the trees were dead and would be used for firewood.

FIGURE 7.15

Fraxinus trees with weeping foliage trained to provide shaded enclosures for diners.

The most important practice, as it was for Dutton, was walking.[22] Korte reckoned that during the years he worked onsite he "walked a lot, sometimes 16 hours per day…[seeing it] it in winter and autumn." From this walking practice, "after years there was a way to work," a method of operating onsite. While Girot's model of "Landing" and "Grounding" incorporates walking,[23] a consultant's visits are very different from the familiarity of being among seasons that change around you, seeing the other "beings" also changing and adjusting as shorts give way to trousers, T-shirts to jumpers, in tandem with the passing seasons. Whereas the landscape architect draws predictions of a future, for Korte, working onsite: "I never thought of it at its end"; instead he worked immediately, according to what he found, responding to what arose from his actions. Because of the scale of the Hombroich, walking there has a dimension, a sense of time, and it is easy to get lost. Korte credits the role of walking with "wellbeing," tied therefore to growth and the other "beings" that make up the site's aesthetic. While walking and making it up as one goes along seems simple, Korte insists that it is not like "three hours in the office," and that the design is very complex—three-dimensional and multi-layered—so that it is perhaps too complex actually to design. Eye-level decisions are thus the most economical way of dealing with such complexity. For Korte, "landscape has a different blood to architecture."

Korte acknowledges that it was not expensive for Müller to build the garden using himself and his team, but maintaining it is much more expensive. He worked in the garden for so long that much of the planting that is characteristic of his initial approach has now gone; however, the bones are still there, he says. While I have been counterpointing Korte's "in the moment" approach to that of predictive office practice, the fact that he approves of things that fit his agenda and not those that do not shows an ownership beyond the sensual, immediate experience of landscape as a space in which to improvise aesthetic decisions. When I ask him how he likes it now, he tells me: "It turned out exactly as I had expected." Inevitably one lives in a dynamic relationship with the future whenever one does anything, so it is not surprising that Korte should have had a vision for the future of the Hombroich, and be proud that it now resembles that vision. In making an argument for the viridic, I am not suggesting that one should abandon the predictive character of design but, rather, that one should treat it in neither absolute nor *laissez-faire* terms operating in a vector between the two. Looking back over the project, after almost forty years Korte finds walking through the Hombroich now to be "like a gift."

THE MANAGER: BURKHARD DAMM, DESIGNING VIA MANAGEMENT

In contrast, a busy man—the current manager of the Stiftung Insel Hombroich, Burkhard Damm—asks to meet me in the Hombroich offices. Located on the rocket station rather than the island, these offices have a contemporary feel, vaguely Ikea-ish, with a meeting room, a bookcase filled with books with identical spines in a diversity of colors lining the walls. They are, I am told, a work of art. Damm is from the next generation of Insel Hombroich, in his forties with the casual air of a designer. We drink coffee, and during the interview Burkhard uses his phone absentmindedly to ensure that he gets the right words in English to communicate his answers, despite being an excellent English speaker. The scrolling sound accompanying his moves through the dictionary create waves of clicks in the background of our recording.

Like Korte, Burkhard Damm studied at Leibniz Universität Hannover; however, he studied landscape architecture rather than horticulture. After graduation he worked first in Hamburg on the HafenCity redevelopment, then in Cologne, and then finally returned to the Neuss area, working for a local council to understand how government functioned. Since joining the Hombroich fourteen years ago he has continued his private practice, undertaking eight projects a year across Germany. He credits his time spent at the Hombroich with enhancing his understanding of his discipline, a gardening-centric version of landscape architecture.

Damm started work at the Hombroich almost by accident: a friend's family was friendly with the family of the sculptor Heerich, who showed him around the rocket station, which was being developed at the time. Later he received a call from Frau Heerich asking him if he wanted to work there. When he started he was the only gardener on Hombroich, and describes being very confused by all the different interpretations of what the landscape should be, since "the things that a gardener must do, you weren't allowed to do here": Heerich wanted clear views of buildings, Korte wanted to cut things, while Müller wanted total naturalness. Damm worked for Müller for seven years before his death, and admired him greatly. Faced with the conflicting approaches to Hombroich, he said, Müller encouraged robust argument, but ultimately told him: "It is your responsibility: you must do what you think is right."

Having interviewed Korte on his experience of working at the Hombroich, and the reasons why he stopped working there, I was curious to hear Damm's reading of the relationship between Korte and Müller when he arrived fourteen years ago. In the genealogy of the project, this was probably ten years after Korte started working on the island and the meadow, but only five years after the later stages of the project, or the terraces above the meadow. Less governed by regulations than the previous areas, Korte's work here was notably more "formal," comprising grids of trees. Undertaken in the early 1990s, this work is characteristic of landscape architecture of the period in its use of disparate grids sitting in an open field of landscape, seen also in the work of the landscape architects who worked with Daniel Libeskind on the Jewish Museum in Berlin, by Müller, Knippschild, Wehberg. This period corresponded to the time in his career when Korte was becoming recognized as a designer rather than simply a gardener, working with architects like his long-time collaborator O. M. Ungers.

According to Korte's broad definition of aesthetics, the difference between the naturalistic treatment of the meadow and the grids of trees is not very significant, since the term "aesthetics" can accommodate divergent approaches in one continuum. However, for Müller—and for Damm, who agreed with him—Korte's switch to formal geometry was Korte "trying to be an artist rather than a gardener." Müller was interested in two types of maker at the Hombroich, both of whom were creative: humans as makers of art, and nature as a maker of growth. But the two were different; thus Heerich described his galleries as not "merely an exhibition space, but...to follow this idea of a dialogue between art and the creative forces of nature...[so that] When one passes through nature's design processes into the buildings then one finds man's peculiar

FIGURE 7.16

Grids of trees that frame outdoor artworks on the terraces did not sit well with Müller's naturalism.

creative power—art."[24] As Louis Le Roy would say: "Man does culture, and nature does nature."[25]

Essentially, Korte's approach transgressed this boundary. Damm supports an interventionist approach as part of the palette of garden design or landscape architecture, but not at the Hombroich—because it is labor-intensive, which can be ill afforded, but largely because it "doesn't look right": a judgment I would agree with, since I found the terrace area less appealing and immersive than the island. However, it is important to remember that Korte, with his aesthetic predilections, did see himself as an artist; this also explains why he was offended by the pay discrepancy between himself and other artists on the site. But as Müller said: "Apparent chaos and excessive growth by the plants is not a process that is killed off, but allowed the greatest possible freedom,"[26] so that for Müller and Damm, the landscape of Hombroich is emphatically not art: it is nature assisted by gardening.

Damm describes the Hombroich as an overgrown mess when he arrived after Korte's departure: fueled by rich soil from the previous pig farm reshaped into the meadow. He was confronted by a thick, unusable plain where paths were like "tunnels" through a mass of nettles two meters high. With his mandate from Müller to "do what he thought was right," he arranged to have them cut down by a local farmer, crucially removing the nutrient-rich material. He reckons that it took six years before the nutrient load was reduced to a manageable level, during which time he also seeded with appropriate indigenous meadow species to develop the vegetation community as the nutrient load tapered off. During this time he also pruned trees to allow pockets of light into the English garden on the island, to stimulate growth there.

As in all his work at the Hombroich, Damm's aim was to create variety in a landscape which tended naturally toward monoculture. He uses the word "variety" a lot, and while he agrees that he means biodiversity, there is also an aesthetic dimension to his notion of variety, as there is to Korte's. At the same time as creating variety, however, Damm also had a guiding "sense," rather than philosophy, perhaps, of what different parts of the Hombroich should be like. Having been there for such a long time, he has had to develop an approach that can outlast changing personnel and living and dying plants, and govern decision-making. This approach comprises the use of a series of "frames," dependent on context. Each area of the garden has a specific frame which he respects, but within which he can make quite significant changes to Korte's design.

It is interesting to hear Damm, as a landscape architect, describe his approach to working at Hombroich; this demonstrates why it is the right case study to end this book on. As a practicing landscape architect, Damm is able to see the difference between landscape architecture and gardening from both perspectives. He brings a conceptual, designerly approach to his decision-making, but uses the tools of gardening to do his work. The emphasis on "decision" here is pertinent, as I argued in chapter 6, because, liberated from representation, design becomes decision in the real-time context of operating as a gardener onsite. Damm uses three concepts, each a metaphor, which do not necessarily sit comfortably with each other, to describe the logic behind these decisions: scale, frame, and dog leash.

Talking about scale, Damm argues that gardening works best at the scale of the body and its sense of immediate, perceptible spaces. Working in a space defined by vegetation and the ambient environment defined by light and microclimate, gardening can compose and manage plants to create rich, luxuriant spaces. However, the relationship between these spaces, and of each space to the whole, needs to be dictated by the strategic design thinking that characterizes landscape architecture. This is not to say that learning from the practice of gardening cannot inform the strategic—indeed it must, because, as Damm says, much of the strategic planning around what must be done (where, when) happens during the process of moving around the site, a by-product of working. For him, this relationship is reminiscent of the baroque, where small spaces require an imagination that is undoubtedly creative—perhaps even artistic, as Korte might suggest; at a "higher scale," however, the willful force of design is required. Recalling Von Clausewitz's difference between strategy and tactics, where a tactical "pyrrhic" victory can mean winning a battle but losing the strategic war,[27] sometimes higher-scale issues require destruction, destroying beautiful areas of the site in response to larger issues. The necessity of cutting the meadow to allow views and circulation through the Hombroich, as against Müller's universal love of growth, is an example of this kind of strategic judgment trumping the tactical.

Damm's concept of frames is important because it is an example of a type of design judgment used in gardening, which supports my argument that gardening can be a design act based on judgment rather than representation. Damm uses two opposite examples to explain this idea of frame, which show that he really means atmosphere or "vibe": the English garden and the meadow. The old English garden on the island, dating from the early nineteenth century, is full of exotic trees, and Damm calls its frame "tropical." While in climatic terms it is far from tropical, this frame provides an evocative atmosphere with clues to future design and management. Crucial to maintaining this atmosphere is almost complete canopy cover: what Damm calls a "roof," with deep shade below. At the same time, however, growth below the canopy requires light. Deciding to diversify the understory, Damm creates small openings in the canopy to let in light right down to the ground, so that there are moments of diverse growth and lushness, but on balance the area is dark. In choosing trees and shrubs to replace dying old ones in the English garden, he does not necessarily replace them with the same species but chooses better-performing trees with large leaves that have that "tropical" feel.

In contrast, the frame for the meadow is openness, with objects such as screened pavilions or isolated pollarded trees, but the balance is in favor of openness. Plant species include indigenous reeds and flowers, but also introduced plants like iris. As I said above, if it were not for constant mowing this space would be subsumed by weed species such as nettles, but if left alone it would also revert to birch forest, a common native landscape type in Germany. This demonstrates that while each frame may have an inherent ecological character, intervention in the ecological system is accepted as a reality, though some level of economy of management is inevitable in the context of so much land. Furthermore, since the meadow is in contrast to the forest in the English garden, the maintenance of one frame consolidates the contrast to the other. The final analogy, the dog leash, relates to nature in the frame. The dog leash to which Damm is referring is the sort that spools out and retracts as required. Nature, Damm says, can be held in tight like the baroque, or let out to become self-organizing

FIGURE 7.17
Damm defines the "frame" of the English garden on the Insel as "tropical" forest, where he uses a strategy of closed canopy with spots of light to the ground to encourage pockets of growth.

FIGURE 7.18
The "frame" for the meadow is a wet base plate of grasses and flowers with clumps of trees and architecture, according to Damm.

wilderness. This attitude to planting design has become very important to the horticulture on contemporary projects like New York's High Line, much of which has been designed by Piet Oudolf, whose aesthetics Korte praised, and who visits the Hombroich often.

Korte, Damm, and later Fischedick all admire the of the work of "the Dutch wave," of whom the best known is Oudolf, but Damm and Fischedick regard Henk Gerritsen's *Essay on Gardening* as the text best typifying their approach,[28] Damm going so far to say: "Just look at Gerritsen: that's how we work here," characterizing his approach in terms familiar from Burle Marx and Dutton: "Look at the conditions, try this, change it next year." In essence the approach is to work with ornamental plants in an ecological way: essentially designing ornamental ecologies, by allowing them to interact as they do in a natural system. The idea of the leash is appropriate because it describes the level of intervention in ecology for ornamental reasons, since natural systems left to themselves will self-organize in ways that may not have aesthetic appeal.

While loath to adopt the "Dutch Wave" moniker, Gerritsen observed that the common denominator between practitioners of the Dutch Wave was "constant renewal." Gerritsen says that Rob Leopold defined its elements as "natural diversity, individual values of perception,"[29] the implication of aesthetics in perception, confirming Kingsbury's caution that while "Piet Oudolf is often portrayed as a leader of an ecological planting movement … ecology … is not the most important … aspect of his work."[30] Nonetheless, Kingsbury places the horticultural and ecological at the core of the Dutch Wave, with its "emphasis on a rich selection of perennials and a desire to enter into a dialogue with nature."[31] He notes a move from "architecturally driven geometries" in Oudolf's work toward "an increasing wildness … exploring an ultimate synthesis of culture and nature" that Oudolf shared with Gerritsen."[32] This synthesis is very different from that envisaged at the Hombroich, where art and nature stand autonomously, albeit in dialogue. In other words, these differences represent different lengths of Damm's leash.

Developing Damm's analogy: the length of the leash can vary according to the context, but the line sets up limits of radii, continuity in any trajectory. The leash is effectively management or labor, reminiscent of

Dutton's philosophy, whereby a more unimpeded natural process requires less energy. This energy could be literal labor, but is not necessarily so, since some activities, like mowing, use machinery that can work large areas at a time, while others, like detailed pruning, can be labor-intensive and take significant amounts of time. This is the basis of some of Damm's critique of Korte's later work, which involves significant tree pruning to produce an effect that Damm considers also antithetical to Müller's approach to nature as creative growth. In order to prune these groups of trees, as well as the pollards, Damm relies on unpaid volunteers from a friends' group, 30–40 people each year, without whom such laborious pruning would significantly impair the ability of the four gardeners to work the entire body of the park. Design decisions—for aesthetic reasons in Korte's case—represent varying maintenance penalties in terms of labor.

While Damm started work as a gardener, he now works largely in an office, gardening with drawings and documents nonetheless. Although he has not yet had time to develop a geographic information system (GIS) for the Hombroich, he has continued over the years to work on an Adobe Illustrator file that locates all the main individual trees onsite, each with a unique identifying number. He and his staff identify these trees from memory, since there are no marks on them for the same reason that there are no labels on the art in the pavilions: intellectual interpretation should not interfere with the appreciation of the works—in this case, the living works: the plants themselves. Of more importance than the drawing is an Excel spreadsheet that acts as a timetable for forthcoming work. Divided up according to all the different material elements that need work, the columns indicate when in the following (and also, therefore, past) years these elements should be maintained. Activities that are critical are shown in red; the period of activity occurs on a range of different time increments, whether seasonally, annually, or biannually. While many tasks comprise pruning and landscape maintenance work, also included

FIGURE 7.19

Groups of volunteers prune these grids of trees annually.

are painting bridges, replacing stone chips on paths, and cleaning outdoor sculpture. The inclusion of these inorganic elements reminds me that the remit of gardening is often the curation of externality as much as it is gardening *per se*. Because the unifying element is the act of moving through the site, activities like rubbish collection or cleaning also provide an opportunity to review the site in a recursive way, always adding new items to the to-do list. For the trees identified on the drawing, another spreadsheet lists all the maintenance for each tree for the last fourteen years; this is given to an external tree consultant, who undertakes pruning and pest control; their work is added to the spreadsheet. Ultimately, Damm says, the most important decisions he made concerned people. He worked outside for the first five or six years before he managed to find the right people: two gardeners, including Fischedick, whom I shall discuss next. Continuing Damm's idea of "frame" and "leash," people are important not because of their skills, which they must of course have, but because of their judgment, their ability to understand and buy into the frame; more importantly, they must be able to make decisions that have effects, operationalizing the leash. On the basis of a design idea they must know what physical acts are needed to catalyze nature to suit the frame for each area. Gardeners must make numerous small decisions, congruent with the frame, that act like pieces in a mosaic, urging nature into filling the frame, holding the leash in to retard it at times, while at others letting it out to allow nature, as process, to do its aesthetic work.

THE GARDENER: KLAUS FISCHEDICK, WATCHING AND WAITING

Whereas I met Korte in a park and Damm in a meeting room, I met Klaus Fischedick at the ticket office at the entry of Insel Hombroich. Damm and Fischedick are both—like me—from generation X: in their forties. A busy man, Fischedick talks quickly and took me to an assortment of places rather than discussing ideas *per se*, using each place to illustrate the diversity of conditions that he must deal with, which in turn define his philosophy for working at the Hombroich. Having worked as a gardener, I recognized his manner of telling the story of the Hombroich via specific instances. Whereas a designer can talk from a plan to orient another designer to what they have done and why, for the gardener the most important thing is what kind of work they do where, and how these collected instances of work aggregate to an overall conception of the place. Place identity arises from a collection of different conditions, a delimited field described through the range of outlying sites and acts that make up a cocktail of what it is. There is no strategy here, just tactics, though Fischedick supports Damm's concept of frames in dealing with the garden.

The first stop we make is down a set of steps behind the ticket office, at the top of the bank where one can see over the meadow. Fischedick says that this is the most important point, because it clearly shows the frame and the parts that make it up: the grassy meadow with wildflowers, the pollarded willows popping up like figures, and the screened pavilions sticking out among them. He reiterates what I know: that it is the "typical view of our region…of grass, water and trees [willows] cut." Struggling to give words to the significance that he feels for what he is saying, he says that Niederrhein means not just "flat" Rhine (referring to the Lower Rhine) but "deep" Rhine. As I was reminded when I talked to Korte, Damm, and now Fischedick, this is a cultural landscape that is in effect also treated as a natural landscape. For a colonial like me, for whom there is a huge divide between nature and people, this merging continues to be somewhat of a revelation. But then Fischedick says forcefully: "But what you see is totally artificial: we mow the grass, we prune the trees, and the watercourses are all pumped to keep them flowing," adding, "but this is only one situation; I'll take you to another reality of my work."

We enter a confusing area of 6-foot-high weeds and broken willow trees: "I call this the disaster area." In 2014 a massive storm, almost a miniature hurricane, hit the Hombroich, and 150 trees came down. Looking at the wildflowers and ferns which he planted after the storm, but are only just coming up, Fischedick says: "When you're working with nature, you have to be open. Working with nature is looking. It's seeing what happens." This approach is universal in the Hombroich. Heerich, designer of the pavilions, observed: "There are many occurrences that do not show what we actually want until the process itself is well under way."[33]

FIGURE 7.20

A key view of the site for Fischedick after entering: the meadow and trees on the Insel.

FIGURE 7.21
Fischedick at the "disaster area" where trees came down during a storm in 2014.

Fischedick describes a model of the decisions he has to make: a triangle, with aesthetics, ecology, and manpower on the corners. He says that there is no time to reconstruct this area; furthermore, he likes what has resulted from the microclimatic change. I ask him how many staff he has, though I know the answer from Damm. He says three, and I say I assume he would like more, but he quickly answers: "No! Three works perfectly because at the Hombroich we don't want to do too much. When there are fewer of you, you have to let nature be spontaneous. You always find places where things are growing that are very interesting when you are doing nothing"—for example, in the "disaster area." As we leave this area, he says: "This is the most extreme edge of our work." He stops, and says that Korte didn't take a long enough view, since the willows will last only fifty years. Pulling some grass apart, he reveals a healthy young oak tree, saying that they planted several and in fifty years this area will be an oak forest, the canopy keeping the vegetation that we now see in check, regulating its life.

Although he got the job as head gardener somewhat by chance—fourteen years ago, while working as a landscaper and stone worker, he saw Damm's advertisement in an industry magazine—Fischedick has very personal reasons for working at the Hombroich, which he already knew and loved. He describes how, in the 1980s, he was part of the "green" movement in Germany, which comprised both environmental and antinuclear protests. At that time, because Germany was a pawn in the NATO network, the area was full of nuclear launch sites as part of the Cold War, this level of military intensity being in stark contrast to the bucolic cultural landscape. It is a poignant memory for him that he had protested at sites like the very rocket station that is now part of the Hombroich: "Thirty years ago we were fighting about having rivers in concrete channels," so that the restoration of the Erft river, even though it is, of course, artificial and pumped, was "part of our [protest] work."

With my mind filled with an image of community and environmental awareness, as we reenter the meadow I am shocked when Fischedick suddenly stops, his ears pricking up like a hunting dog's, and, changing from English suddenly, shouts in German at a couple who are photographing a flower by a stream to "get back onto the path." He tells me, with light-hearted vehemence: "I am a misanthrope. I hate people. Men. Women. They destroy everything. They think it's just 'freedom'! They just destroy nature. They see a wildflower over there and destroy other plants on the way just to see one fucking plant. And no one sees this fucking photo." His response reminds me of Korte's characterization of him as treating the Hombroich as an ecological project. I tell him that this attitude to people seems contradictory to his previous protest views and his cultural landscape approach, and he replies that if he had his way, the Hombroich would be locked up and accessed only once a year by 20 people, rather than the 100,000 a year that now visit it. For Fischedick, as one might imagine, nature is at the center of Hombroich, and while he is allowed to interfere in it—only in a limited way, of course—it should proceed without human intervention. While this is the approach one might take in a national park, where species that are rare or becoming extinct need to be preserved for the sake of biodiversity, as Fischedick acknowledges, the Hombroich is artificial, and the species growing there are not rare. While one could make environmental claims to its value for carbon sequestration to combat climate change, or wildlife corridors, in fact Fischedick is interested in nature as a kind of performance; in the end, this is not so different to Korte's idea of an "aesthetics of beings" at the Hombroich. Judging from Fischedick's reaction to the photographers, clearly humans are not part of this aesthetic: an attitude I suggest Korte would share.

As we walk across the meadow to the old park, we discuss the management of the transition, and I am reminded of Damm's idea of the leash. Whereas in the "disaster area" the leash had been let right out, while in the meadow it had been wound in quite tight, the edge between meadow and forest was a gradient between the two: perhaps the moment when the leash is spooling out before it is stopped at either extent. As Damm had told me, mowing was the tool to keep the meadow free of trees and nettles. Fischedick further uses carefully timed mowing to stop certain weed species from developing flowers and seeds, cutting them off just before they do so. Recalling Olmsted's construction of graduated forest edges in Central and Prospect Park, Fischedick similarly uses mowing to control the spread of the forest into the meadow: in effect, the machine is used to push back the forest edge, to regulate it, in a not dissimilar way to how it was done at Courances, though there the tool was a hedging attachment to the tractor rather than a mower. However, while this makes the forest sound like a mass pushing out, in the interior of the old park it is in fact the canopy that regulates growth by determining how much light meets the forest floor. In effect, while it is impossible to call nature stable, or in a state of ecological climax, the forest on one side and the meadow on the other are close to being so: the former because of control by light, the latter because of control by mowing. The zone of flux, rather, is the margin between these two, a phenomenon well described in landscape ecology. Although both Fischedick and Damm tell me that they don't really prune trees, in this intermediate zone between the meadow and the old garden, Fischedick tells me that he loves the view into the forest between the mown meadow and the low-hanging pruned limbs of the trees that edge it. These produce a frame for other plants in the distance, other spaces. As we enter the forest I ask him about dead limbs on the ground and he says that he loves them, that they are "part of the game," recalling Henk Gerritsen's use of a game of chess as an analogy for the gardener's relationship with nature: "even though nature is a reliable and transparent adversary, it sometimes makes moves that are beyond a human being's comprehension."[34]

Inside the forest we move to an area that characterizes the kind of work that Fischedick describes as "his favorite thing." Pointing to a patch of nice understory vegetation below the canopy, he tells me that when he started working there fourteen years ago the area was dominated by maples, *Acer* spp., which he removed, then planted hellebores and a fern. Then: "the only thing I did was weed and wait," and within ten years the species had naturalized: "This is the kind of gardening I love."

FIGURE 7.22
Tractor mowing is used to push back the forest edge and keep the interface to the meadow open.

FIGURE 7.23
Although it does not look artificial, Fischedick has weeded and naturalized plants into this understory to create a new ecology: his "favorite thing."

To explain this difference of approach further, he uses his home garden at the block of flats where he lives as an example. The gardener who worked there "was cutting everything: he was 'cleaning' the garden...he was under stress, sweating."[35] Instead Fischedick suggested simply a little weeding four times a year, to "wait and see" what was already in the garden, after which time they had "a garden of wildflowers." Because these plants are now outcompeting the weeds, they now work in the garden only twice a year. This is an interesting approach, because it catalyzes the inherent momentum of nature and its "natural" movement toward growth, then curates the resulting growth on an aesthetic basis, working with what is latent in the ground. Fischedick calls this meditative or slow approach "sit and see," which encapsulates the difference between office practice and gardening: predictive versus experiential. In this real-time process we can see what Müller called "the essence of the island...constant change and transformation" during which "the participants have no conception of progress or aims."[36]

Key to Gerritsen's approach is an attribute that Fischedick mentions often: letting time pass. Gerritsen contrasts his view of the "the natural garden," which "focuses in particular on beauty and the inherent merits of plants and animals"[37]—reminiscent of Korte, but with an ecological emphasis—to a garden where "the gardener makes a once-only intervention and then leans back to see what Mother Nature thinks of his ideal image."[38] For this type of garden, Gerritsen foresees that "one by one, the objects of his love get the shorter end of the stick and [will] be supplanted by perennial herbs, grasses, rampant perennial weeds, bushes and finally trees: the natural succession which invariably leads to forest formation, the natural 'climax vegetation,'" though he notes that climax suggests a "stand-still or final stage," which is untrue.[39] In essence, Gerritsen argues that this latter type of gardener "may as well never have started."[40]

Gerritsen talks about a plant's "ecological amplitude," or range, which "encompasses the conditions under which it will still grow," which for most garden plants is quite wide. Using this idea of ecological amplitude as a model, he argues for working with the *minimum* conditions that a plant needs rather than the maximum, as we might expect, since he uses soil fertility to regulate growth, where less growth equals less maintenance.

In this model, "plants would grow slowly and relatively small," also affecting competing plants or weeds that would otherwise overgrow them in rich soil.[41] Faced with the succession cycle, Gerritsen suggests that "the most important trick to keep maintenance to a minimum is to limit fertility," which in a naturally fertile soil means to "*never* add fertiliser, remove leaves and stems of dead plants … [and to] use compost sparingly."[42] From this approach Gerritsen derives four rules: 1. Use of fertilizers and chemical herbicides is a sin: weed; 2. Try to disturb the soil as little as possible; 3. Be frugal with water; 4. Don't whinge. This is because "Gardens are by definition dynamic environments [due to] constant interventions, the natural succession … is repeatedly interrupted. … Therefore gardens are a paradise for rampant plants and a source of desperation for their owners."[43] Instead, what he is saying is quite simple: use plants that have an ecological amplitude matching the existing, unimproved environment, which, with an eye on the level of dynamism in their environment, will outcompete undesirable species.

On our way from the English garden to the Zwölf-Räume-Haus where we are heading to visit one of Fischedick's perennial gardens, we move up into "the terraces" where Korte undertook the later "artistic" work that caused his clash with Müller. This work is clear and interesting in the aerial photograph, contrasting grids to the seemingly natural groupings elsewhere. Because it had been on the basis of these horticultural manipulations that my friend had recommended Hombroich as a subject, and because of my desire to build an argument that formal manipulation, like the baroque, was not unnatural, I had been trying to get a handle on these areas when I met Damm. However, as I spent time with Fischedick, walking through the garden, I recognized a gardening logic that I knew from my own time as a gardener, and I enjoyed the way he positioned nature in relationship to it; this caused me to lose some of my interest in Korte's later work.

Walking past one of these grids, however, I was struck by a spatial effect that reminded me of the Miller Garden, with a clear architectonic logic. Like the Honey Locust Allée, this grid of 10 x 10 trees acted as a filter between the space of the island and its English garden at the lower level, and the upper level of the terraces. This grid sits like a like a sticking

FIGURE 7.24

One of Korte's grids of trees acting as a filter to look through; Fischedick grudgingly acknowledges its effectiveness.

plaster between two other groups of vegetation, filling in the gap. When I was actually confronted with it, rather than considering it in the abstract as a caricature of Korte's later approach, I asked Fischedick if he liked it, and he answered grudgingly: "Sometimes I do and sometimes don't. I like it when I can look through."

To have visibility through or not is a maintenance question, and we talk again about how this space is pruned by the volunteers on one day a year. Considering that Fischedick likes the view under trees through the meadow, and the view here, we are confronted by the latent aesthetic predilections of his approach to nature: that it somehow must look natural. This reveals an interesting sliding scale, or perhaps a seesaw, where manipulation in a cultural landscape sense, like the pollards, is treated as on a par with nature, while when it is formed from a spatial perspective using geometry, it is somehow "trying too hard." This is a contradiction that Gerritsen talks about in his own work: a desire for topiary, but a love of naturalness. For my part, I wondered if treating this vegetation as a band all along the edge between the lower and upper landscape might have had a strategic effect: announcing the transition, rather than leaving the grids floating in space—art for art's sake by the transgressive gardener, as Müller considered Korte to be.

Moving past this spatial transition, walking to one of the perennial gardens that he wants to show me, Fischedick, after much questioning,[44] turns to me and says: "I want to ask *you* a question: what do you think of this edge?" He is pointing to a gravel road that enters the base of Heerich's Tadeusz Pavilion, with a straight edge on one side and a curved one on the other. I like both edges, the straight one addressing the geometry of the building and the other the topography. "Exactly," says Fischedick, "but Burkhard wants them both straight. Makes no sense to me." At this moment I am reminded of the incongruities I faced as a young landscaper in building the designs of landscape architects: the designs seemed to contradict the way the site was working. Inasmuch as Damm followed a "Dutch wave" approach, this was clearly a formal element for him. I thought Fischedick's curved transition rather elegant.

Behind the Zwölf-Räume-Haus, Fischedick takes me to one of his favorite areas where he is working with perennials, which I remember

FIGURE 7.25

A perennial garden that Müller wanted after seeing Giverny; Fischedick has now developed it in the style of Oudolf.

Korte describing as resulting from Müller's desire to "have" Monet's garden at Giverny after a visit there. By both Korte's and Fischedick's account, the site chosen was unacceptable, but Fischedick has nonetheless colonized Korte's design with a perennial garden in the style of Oudolf and Gerritsen, working one section demarcated by Korte's geometry after another. Together with the cloister at the rocket station, these two gardens are clearly some of Fischedick's favorites, perhaps even an addiction, so that in the face of all the work to be done at the Insel and the rocket station, Fischedick has to make sure he doesn't do too much, since the more he does, the more he will have to do. I am reminded of Korte's throwaway remark that Fischedick is more interested in maintaining the cloister than the Hombroich.

As in his home garden, Fischedick's approach is to mow a section once a year and simply see what comes up, then to weed the result at a later stage. He points to a "beautiful flower," recalling Korte's emphasis on aesthetics at the expense of everything else, and says: "It's common here. But everyone else is shocked, since it's a weed." Acknowledging the inherent weediness of the plant, he adds: "It's not a problem, I cut half one year, half the other." If we take the main criterion of Fischedick's approach to be "see what comes up," then essentially one gets a garden of weeds, or partly so, since the *OED* describes a weed as, on the one hand, "a wild plant," which the plants in this garden undoubtedly are; on the other hand, they are not weeds because they are not—as the dictionary description goes on—"in competition with a cultivated plant," because none of these plants is essentially cultivated, they are all spontaneous; furthermore, they are not "growing where [they are] not wanted." That being said, once Fischedick starts weeding, the plants that remain are in effect cultivated. He says: "It's not a garden. We don't have a plan. Over the years I learn which plants work and which don't; trial and error. After fourteen years I know. I don't have to do much." He says that 90 percent of gardening is "just for [the sake of] doing something." At the same time, this waiting can be a stressful process, a counterintuitive holding back, since "I do have a moment where I think: I've gone too far," adding: "you have to have courage."

FIGURE 7.26

The cloister at the rocket station, where Fischedick has created a productive garden that grows vegetables which are served at the cafeteria.

CONCLUSION

Ending the book on management and the range of players involved in a project like this reminded me of my experiences as a gardener at the bottom of the food chain, and how the roles of different professionals inform their view of a project. The place itself becomes a pivot, and the disciplinary agenda, mode of practice, and physical location inform a different sense of what it is, and therefore how it should be managed. As one player influences another, the mandate for each player and the type of engagement change, and all this ultimately has physical effects on a landscape.

The common tool for landscape architects working with projects over time is the "Plan of Management," which generally uses a timeline and a key to locate what should happen where and when. While this can be used to allocate funding at a client level, for the gardener or landscaper on the front line, more often than not, if they see such a document at all, it ends up in the drawer underneath the tea bags in the site shed, totally divorced from their day-to-day practice. The top-down nature of such documents does not marry with their "sense" of what they are doing.

Discussing management at Insel Hombroich shows us another way of practicing with the viridic as a design language that operates through regulation. Management processes undertaken onsite regulate existing site processes, such as those described by Fischedick and Gerritsen. Since forms that might be valued in design terms are always in a constant state of transition, potentially into a form that differs from the original design, management selectively intervenes, or not, since it knows the forces in the system that have caused the deviation to arise. If we look at Gerritsen's model again, too much attention is as much a problem as not enough. Increasing disturbance for the right reasons will inevitably also catalyze the undesirable.

This view of form as the result of the regulation of natural processes by management provides a key to the way landscape architecture and gardening can come together in practice. The development of a common language like the viridic, which sees growth always as form and process simultaneously, can allow for a respectful and productive negotiation between landscape architecture—which can provide a strategic overview and formal ambitions—and gardening—which uses tactical judgment to regulate natural processes of growth. This *rapprochement* will allow the realization of a unique type of design that is constantly in a state of change, with materials that have a life, just as we do, and are ultimately our key collaborators in any landscape design.

CHAPTER 8

Conclusion: A Manifesto *for the* Viridic

PLANTS REPRESENT a unique material language for landscape architecture as distinct from architecture, a language that is inseparable from a practice that I have been calling "the viridic." I have used the case studies in this book to explore aspects of this practice, and in lieu of a summative conclusion I shall instead opt for a formative one, laying down a series of positions that can inform a new practice for landscape architecture that optimizes the exciting properties of plants through changing the way landscape architects work.

In landscape architecture over the last twenty years, the process discourse has exhibited the stridency of the architectural avant-garde, utilizing a muscular language full of instrumental terms like infrastructure and systems, while also aggressively criticizing landscape architecture, which it seeks to replace with ecological urbanism; even the word landscape has disappeared. In contrast to this, plants and gardening can seem flaccid and soft, or dismissed as feminine, as Meyer noted of landscape architecture in relation to modern architecture.[1] In fact, there may be much more to plants than meets the eye. In the Amazon, indigenous shamans believe that plants have consciousness, and are fickle and jealous; they consume psychotropic substances like ayahuasca in order to have a literal engagement with plants as spirits. Similarly, Patrick Blanc,[2] and more recently Luce Irigaray and Michael Marder,[3] have begun to speculate on the sexuality of plants: their desires. All this is to say that when it comes to plants, we don't really know what is going on, but as soon as we really look at them, and try to engage with them, their "plantness" comes to the fore.

In developing this practice of the viridic, I have demonstrated how excitingly fluid and dynamic plant growth is as a formal and spatial language, and the serious, and liberating, implications of reconceiving landscape architecture based on this language. I will end with a manifesto for the viridic, and propose that a radical rethinking of landscape architecture is required, based on plants. In setting out such a manifesto I will, by way of conclusion, rebuild my case via my key claims, then lay out their implications for a new practice of landscape architecture.

THE VIRIDIC MAKES PLANT AND DESIGNER EQUALS

While the architectonic and representational practice of landscape architecture treats plants as objects, humans have more in ῾common with plants than they do with the "muscular" materials of landscape architecture—like paving, walls, or structures—that are treated as "real" design, where design equals form. Humans and plants share the DNA, and metabolic and sexual processes, common to all living things, and interact with their environment in a similar way.

Both plants and people exist in the same temporal continuum in terms of growth and change; both have similar life cycles. Taking this idea seriously involves developing a nonromantic empathy with plants that will also help them to grow, since humans can use their own experience and life requirements to make decisions about plants. Also, since plants live in a community, as do humans, using the analogy of the social allows for designs to be set up as "communities" rather than as containers for autonomous objects.

> *Utilizing the viridic involves breaking the subject/object split between human and plant; instead, both are in an intersubjective relationship in the garden. Treating the viridic as a relationship embeds landscape architecture in the growth of the landscape as a subject.*

PLANT MATERIAL IS GROWTH IN THE VIRIDIC

Planting design treats plants as static objects, because they are specified in terms of name and location. Embedded in this act is a prediction about a plant's future condition in terms of size and form at maturity. Such a view assumes that a plant has just two states: a pot at installation and tree at maturity. In between, it is considered to be in transition, undervalued because it is in waiting for its maturity.

Along the way, however, the plant grows: its foliage, branches, flowers, roots, etc., keep on developing. Nevertheless, it is the same plant at every stage, right up to its mature state. Growth is the literal material of the plant, but it is seldom considered for its own sake. The plant at maturity is the growth that happened before. When we talk about a plant, we are really talking about growth.

The assumption of growth destabilizes the categories of conventional planting design in an exciting way. "Form" becomes dynamic and changeable, and has many more configurations than a single category, moving from potential plant to shrub to tree; "texture" emerges as a characteristic with ecological or physiological rationales in relation to growth, such as avoiding transpiration or predation; and "color" is something that actually registers time, as changes of season or changes in habit from juvenile to mature.

> *The viridic constitutes a recognition that the plant is growing, and that growth is the material nature of the plant. An interest in the viridic is an interest in—even an awe of—growth. The implication of this is that all the intermediate states that the plant goes through along the way represent a multitude of emerging and changing qualities all from the same plant, each intermediate state valued in design terms as much as the mature condition. Taking on board such changing qualities creates a dynamic form language for landscape architecture, very different from architecture.*

MAINTENANCE MUST BE EXPLICIT IN LANDSCAPE DESIGN WITH THE VIRIDIC

Due to the assumption of a mature plant in specifying location in plan, growth is implicit but unacknowledged in planting design. The fact that the plant must grow over time to reach maturity means that maintenance, in the form of gardening, is also implicit and assumed in the future of the plant, and therefore the project.

A viridic practice means making the implicit assumptions about maintenance or gardening explicit, and involving them actively in the design process. There are two obvious ways for the designer to work explicitly with the viridic to achieve a plant's desired mature condition: contingency in design and gardening in practice. For the former, contingency means acknowledging the ecological effects of planting decisions and using increased density, sacrificial crops, microclimate, or other "hacks" to influence growth beyond simply predictive spacing, so that the growing process is catalyzed. For the latter, as I will argue below, changing conventional landscape-architectural practice will be required to involve a physical gardening role later in the project's development.

REGULATE AND ACCEPT THE ENVIRONMENT TO CULTIVATE VIRIDIC QUALITIES

Historically, gardens and parks have been places for recreation, where plants contribute to the qualities of spaces. Plant growth is the material of those qualities, and plants grow or do not grow on the basis of the environment as ecology. Thus a beautiful park or garden is beautiful because plants are growing, and plants are growing only because the ecological environment is functioning, regardless of whether that functioning is artificial or natural in terms of products like fertilizers or pesticides. Landscape design and gardening are the tools that set up the effectiveness of that environment as a place of growth, calibrating plants to the environment on the basis of grooming conditions which facilitate material qualities. Gardening actions, in effect, also act ecologically, because they simulate natural disturbance and thereby evoke from the plant responses that reflect evolutionary success mechanisms.

A viridic practice of landscape design with gardening involves treating designed and maintained spaces first as an ecology, but one that is tailored to the particular formal and material qualities that interest the designer. From the opposite direction, it also means potentially fostering aesthetic qualities by manipulating the ecology of the environment, by using design to regulate ecological systems that may not be obvious.

THE VIRIDIC IS ABOUT ENERGY

Thermodynamics describes the movement of energy through the universe, and every material is tied to it: human beings as much as plants. Energy moves through the environment into us and plants in numerous forms, including nutrition, water, and light, then leaves us to reemerge into the environment in a fluid process. These processes of metabolism and physiology result in growth.

Since growth is the focus of the viridic, any interest in it is also an interest in energy, and any desire to manipulate the viridic is first and foremost a question of energy: the energy that can be put into the system, by the gardener and by the ecological resources they can muster, and the plants' responses to those insertions; such responses are also insertions into the system.

To work with the viridic is to see design as the insertion of energy into a system, with an eye to what will come out of that system as a result of growth. Gardening is the process of optimizing what emerges from insertions of energy, as it arises. A key consideration for a viridic approach to design would be whether inputs into systems create more material outputs than the energy that was put in, using the momentum of the system in such a way that inputs are value-adding.

ACTIONS TRIGGER LATENT EFFECTS IN THE VIRIDIC

Plants, like humans, have evolved not just to survive but to thrive due to environmental stresses, through what is called "hormesis." Such a response is not always negative, so long as it is survived, but can be productive: a quality that Nicholas Nassim Taleb calls "antifragility,"[4] which he opposed to "resilience." Examples of such stress in plants can include predation or damage due to climate events like storms.

Plants generally respond to such stresses by producing new juvenile foliage, but flowering is another response. In design terms, the production of juvenile foliage represents a latent material quality of plants that can make a plant look different from its characteristic appearance. Like plant succession, since these changes are transitional, a change of leaf form in the first instance precipitates the next morphological state, where a different plant architecture results. Thus, in a process over time, a state change in leaf material leads to changes of plant form, which have spatial outcomes in relation to other plants in the original and evolving design.

A viridic approach uses gardening techniques that simulate stresses to which plants have evolved to respond. These stresses create a material change in the plant at different times during its development, effectively renewing a juvenile state in parts, since it is possible for the plant to have both mature and juvenile material on it simultaneously. To fully exploit the viridic as a language of plants would be to take a curatorial approach to the plant, and manage it to bring out changes in material quality due to maintenance at different stages during its overall growth—ironically, a process not dissimilar to hairdressing. In this way plant qualities are manipulated to dynamically influence developing spatial and organizational effects, endowing them with different qualities as time goes on.

THE VIRIDIC IS FORM
AND PROCESS SIMULTANEOUSLY

In an effort to provide a substance to form, process has become the dominant paradigm for landscape-architectural design. The process discourse characterizes an interest in form as "formalism," preferring to treat form as an outcome rather than something pursued in its own right. This is disingenuous, because there are still formal predilections in the outcomes of a process-led design, despite the fact that it appears non-formal.

Plants destabilize what I argue is a false dichotomy between form and process, because manipulation of plant form at a particular point in time must be undertaken in order to initiate or develop a process outcome later. Correspondingly, in a recursive fashion, form is the result of growth, and changes in form result in changes in growth. The qualities of plants used in design arise from processes as simultaneously formal and material.

> *Beyond selection and location during design, any viridic property of plants, such as material quality or form, is always the result of a process that happens after planting. At the point where process actions occur, the viridic is always a formal language because the plant is shaped as a form, regardless of the fact that the form will have process effects. Correspondingly, the viridic is always both a formal and a process material at one and the same time. This has implication for planting design that treats plant qualities as static.*

BIOLOGY AND AESTHETICS
ARE NOT SEPARATE IN THE VIRIDIC

The look of a plant is the external manifestation of its physiological and morphological processes. The convention for describing such processes is in terms of biology and botany. The morphology of a plant, however, can be considered in aesthetic terms, autonomous from its scientific description, such as in common aesthetic qualities used in planting design: texture or form, for example. However, even as they are considered thus, such qualities will only ever be present due to growth, and therefore maintenance, so it is dangerous to separate biology and aesthetics.

Since aesthetic qualities arise from biological factors, gardening is a tool for manipulating such qualities, since its actions affect the biological factors that bring them to fruition. Correspondingly, there is no reason to separate the aesthetic and the biological; in fact, taking a biological approach to the aesthetic enables the factors that cause qualities to be manipulated for aesthetic effect.

Gardening manipulates plant biology for aesthetic outcomes in the viridic, and merges the biological and the aesthetic. Conversely, utilizing aesthetic criteria in the maintenance of plants can also catalyze the biological in the viridic. Thus, in the viridic, biology and aesthetics are interchangeable and mutually imbricated.

THE VIRIDIC IS ABOUT ACTION RATHER THAN REPRESENTATION

Representation of plant material can only ever either specify a start or provide set reactions to predicted contingencies. Any specification for maintenance must predict potential situations; this makes it the same as the planting plan in that it simulates a future, even if that future is a catastrophic one.

However, if we accept that growth is the material of plants, such an approach to change is negative and pessimistic. Since a plant will never end up looking exactly as predicted, because each plant is a genetically different individual, emerging characteristics and traits during the growth process should be encouraged and engaged with. Nevertheless, representation will never be the key to this. Instead, real-time action in response to the plant, also known as gardening, provides a better tool to optimize serendipitous characteristics emerging from growth. Representation, where it is used, should instead be post-factum, as a means of documenting effects to allow for a learning process to inform later practice.

The viridic, like the tectonic, is not about material as an object, but an active shaping interaction between the material and the person shaping it. The material becomes catalyzed—in fact, becomes the material—on the basis of that shaping. For the viridic this means undertaking direct actions over time that physically shape the plant in response to its state at a specific point in time, rather than trying to cover contingencies in representation.

A VIRIDIC PRACTICE IS A LEARNING PRACTICE

Plants grow, and gardening happens, in real time. Plants change due to gardeners' actions, and gardeners learn by observation of the effects of their previous actions. Because plants and gardeners live together in time, they learn from each other. By producing certain effects that are desirable for gardeners, plants gain an evolutionary advantage, and by facilitating growth, gardeners enable plants to live and flourish.

A viridic practice is always to some extent didactic, since failure to learn results in plant death. Learning is also a fundamental aspect of human nature, and the role of gardens as a learning environment adds to their therapeutic effects. The viridic is therefore beneficial.

THE VIRIDIC MERGES GARDENING AND DESIGN THINKING

The viridic requires changes to both landscape architecture and gardening in terms of hidden but implicit class implications by each about the other. For landscape architecture, it requires a change of practice from representation to physical work in order to exercise design judgment or control over what is emerging over time, while for gardening it involves bringing a level of spatial and abstract design thinking to gardening decisions. The implication of the viridic is the liberation of design from the predictive graphic artifact to design judgment in real time about emerging conditions and the next stages sought from the growth process.

Gardening involves a different type of decision-making process to design, but design thinking can offer powerful opportunities to the gardener to enhance the spatial and material quality of their garden, At the same time, gardening also always has a spatial dimension in how gardening decisions adapt to, and adapt, emerging formal characteristics of plants, offering an additional level of control to designers. The viridic deploys both types of judgment simultaneously.

THE VIRIDIC USES GARDENING AS A FEEDBACK TOOL

The linear process of design, to construction and then to maintenance by others, treats designs and everything in them as objects. While the ambition may be for the design to eventually work out in a certain way, the real ability to influence it over time is limited by the convention that design and maintenance are separate. Even where maintenance exists, its aim is to realize the original vision at the commencement of the design process, which in effect still makes the process linear.

In contrast, if one assumes that part of embracing growth is an appreciation and, indeed, a welcoming of qualities that arise during the growth process, then beyond maintenance a feedback process is required which can bring novel qualities that arise back into the design process in such a way that the original design can also change, not simply that changes can be pulled back to meet the earlier proposition as envisaged. Gardening is the best tool to facilitate feedback between original design and resultant change, and the modification of each.

The nature of the viridic is inherently recursive and iterative, constantly moving from cause to effect, whereby the latest effects cause subsequent ones. A viridic approach requires—indeed, encourages—a recognition that the original design is dynamic, and changes as growth occurs. Gardening in this context becomes the secret weapon for feedback in the landscape design process.

THE VIRIDIC ENTAILS A CHANGE IN PRACTICE

Gardening and landscape architecture have become separate from one another, because the professionalization of the former means that it has become the latter. With this professionalization has come a loss of expertise in both directions: gardening has become "practical," landscape architecture "theoretical." Gardening has lost its sense of creativity or design, while landscape architecture has lost its ability to work with the real nature of its materials.

The gulf between indoor and outdoor, between designing and doing, is almost insurmountable, because with it comes a political and social change implied in "getting one's hands dirty." Convention correspondingly provides the most significant impediment to a practice that is engaged with growth. Design practice is also economical, since working at scale allows for an increased territorial control even as it can miss emergent characteristics. This is why the viridic is most closely tied to a site-specific practice of landscape architecture, which would allow for the most immediate way of moving to a viridic practice.

> *Rejecting classism and a blue-collar/white-collar separation is key to a viridic practice of landscape architecture, though little is really at stake in doing so. Developing landscape maintenance as a part of landscape-architectural practice is a vital and exciting mechanism for engaging the viridic, and might also allow for a reinvigoration of the profession of landscape architecture, as it can then also feed off the growth of its key material: plants. Working in a site-specific manner as a landscape architect, and increasing site visits and the duration of contracts to allow for management, would be the first step into a viridic practice.*

NOTES

FOREWORD

1. Richard Weller and Billy Fleming, "Has Landscape Architecture Failed?," *The Dirt: Uniting the Built and the Natural Environments* (blog, 2016; accessed 2018).
2. Luce Irigaray and Michael Marder, *Through Vegetal Being: Two Philosophical Perspectives* (New York: Columbia University Press, 2016).
3. Michael Marder, *Plant-Thinking: A Philosophy of Vegetal Life* (New York: Columbia University Press, 2013).
4. Craig Holdrege, *Thinking Like a Plant: A Living Science for Life* (Great Barrington, MA: Lindisfarne Books, 2013).
5. Stephen Harrod Buhner, *Plant Intelligence and the Imaginal Realm: Beyond the Doors of Perception into the Dreaming of Earth* (Rochester, VT: Bear & Company, 2014).

CHAPTER 1: INTRODUCTION

1. For example, Michael Pollan, *Second Nature: A Gardener's Education* (London: Bloomsbury, 1991).
2. Stanislaus Fung, "The Interdisciplinary Prospects of Reading Yuan Ye," *Studies in the History of Gardens and Designed Landscapes* 18, no. 3 (1998), 211–231.
3. Geoffrey Jellicoe and Susan Jellicoe, *The Landscape of Man: Shaping the Environment from Pre-History to the Present Day* (London: Thames and Hudson, 1975).
4. For a historical sequence to the development of the term "landscape architect," see Charles Waldheim, *Landscape as Urbanism: A General Theory* (Princeton: Princeton Architectural Press, 2016).
5. Though real botanists like Patrick Blanc do not like him described as such, even if they appreciate his work. Francis Rambert, "In Praise of a Plant Amateur: Interview

with Patrick Blanc," in Lauro Cavalcanti, Farès El-Dahdah, and Francis Rambert, eds., *Roberto Burle Marx: The Modernity of Landscape* (Barcelona: Actar, 2011).

6. Charles Waldheim, ed., *The Landscape Urbanism Reader* (New York: Princeton Architectural Press, 2006).

7. Astronomer Arthur Eddington used the phrase "arrow of time" to refer to the asymmetry of time: that it is one-directional, and it is impossible to go backward.

8. For an exciting approach that acknowledges this critique, and looks at real-time feedback in landscape-architectural design, see Bradley Cantrell and Justine Holzman, *Responsive Landscapes: Strategies for Responsive Technologies in Landscape Architecture* (London: Routledge, 2016). I have written about the evolution of the digital recently; see J. Raxworthy, "The Discourse of the Digital in Contemporary Landscape Architecture," *Journal of Landscape Architecture* 12, no. 2 (2017), 88–93.

9. Teresa Galí-Izard examines gardening strategies as a design practice (Teresa Galí-Izard, *The Same Landscapes: Ideas and Interpretations* [Barcelona: Editorial Gustavo Gili, 2006]), including those of the master of using gardening techniques to create landscape designs, Gilles Clément—as in his *Gardens of Movement* at the Parc Citroën in Paris and Parc Henri Matisse in Lille. His approach is described in depth in Gilles Clément, *Le jardin en mouvement* (Paris: Sens & Tonka, 2007), with extracts in an English-language monograph on his work: Alessandro Rocca, ed., *Planetary Gardens: The Landscape Architecture of Gilles Clément* (Basel: Birkhäuser, 2007). Another contemporary landscape architecture practice that incorporates gardening is that of Atelier Le Balto; see Brigitte Franzen, *Atelier Le Balto: Les pieds sur terre* (Frankfurt: Walther König, 2010).

10. Mark Wigley, *The Architecture of Deconstruction: Derrida's Haunt* (Cambridge, MA: MIT Press, 1993), 35.

11. Michael Laurie, *An Introduction to Landscape Architecture*, 2nd edn. (New York: Elsevier, 1986), 9.

12. Brian Hackett quoted in ibid., 10.

13. Wigley, *The Architecture of Deconstruction*, 35.

14. Ibid., 214.

15. Marc Treib, "Formal Problems," *Studies in the History of Gardens and Designed Landscapes* 18, no. 2 (1998), 71. Though, as Treib notes, "rarely, if ever, do we encounter the presence of the formal independently of the informal"; the "formal"/informal (or *l'informe*, as the French call it) split is a distinction that is as convenient as it is obvious.

16. Oxford Dictionaries, "Growth," Oxford University Press, <http://www.oxforddictionaries.com/definition/english/growth>.

17. Adrian Forty, *Words and Buildings: A Vocabulary of Modern Architecture* (London: Thames and Hudson, 2000), 256.

18. Forty quotes Adolf Hildebrand (ibid., 259).

19. Forty quotes Semper (ibid., 260).
20. Sven-Ingvar Andersson, "Letter from My Henyard," in Steen Høyer, ed., *Sven-Ingvar Andersson: Garden Art and Beyond* (Copenhagen: Arkitektens Forlag, 2002), 107.
21. Forty quotes Hildebrand (Forty, *Words and Buildings*, 260).
22. Ibid., 271.
23. Roberto Burle Marx, "The Garden as Art Form" (1962), in Cavalcanti, El-Dahdah, and Rambert, *Roberto Burle Marx*, 122.
24. Garrett Eckbo, "Small Gardens in the City: A Study of Their Design Possibilities," *Pencil Points* 18, no. 9 (1937), 573.
25. Ibid.
26. Gregg Bleam, "The Work of Dan Kiley," in Marc Treib, ed., *Modern Landscape Architecture: A Critical Review* (Cambridge, MA: MIT Press, 1993).
27. Dan Kiley, "Miller House," in *Landscape Design: Works of Dan Kiley* (Tokyo: Bunji Murotani, 1982), 21.
28. R. E. Wörle and H. J. Wörle, *Designing with Plants* (Basel: Birkhäuser, 2008) describes this approach as planting to produce "Spatial Structure."
29. James C. Rose, *Creative Gardens* (New York: Reinhold, 1958).
30. James C. Rose, "Plants Dictate Garden Forms" (1938), in Treib, *Modern Landscape Architecture*.
31. Gaston Bachelard, *The Poetics of Space* (Boston: Beacon Press, 1969).
32. R. E. Somol, "12 Reasons to Get Back into Shape," in Rem Koolhaas and Brendan McGetrick, eds., *Content* (Cologne: Taschen, 2004), 86.
33. Ibid.
34. D'Arcy Wentworth Thompson, *On Growth and Form* (Cambridge: Cambridge University Press, 1945), 16.
35. Sanford Kwinter, "Who's Afraid of Formalism?," in Cynthia Davidson, ed., *Far from Equilibrium: Essays on Technology and Design Culture* (Barcelona: Actar, 2008), 146.
36. Ibid.
37. Ibid., 147.
38. Ibid.
39. Adrian D. Bell, *Plant Form* (Portland: Timber Press, 2008), 35.
40. Ibid., 258.
41. Ibid., 292.
42. Stefan Buczaki, *Ground Rules for Gardeners: A Practical Guide to Garden Ecology* (London: Collins, 1986), 183.
43. G. R. F. Ferrari, "The Meaninglessness of Gardens," *Journal of Aesthetics and Art Criticism* 68, no. 1 (2010), 34.
44. Ibid., 37.

45. Ibid., 41.
46. Ibid., 39.
47. Michael Marder, *Plant-Thinking: A Philosophy of Vegetal Life* (New York: Columbia University Press, 2013), 10.
48. Ibid., 8.
49. Ibid.
50. Ibid., 4.
51. Ibid., 8.
52. Buczaki, *Ground Rules for Gardeners*, 16.
53. Ferrari, "The Meaninglessness of Gardens," 35.
54. Ibid.
55. Marder, *Plant-Thinking*, 4.
56. Ibid.
57. Oxford Dictionaries, "Gardener," Oxford University Press, <http://www.oxforddictionaries.com/definition/english/gardener>. Compared to "Landscape Architecture," Oxford University Press, <http://www.oxforddictionaries.com/definition/english/landscape-architecture?q=landscape+architect#landscape-architecture__5>.
58. Ferrari, "The Meaninglessness of Gardens."
59. Mateusz Salwa, "The Garden as Performance," *Estetika* 8, no. 1 (2014).
60. Nonetheless, landscape architects are increasingly interested in factoring maintenance into their designs, notably in the growing role of gardeners in consultant teams, such as Piet Oudolf (whom I discuss in chapter 7 below) on the High Line team, and the incorporation of gardening in Olin's Apple campus landscape design and Michael Van Valkenburgh Associates landscape of the Obama Presidential Center, both in progress at the time of writing.
61. Timothy C. Baird and Bonj Szczygiel, "Sociology of Professions: The Evolution of Landscape Architecture in the United States," *Landscape Review* 12, no. 1 (2007).
62. Edward Hyams, *A History of Gardens and Gardening* (New York: Praeger, 1971), 239.
63. J. C. Loudon, *The Landscape Gardening and Landscape Architecture of the Late Humphry Repton, Esq.* (Edinburgh: Longman & Co, 1840).
64. Ibid., 2.
65. Waldheim, *Landscape as Urbanism*, 161.
66. Loudon, *The Landscape Gardening and Landscape Architecture of the Late Humphry Repton*, 29.
67. Baird and Szczygiel, "Sociology of Professions," 8.
68. Loudon, *The Landscape Gardening and Landscape Architecture of the Late Humphry Repton*, 29.

69. Ibid., 30.
70. Ibid., 3.
71. Ibid.
72. Baird and Szczygiel, "Sociology of Professions," 6.
73. Ibid., 9.
74. Loudon, *The Landscape Gardening and Landscape Architecture of the Late Humphry Repton*, 2.
75. Ibid.
76. Sally-Ann Murray, "The Idea of Gardening: Plants, Bewilderment, and Indigenous Identity in South Africa," *English in Africa* 33, no. 2 (2006), 56.
77. Jenni Gobind, Graham du Plessis, and Wilfred Ukpere, "Minimum Wage and Domestic Workers' Right to Basic Conditions of Employment: Are Employers Complying?," *African Journal of Business Management* 6, no. 47 (2012), 11685.
78. In a township, an initiation was once offered to me as a way to make me a man. This demonstrates how the idea that black garden workers are referred to as boys clearly insulting.
79. Despite this, however, in research I am undertaking currently I have found that although ornamental gardens are not a feature of Xhosa culture, many gardeners employed by white homeowners are now developing their own gardens for pleasure in townships in Cape Town.
80. Gobind, du Plessis, and Ukpere, "Minimum Wage and Domestic Workers' Right to Basic Conditions of Employment," 11683.
81. Jeffrey du Preez et al., "The Employment Relationship in the Domestic Workspace in South Africa: Beyond the Apartheid Legacy," *Social Dynamics* 36, no. 2 (2010), 406.
82. Alvaro Huerta, "Looking Beyond 'Mow, Blow and Go': A Case Study of Mexican Immigrant Gardeners in Los Angeles," *Berkeley Planning Journal* 20, no. 1 (2007).
83. Du Preez et al., "The Employment Relationship in the Domestic Workspace in South Africa," 406.
84. Baird and Szczygiel, "Sociology of Professions," 11.
85. Eckbo, "Small Gardens in the City," 574. It should be noted that this project featured plants only in a limited way.
86. John Dixon Hunt, "The Idea of a Garden and the Three Natures," in Hunt, *Greater Perfections: The Practice of Garden Theory* (London: Thames and Hudson, 2000), 32–75.
87. Mark Francis, "The Everyday and the Personal: Six Garden Stories," in Mark Francis and Randolph T. Hester, eds., *The Meaning of Gardens* (Cambridge, MA: MIT Press, 1992), 206 (original emphasis).
88. Oxford Dictionaries, "Maintain," Oxford University Press, <http://www.oxforddictionaries.com/definition/english/maintain>.

CHAPTER 2: THE PERSISTENCE OF A LINE

1. The current owner of Courances, Valentine de Ganay, supports Françoise Boudon's questioning of the description of French gardens as baroque.
2. Allen S. Weiss, "Vaux-le-Vicomte: Anamorphosis Abscondita," in Weiss, *Mirrors of Infinity: The French Formal Garden and 17th-Century Metaphysics* (New York: Princeton Architectural Press, 1995). This fascination with the visual spectacle of the baroque was a trope of the time, also seen in Peter Greenaway's film *The Draughtsman's Contract*. Chantal Cornut-Gentille D'Arcy, "Landscape Design and Drawing in *The Draughtsman's Contract*: Peepholes to an Age," *Miscelánea: A Journal of English and American Studies* 14 (1993).
3. Gregg Bleam, "The Work of Dan Kiley," in Marc Treib, ed., *Modern Landscape Architecture: A Critical Review* (Cambridge, MA: MIT Press, 1993).
4. I did not return to France for ten years, since I was focused on projects and teaching, until my father died and I decided to visit Paris, a city that he loved and had played jazz in in the 1950s. A colleague, Richard Weller, had further advised: "Rackers, you have to do the grand tour, you have to visit all that old stuff," so I leased a Renault Clio, picking it up in Rome and dropping it off in Amsterdam three months later.
5. H. W. Lawrence, "Origins of the Tree-Lined Boulevard," *Geographical Review* 78, no. 4 (1988), 363. Lawrence suggests that "This type of avenue [the tree-lined allée] served as a model in the large-scale spatial planning by later urban designers."
6. Penelope Hobhouse and Patrick Taylor, *The Gardens of Europe* (London: George Philip, 1990), 77. Although it is often attributed by default to André Le Nôtre, Courances is a much older example of what are traditionally known as French formal gardens. Thierry Mariage includes Courances in his inventory of gardens already established before Le Nôtre (Thierry Mariage, *The World of André Le Nôtre* [Philadelphia: University of Pennsylvania Press, 2010], 18–19), with its main features in place, and uses Courances as an example of how ideas and techniques attributed to Le Nôtre preexisted him. In the Foreword to the English edition, the editor, John Dixon Hunt, felt compelled to reassure readers that "Le Nôtre's genius in not in dispute," because the book potentially destabilizes the narrative of Le Nôtre; nonetheless, he noted that "Le Nôtre has achieved a stature and significance that celebrates his œuvre above everything else." Similarly, the current owners assert that Le Nôtre did not have a role in designing the garden, and show as evidence a letter from Jean Le Nôtre, André Le Nôtre's gardener father, providing a quotation for maintenance of the existing garden, which had been developed between 1548 and 1622 (André Le Nôtre lived between 1613 and 1700). The quotation was not accepted, and the current owners suggest that Courances may instead have been influential for the young Le Nôtre. Ironically,

even while debunking Le Nôtre, a member of the family, Count Ernest de Ganay, was one of his biographers (Ernest de Ganay, *André Le Nostre* (Paris: Vincent Fréal, 1962).

7. Vincent Scully, in J. Baubion-Mackler, ed., *French Royal Gardens: The Designs of Andre Le Nôtre* (New York: Rizzoli, 1992), 112.

8. I recognize that this is an unusual conflation of the modern use of the term *parti* and an abstraction of the conventional meaning of the *parterre* as a figure made of vegetation, but I beg the reader's forbearance in judging it not on its provenance but on the relationship it describes.

9. Andrea Simitch and Val Warke, *The Language of Architecture: 26 Principles Every Architect Should Know* (Beverly, MA: Rockport Publishers, 2014), 34.

10. *Oxford English Dictionary*.

11. Mariage, *The World of André Le Nôtre*, suggests that Renaissance and baroque *parterres* were actually composed of much simpler motifs, but became complex in historic restoration by later garden writers such as André Mollet.

12. Marc Rumelhart, reading my manuscript, suggests that it is important to note that my use of *parterre* is an abstraction of the term, since the *parterre de broderie* is its strict definition.

13. Michel Corajoud, "The Landscape Project: Letter to the Students," in Germán T. Cruz, ed., *The French Mind on the Landscape* (Bloomington: Xlibris, 2012), 139.

14. Or "regimes of care," as Professor Leon van Schaik from RMIT University in Melbourne referred to them. This usage is intimate and personal, like Foucault's notion of the "care of the self," to which I was introduced by Peter Connolly in his wedding speech.

15. Although I am suggesting that the *parti-parterre* relationship is a landscape process, it is also urbanistic, because the *parti* operates like a landscape phenomenon. An incremental series of figures in Aldo Rossi's *Architecture of the City* (Cambridge, MA: MIT Press, 1982) describes the propensity of graphic figures over a certain size to exert force on their context over time, as the context is forced to adjust to them. In the first figure it is a Roman theater, a pristine setting for events floating clearly in a dense organic fabric. In the second, after time has passed and the civic unrest of the Dark Ages has completely changed the political and physical milieu, the theater has been appropriated to operate as a defensive urban wall, and the town has withdrawn into the interior for protection from raiding. In the final figure, much time has passed and the theater has disappeared completely, but the systems of land tenure and ownership it established have caused its oval shape to become the street layout and plot structure. During the preceding ten years of the process discourse, I frequently employed this series of figures to show that the vilification of form by denigrating it as effect result rather than elevating it as cause was arbitrary. In Rossi's series we see that time does things to objects, but also that

objects inflect time. Keeping both in hand is important, and the recognition that in this sense architecture is more geological than biological is a useful emerging discourse. Stan Allen, "From the Biological to the Geological," in Stan Allen and Marc McQuade, eds., *Landform Building* (Zurich: Lars Müller/Princeton University School of Architecture, 2011). Key symposia like "The Geologic Turn: Architecture's New Alliance," February 10–11, 2012 (<http://anexact.org/The-Geologic-Turn>) have explored the geological in architecture.

16. Thierry Mariage, "Parks, Forests and Planning," in *The World of André Le Nôtre*.
17. I will be relying on drawings, photographs, and essays from the Courances book as evidence, and comparing these to other accounts of French baroque avenue and arboriculture practices during the period.
18. Oliver Poncet, "The Owners," <http://www.courances.net/histoires5UK.htm>.
19. Mariage, *The World of André Le Nôtre*, 20.
20. Françoise Boudon, <http://www.courances.net/histoires2UK.htm>. This garden type was common across the lowlands of Europe, particularly in the Veneto in the sixteenth century, and was further developed in France by King François I in the 1540s in the Grand Jardin and the Pine Garden at the Château de Fontainebleau.
21. Ibid.
22. Françoise Boudon, "Courances à la Renaissance: Mise en scène progressive de l'eau," in Valentine de Ganay and Louis Le Bon, eds., *Courances* (Paris: Flammarion, 2003), 56. Courances is featured in Androuet du Cerceau's survey of châteaux, *Livre d'architecture* (1582), and both Boudon and Mariage analyze its oblique drawings to model the development of Courances.
23. Cosme's grandson François Clausse was Grand Maître des Eaux et Forêts (Grand Master of Water and Forests) for Bourgogne, which might also explain some of the garden's innovative land practices.
24. Boudon, 68: "Gallard s'intéressait aux végétaux. Il avait une pépinière, qualifée de 'vieille' en 1643, qu'il projetait alors de remplacer ou de doubler par une nouvelle. Il avait le goût de l'innovation: des cyprès avaient été associés aux 'palissades d'épines' le long des canaux longeant l'avenue d'arrivée. En 1645, les épines sont toujours là mais des cyprès, il n'est plus question; auraient-ils étés arrachés parce qu'ils étaient morts?" [Gallard was interested in vegetation. He had a nursery that was old in 1643, and planned to replace it with a new, better one. He had a taste for innovation: he put the cypresses associated with the wall of thorns along the entry canal. In 1645 the thorns remained but not the cypresses: were they dug up because they were dead?]
25. Rumelhart describes the etymology of the palisade in French language and horticulture (Marc Rumelhart, email to author, February 26, 2010): "For ancient authors, a 'palissade' is a living hedge, usually clipped or trimmed. They had been named 'palissades' because originally they could/had to be attached to a 'dead'

woody structure (crossed posts and canes ['palissées']). "Pal" is an Old French word for stick or picket, post, pale." While Rumelhart suggests that the species used could have been either *Prunus spinosa* ("épine noire," prunellier) or *Cornus sanguinea* (cornouiller sanguin), these would not have been appropriate because "they are unable to keep their feet at the place you placed them (such bad behavior for marking a property's limit!)." Instead he agrees with me that it was most likely crab apple or *Crataegus monogyna* ("épine blanche," aubépine commune). The use of cypresses for the trees above the palisade is unusual, and is not discussed by Adams (William Howard Adams, *The French Garden 1500–1800* [London: Scolar Press, 1979]), who, from his reading of Boyceau, suggests that during the seventeenth century the most common species used in allées were lime (*Tilia* spp.), beech (*Fagus sylvatica*), hornbeam (*Carpinus betulus*), and horse chestnut (*Aesculus hippocastanum*). These species are also mentioned in Sarah M. Couch, "The Practice of Avenue Planting in the Seventeenth and Eighteenth Centuries," *Garden History* 20, no. 2 (1992) in her discussion of the adoption of French avenue planting in Britain during the seventeenth and eighteenth centuries.

26. This does not surprise Rumelhart, who says that Mollet "mentions a hard winter (1608?) when all the formal hedges froze in the King's [Henri IV's] garden. They were made of cypress (*Cupressus sempervirens*) by imitation of Italian Renaissance gardens, and cypress, which is not hardy in the Paris region. Claude Mollet tells that he was compelled by this disaster to use box (*Buxus sempervirens*), which they knew to be native in southwest Europe, but which produces a strange smell in winter and was perhaps not exotic enough."

27. Numerous other canals at the rear of the garden currently exist in such a utilitarian manner, notably behind the Allée de Moigny, where canals run at the back of the palisade through the forest in the park.

28. Monique Mosser suggests that these double rows of trees were lime trees (*Tillia* spp.)—during the time of Anne Marguerite Nicolay, who died in 1772, a common feature of baroque gardens of this period. This is the form of the *contre-allée* at St Germain-en-Laye, renovated by Le Nôtre, where multiple rows of lime run toward the edge of the famous terrace overlooking Paris, creating a series of long plazas oriented toward the view. (Monique Mosser, "From the XVIIIth until Today," http://www.courances.net/histoires3UK.htm, accessed January 21, 2010).

29. Mosser, "From the XVIIIth until Today."

30. I was saddened to hear that Comte Jean de Ganay passed away recently (<http://www.telegraph.co.uk/news/obituaries/10183320/Jean-Louis-de-Ganay.html>) and remembered his generosity in giving my partner and me a lift back to Paris during a rainy winter visit to Courances. He was going to the opera, and his driver put newspaper on the seats where we sat in his Citroën. Since the family came

from Argentina, we had a great conversation about Brazil, and he told us of the multicolored parrots he had seen in the Amazon.

31. Pascal Cribier, "Impressions d'un promeneur assidu," in de Ganay and Le Bon, *Courances*, 19–22. "Ou l'énorme branche horizontale du platane au bout de l'Allée d'Honneur qui aurait dû casser mille fois mais qui résiste, défiant toutes les lois de l'apesanteur."
32. With the advent of a universally accessible Google Maps, some of the romance of the idea of "territory" has dissipated, since we can now almost visualize the landscape as if we too were satellites.
33. In 35-degree heat I rode 22 kilometers between the station and Courances, and 22 kilometers back, on my Brompton folding bike.
34. Olivier de Serres, *Le Théâtre d'Agriculture et Mesnage des Champs* (Arles: Actes Sud, 2001).
35. As a caveat, I should note that mechanization has again reduced the costs and time of maintaining a garden like this, but at the price of a homogenization of treatment compared to the finer-grain treatments possible with individual laborers and hand tools.
36. Is the garden a garden if no one is there to experience it? Since the garden mobilizes plants for aesthetic experience, without people the garden is really simply a natural environment with ecological characteristics.
37. Giulia Pacini, "A Culture of Trees: The Politics of Pruning and Felling in Late Eighteenth-Century France," *Eighteenth-Century Studies* 41, no. 1 (2007), 3.
38. While in the 1990s it was understood that the idea of nature was constructed, an increased interest in indigenous plants means I have to note that when I talk here about "natural regeneration," I really mean spontaneous vegetation, and ecology proceeding as it does, not on the basis of any human construct about a pristine condition. Indeed, the vegetation in the forests of baroque gardens like Courances is entirely cosmopolitan, with a mix of agricultural weeds, garden escapees, and native species.
39. While there were probably planted trees in among the thick regenerating vegetation, another strategy for producing forest could be to cut rows, as they did at Courances, and use this as a process for selecting trees, allowing any trees in the uncut row to remain. This would give a looser but still visible row made up of strong but diverse species: another method of producing a forest.
40. Boudon, "Courances à la Renaissance," 61. (My translation.)
41. Fletcher Steele, *Gardens and People* (Cambridge, MA: Riverside Press, 1964), 128.
42. Adrian D. Bell, *Plant Form* (Portland: Timber Press, 2008), 344.

CHAPTER 3: ARCHITECTURE WITH PLANTS

1. Steven R. Krog, "The Language of the Modern," *Landscape Architecture* 75, no. 2 (1985), 56.
2. I recognize that this is a critique that could also be applied to this book, with its emphasis on form and technique rather than the political, and it would be fair. As I write this in Africa, from research I brought with me, how these First World discourses apply in the Global South is a question that I am still considering, and will address in future publications.
3. While I too admire Kiley's work at the Miller Garden, his work with Saarinen on the arch in St. Louis is to my mind even more sophisticated: the same trees, with the same rigid spacing, create multiple different types of landscape spaces as their alignment changes, converging to cover plazas and separating to frame grassed areas.
4. Elizabeth K. Meyer, "Kiley and the Spaces of Landscape Modernism," in Reuben M. Rainey and Marc Treib, eds., *Dan Kiley Landscapes: The Poetry of Space* (Richmond, CA: William Stout, 2009), 128.
5. Ibid., 189.
6. Gregg Bleam, "Modern and Classical Themes in the Work of Dan Kiley," in Rainey and Treib, *Dan Kiley Landscapes*, 234.
7. Bradley C. Brooks, "A Journey through Miller House and Garden," in Brooks, ed., *Miller House and Garden* (Indianapolis: Indianapolis Museum of Art, 2011), 23.
8. The Henry Moore sculpture was sold by the Millers' estate prior to the property's handover to the IMA in 2006.
9. Emphasis added.
10. Bleam, "Modern and Classical Themes in the Work of Dan Kiley," 231.
11. Ibid., 221.
12. Alexander T. Shulgin, "How Similar Is Substantially Similar?," *Journal of Forensic Science*, no. 35 (1990). This definition comes from the realm of psychedelic drugs. Shulgin, a brilliant chemist, was affected by President Reagan's Anti-Drug Abuse Act (1986). One of the several sections of this Act, known as the "Controlled Substances Analogue Enforcement Act of 1986," concerned him because he was synthesizing analogues for MDMA (ecstasy), including the psychedelic phenethylamine 2CB, as part of his academic research.
13. Gary R. Hilderbrand, *The Miller Garden: Icon of Modernism* (Washington, DC: Spacemaker Press, 1999), 24.
14. Marc Treib, "Axioms for a Modern Landscape Architecture," in Treib, ed., *Modern Landscape Architecture: A Critical Review* (Cambridge, MA: MIT Press, 1993), 43.
15. Bleam, "Modern and Classical Themes in the Work of Dan Kiley," 235.
16. Meyer, "Kiley and the Spaces of Landscape Modernism," 125.

17. Caroline Constant, "1990," *AA Files*, no. 20 (Autumn 1990), 47.
18. Meyer, "Kiley and the Spaces of Landscape Modernism," 125.
19. Ibid., 127.
20. Ibid., 125.
21. Frederick Gutheim, "Natural Responses to Architectural Statements," in *Landscape Design: Works of Dan Kiley*, Process: Architecture (Tokyo: Bunji Murotani, 1982), 63.
22. Brooks, "A Journey through Miller House and Garden," 20.
23. Treib, "Axioms for a Modern Landscape Architecture," 39.
24. Richard Becherer, "Past Remembering: Robert Mallet-Stevens's Architecture of Duration," *Assemblage*, no. 31 (1996), 19.
25. Treib, "Axioms for a Modern Landscape Architecture," 39.
26. James C. Rose, "(1938) Freedom in the Garden," in Treib, *Modern Landscape Architecture: A Critical Review*, 70.
27. James C. Rose, "(1939) Why Not Try Science?," in Treib, *Modern Landscape Architecture: A Critical Review*, 77.
28. Rose, "(1938) Freedom in the Garden," 70.
29. Rose, "(1939) Why Not Try Science?," 77.
30. Rose, "(1938) Freedom in the Garden," 70.
31. James C. Rose, "(1938) Articulate Form in Landscape Design," in Treib, *Modern Landscape Architecture: A Critical Review*, 75.
32. Rose, "(1938) Freedom in the Garden," 70.
33. Rose, "(1939) Why Not Try Science?," 77.
34. Ibid.
35. James C. Rose, "(1938) Plants Dictate Garden Forms," in Treib, *Modern Landscape Architecture: A Critical Review*, 72.
36. James C. Rose, *Creative Gardens* (New York: Reinhold, 1958).
37. Meyer, "Kiley and the Spaces of Landscape Modernism," 126. Meyer notes that Rose's taxonomy was first published in in another book, *Designs for Outdoor Living*, by Margaret O. Goldsmith.
38. Rose, "(1938) Freedom in the Garden," 69.
39. Reyner Banham, *Theory and Design in the First Machine Age* (Cambridge, MA: MIT Press, 1980), 266. As an aside, both Taut, in his drawings of the Katsura Royal Villa, and Rose, in his writing on Japanese gardens, demonstrated an interest in Japanese spatial notions. However, Dean Cardasis, head of the James Rose Center, notes that when Rose was regularly asked to design a Japanese garden by prospective clients, he would answer: "Certainly, which part of Japan do you live in?" (Dean Cardasis, "Later Works—James Rose Center for Landscape Architectural Research and Design," <http://jamesrosecenter.org/about/about-james-rose/later-works>).

40. Colin Rowe and Robert Slutzky, "Transparency: Literal and Phenomenal," in Rowe, *The Mathematics of the Ideal Villa and Other Essays* (Cambridge, MA: MIT Press, 1983), 161; original emphasis.
41. Rose, *Creative Gardens*, 196.
42. György Kepes, quoted in Rowe and Slutzky, "Transparency: Literal and Phenomenal," 161.
43. OED online.
44. Rose's drawings use the same style to indicate plant or gap, so I am really using his term fenestration to assume that the shape shown between vertical elements is really a gap rather than a plant, since the term would be a misnomer if the whole surface were continuous.
45. Rose, "(1938) Plants Dictate Garden Forms," 72.
46. Ben Wever's first job was at the Miller Garden 1996, when he was 16, though he had been visiting the garden "since I can remember" with his grandmother, who worked for the Millers for 47 years. After a trade education in horticulture, he began working there full-time from 2000 as a groundsman under his "mentor" Jim Shearn, who had worked at the garden since it was first established. Wever's long history in the Miller Garden is an invaluable resource for understanding the development of the allée over time. Wever discussed my questions with Shearn before I interviewed him to get his perspective over the whole life of the garden, and to cross-check his own answers.
47. Langworthy Garfield (1955), IMA Archives, http://archive.imamuseum.org/results.html?query=miller+house+and+garden.
48. Dan Kiley (1955), IMA Archives.
49. Eric Paepcke (1955); James A. Maschmeyer (1955), IMA Archives.
50. O. D. Hungerford (1975), "Honey Locust and Horse Chestnut Tree Problems, Correspondence," IMA Archives.
51. IMA Archives (1977), "Memorandum: Maintenance Project Status Report to Xenia S. Miller and J. Irwin Miller."
52. IMA Archives (1978).
53. Ibid.
54. O. D. Hungerford (1983), IMA Archives.
55. O. D. Hungerford (1980), "2760 Trees & Shrubs," IMA Archives.
56. Jack Curtis (1985), IMA Archives.
57. IMA Archives (1986), "Renovation Plan Miller Residence (Annotated) 12th February 1986."
58. IMA Archives (1986), "Observation Report"; emphasis added.
59. IMA Archives (1997).
60. Beverley V. McDermott (1999), "Memorandum: Irwin and Miller Garden Tree Problems, Memorandum with Diagram," IMA Archives.

61. James Shearn (1999), "Survey of Locust Trees in Allée," IMA Archives.
62. Jack Curtis (2004), "Memorandum: Replacement Trees for Mhg and Irwin Garden," IMA Archives.
63. Bleam, "Modern and Classical Themes in the Work of Dan Kiley," 235.
64. Meyer, "Kiley and the Spaces of Landscape Modernism," 125.
65. Ibid.
66. Peter Walker and Melanie Simo, *Invisible Gardens: The Search for Modernism in the American Landscape* (Cambridge, MA: MIT Press, 1994), 191.
67. There are exceptions to this rule. For certain architectural periods or styles, weathering of materials is welcomed (see Mohsen Mostafavi and David Leatherbarrow, *On Weathering: The Life of Buildings in Time* [Cambridge, MA: MIT Press, 1992]). For other famous projects that deviated from their design, like Utzon's Sydney Opera House, preservation involves renovating the project to implement the original design, which was not realized at the time of construction.
68. Martin Filler, "Indiana: Modern," *Magazine Antiques* 175, no. 4 (2009), 111.
69. Gutheim, "Natural Responses to Architectural Statements," 66.
70. Hilderbrand, *The Miller Garden: Icon of Modernism*, 23; emphasis added.
71. Ibid., 18; emphasis added.
72. The continuing novelty of vegetative architecture persists in the ongoing fascination with green, or "living," walls, for example.
73. G. R. F. Ferrari, "The Meaninglessness of Gardens," *Journal of Aesthetics and Art Criticism* 68, no. 1 (2010), 34.
74. Ibid., 35.
75. I must acknowledge an MLA student at the University of Cape Town, Frank Kleinschmidt, in a tutorial on Ferrari's reading, for pointing out that, according to Ferrari's definition, the Miller Garden is not a garden.

CHAPTER 4: CHANGING ROOMS

1. Mark Francis and Randolph T. Hester, "The Garden as Idea, Place and Action," in Francis and Hester, eds., *The Meaning of Gardens* (Cambridge, MA: MIT Press, 1992), 2.
2. Michel de Certeau, *The Practice of Everyday Life* (Berkeley: University of California Press, 1984).
3. Anne Whiston Spirn, *The Granite Garden: Urban Nature and Human Design* (New York: Basic Books, 1984).
4. Ibid., 168.
5. Most prominently in the widespread interest in Roland Barthes and signs during the period.

6. Anne Whiston Spirn, *The Language of Landscape* (New Haven: Yale University Press, 1998), 124.
7. Ibid., 181.
8. "Q&A with Landscape Architect Martha Schwartz," *Newsweek*, <http://www.newsweek.com/qa-architect-martha-scwartz-312920>.
9. Derek Jarman, *Derek Jarman's Garden* (New York: Overlook Press, 1996).
10. From Spirn's response to my draft: "The word for chickens in Danish is kyllinger … [generally] Sven Ingvar always uses the Danish word for hen not chicken," adding as an aside: "Hen is a more inclusive word, and in the end, he shaped them more like doves than chickens.… Hen is a more poetic word than the prosaic chicken."
11. Spirn, *The Language of Landscape*, 192.
12. Ibid.
13. Spirn commented, in her review of my draft, that despite Andersson's description of them as such: "in fact, they are not chicken shaped, but rather resemble the birds in traditional Danish (and presumably Scandinavian) embroidery."
14. Comment from Spirn on draft.
15. Discussing the plans, Spirn suggests not placing too much faith in them, noting: "there are at least two plans. One, quite schematic, was published in 1967; the other with more detail much later. But the latter plan is quite idealized and in some aspects, like the placement of hens, does not conform to the actual garden." (Comment from Spirn on draft.)
16. I owe this point to Spirn, from her comments on my draft.
17. Sørensen is regarded as one of the great modernist innovators in Danish landscape architecture, as well as a significant theorist and historian, despite the fact that he was Swedish, like Andersson. His (and Andersson's) use of the ellipse became a characteristic of Scandinavian landscape architecture.
18. Anne-Marie Lund, "Andersson, Sven-Ingvar," in Patrick Taylor, ed., *The Oxford Companion to Gardens* (Oxford: Oxford University Press, 2006), <http://www.oxfordreference.com/views/ENTRY.html?subview=Main&entry=t215.e0049>.
19. Discussed in both Marc Treib, "Sven-Ingvar Andersson, Who Should Have Come from Hven," and Dusan Ogrin, "Sven-Ingvar Andersson and the Quadrature of the Ellipse," both in Steen Høyer, Annemarie Lund, and Susanne Møldrup, eds., *Festskrift tilegnet Sven-Ingvar Andersson* (Denmark: Architektens Forlag, 1994).
20. Sven-Ingvar Andersson, "Letter from My Henyard," in Steen Høyer, ed., *Sven-Ingvar Andersson: Garden Art and Beyond* (Copenhagen: Arkitektens Forlag, 2002).
21. Stefan Boris, "Gardens of Situations: Learning from the Modern Danish Landscape," PhD working paper, 2009.

22. Not too dissimilar to his prediction that perhaps in the future he might live next door to a rocket-launching station (Treib, "Sven-Ingvar Andersson, Who Should Have Come from Hven," 76).
23. Andersson, "Letter from My Henyard," 108.
24. Ibid., 107.
25. Ibid.
26. Comment from Spirn on draft.
27. Andersson, "Letter from My Henyard," 105.
28. Ibid., 107.
29. Elizabeth K. Meyer, "Kiley and the Spaces of Landscape Modernism," in Reuben M. Rainey and Marc Treib, eds., *Dan Kiley Landscapes: The Poetry of Space* (Richmond, CA: William Stout, 2009), 126.
30. "Medium" is defined in the *Oxford English Dictionary* as "an agency or means of doing something" more than as "the material or form used by an artist, composer, or writer."
31. Clement Greenberg, "Modernist Painting," <http://web.archive.org/web/20060105194921/http://www.sharecom.ca/greenberg/modernism.html>.
32. Hal Foster et al., *Art since 1900* (London: Thames & Hudson, 2004), 441.
33. Rosalind Krauss, *Under Blue Cup* (Cambridge, MA: MIT Press, 2011), 4.
34. Margaret Iversen, "The Medium Is the Memory," *Art History* 36, no. 2 (2013), 460, quoting Krauss.
35. Greenberg, "Modernist Painting." (Emphasis added.)
36. G. R. F. Ferrari, "The Meaninglessness of Gardens," *Journal of Aesthetics and Art Criticism* 68, no. 1 (2010).
37. Ibid., 40.
38. Krauss, *Under Blue Cup*, 127.
39. Ibid., 7.
40. Ibid., 17.
41. Kenneth Frampton, "Introduction: Reflections on the Scope of the Tectonic," in Frampton, *Studies in Tectonic Culture: The Poetics of Construction in Nineteenth and Twentieth Century Architecture*, ed. John Cava (Cambridge, MA: MIT Press, 1995), 2.
42. Ibid., 5.
43. Ibid., 4.
44. Ibid., 18.
45. Gottfried Semper, *Style in the Technical and Tectonic Arts* (Los Angeles: Getty Publications, 2004), 107. (Emphasis added.)
46. Michel Pastoureau, *Green: The History of a Color* (Princeton: Princeton University Press, 2014).
47. Ibid.

48. Semper, *Style in the Technical and Tectonic Arts*, 107.
49. Andersson, "Letter from My Henyard," 107.
50. Stefan Buczaki, *Ground Rules for Gardeners: A Practical Guide to Garden Ecology* (London: Collins, 1986), 183.
51. R. E. Wörle and H. J. Wörle, *Designing with Plants* (Basel: Birkhäuser, 2008), 64.
52. Andersson, "Letter from My Henyard," 106.
53. Julian Richard Raxworthy, "Landscape Symphonies: Gardening as a Source of Landscape Architectural Practice, Engaged with Change," paper presented at the PROGRESS conference of SAHANZ, University of Sydney, 2003.
54. W. H. Dowdeswell, *Hedgerows and Verges* (London: Allen & Unwin, 1987), 1.
55. Treib, "Sven-Ingvar Andersson, Who Should Have Come from Hven," 63. Spirn notes in her comment on my draft that "despite being in Sweden, the Marnas garden is in the southern province of Skåne, which shares a similar geology and physiography to Denmark."
56. Andersson, "Letter from My Henyard," 107.
57. Ibid.
58. Chromosomes are long strands of DNA, made up of a material called chromatin. Chromatin is a complex of DNA wrapped around proteins called histones. DNA—therefore, chromosomes—encode and direct the development of proteins. While there are highly specific chromosomal responses, which involve both mutation and genetic invariance, more additional information persists (sometimes called "junk" DNA) than is used at the moment of cell division.
59. Spirn, *The Language of Landscape*, 177.

CHAPTER 5: A MOVING WORK OF ART

1. Parc de la Villette continues to be the touchstone for a "radical" park design, such as the work of Australian landscape architects Taylor Cullity Lethlean in their Australian Garden. Students, too, discovering Parc de la Villette, tend to feature point grids and exaggerated curves juxtaposed in their studio projects.
2. Including in the recent monograph by Catalan design publisher Actar: Lauro Cavalcanti, Farès El-Dahdah, and Francis Rambert, eds., *Roberto Burle Marx: The Modernity of Landscape* (Barcelona: Actar, 2011).
3. Valerie Fraser, "Cannibalizing Le Corbusier: The Mes Gardens of Roberto Burle Marx," *Journal of the Society of Architectural Historians* 59, no. 2 (2000).
4. In Sydney, much of the work of Aspect Studios, such as Alumni Square, features this language, as does the work of Stig Andersson of SLA, for example in his courtyard for Charlotteshaven in Copenhagen.
5. Sima Eliovson, "Biographical Notes on Roberto Burle Marx, a Unique Personality," *Journal of the Adelaide Botanic Garden* 1 (1979), 270.

6. Discussed in James Gleick, *Faster* (London: Picador, 1998).
7. Burle Marx, quoted in Roberio Dias, "O Sítio Santo Antônio da Bica: um laboratório paisagístico," on his website *Escritos na paisagem*, 2008, <http://escritosnapaisagem.blogspot.com/2009/11/o-sitio-santo-antonio-da-bica-um.html>.
8. Dias noted in his response to my draft of this chapter (which he was unhappy with; his comments form the basis of its revision) that Burle Marx said: "I have made gardens for many people but I don't have one, [since] the Sítio is my place for experiments in landscape design."
9. Sally-Ann Murray, "The Idea of Gardening: Plants, Bewilderment, and Indigenous Identity in South Africa," *English in Africa* 33, no. 2 (2006).
10. Roberto Romão et al., "Brazilian Biodiversity for Ornamental Use and Conservation," *Crop Breeding and Applied Biotechnology* 15, no. 2 (2015), 102.
11. P. M. Bardi, *The Tropical Gardens of Burle Marx* (Rio de Janeiro: Colibris Editoria, 1964).
12. Michael Parfit, "A Brazilian Master Who Finds the Art in Nature's Bounty," *Smithsonian* 21, no. 4 (1990).
13. Eliovson, "Biographical Notes on Roberto Burle Marx," 268.
14. Romão et al., "Brazilian Biodiversity for Ornamental Use and Conservation," 102.
15. I visited Sítio Roberto Burle Marx and documented my visit photographically; some of my photographs may be viewed on my Flickr feed: <https://www.flickr.com/photos/julian_raxworthy/sets/72157648484783738/>.
16. Marta Iris Montero, *Roberto Burle Marx: The Lyrical Landscape* (Berkeley: University of California Press, 2001), 47.
17. Eliovson, "Biographical Notes on Roberto Burle Marx," 270.
18. Romão et al., "Brazilian Biodiversity for Ornamental Use and Conservation," 104.
19. Permanent Delegation of Brazil to UNESCO, "Unesco World Heritage Tentative Listing: Sítio Roberto Burle Marx," <http://whc.unesco.org/en/tentativelists/6001/>.
20. Responding to the draft of this chapter, Dias said in an email about the Lago: "When I arrived as director, in 1995, all the plants at the Lago were *Pontederia cordata*. During the long infirmity, 10 years after Burle Marx passed away, the Sítio had been uncared for. This maltreatment of the garden let that one species dominate. The replanting I made at the Lago was to put back the aquatic vegetation of the Sítio. I had to take out a fig tree that spontaneously appeared, so big that it had blocked the view of the majestic rock on top, the reason Burle Marx bought that strip of land in the first place."
21. Burle Marx, quoted in Dias, "O Sítio Santo Antônio da Bica." All quotations from this essay on Dias's webpage are my own translation from the Portuguese, checked with the author; I have included the original text in case the reader wishes to check my translations (here, "'O Sítio é meu lugar de experiências em paisagismo'").

22. Dorothée Imbert, "Review: Roberto Burle Marx: La Permanence de l'instable," *Journal of the Society of Architectural Historians* 71, no. 2 (2012), 247.
23. Montero, *Roberto Burle Marx*, 27.
24. Romão et al., "Brazilian Biodiversity for Ornamental Use and Conservation," 100.
25. Dias disagrees with Fraser on this point: "Maybe in his youth [Burle Marx believed in socialism], but not by the time I knew him."
26. Fraser, "Cannibalizing Le Corbusier," 184.
27. On reading the draft of this manuscript, Dias further suggested that "Gardeners (not all of them) were angry because I made them work. When Burle Marx was ill, they let the spontaneous vegetation grow, and many small plants that could be eradicated with one hand, by the time I came, had become trees blocking the views and ruining the compositions. This is the real reason why some of them, instigated by their Union, were against me."
28. I interviewed Roberio extensively in Brazil on March 31, 2015.
29. Dias disagrees with characterization of the Sítio as a studio: "His studio was in Laranjeiras, 50 kilometers away, where he went every day, morning and afternoon, to work on his projects. The Sítio was more like the place where he augmented his botanical vocabulary and tested his plants," though, as I argue later in this chapter, the plants are being tested for design reasons.
30. Imbert, "Review: Roberto Burle Marx: La Permanence de l'instable," 248.
31. Roberio's response here is also interesting, and worth including in its entirety: "Burle Marx had the clear notion that landscape design and ecology have less in common than people today are driven to think. The way landscape design influences positively ecology is indirect: by making people love, or be in favor of, plants and nature. The ecology involved in landscape design is minimal: if you can make one plant live with another, all right. The Sítio has lots of species from many countries, brought by Burle Marx on every international trip he made. All the species in the Copacabana beach project, excepting two or three, exotic. It is ot so very different in Aterro do Flamengo. He imported and brought lots of foreign plants and treasured them as much as the indigenous vegetation he loved. The natural association that the botanist Mello Barreto taught him was taken mainly by the aesthetic side. He knew that it was not possible for landscape projects to preserve ecosystems. Instead, he always tried to foster laws and influence politicians to act and defend nature."
32. Yuriko Saito, "Everyday Aesthetics," *Philosophy and Literature* 25, no. 1 (2001), 88.
33. Romão et al., "Brazilian Biodiversity for Ornamental Use and Conservation," 102.
34. Dias, "O Sítio Santo Antônio da Bica." ("Podemos dividir, então, as ditas experiências em dois grupos básicos: as de ter e as de usar.")
35. Oscar Bressane, interviewed by author, September 24, 2014.
36. Ibid.

37. Dias, "O Sítio Santo Antônio da Bica." ("Como seus troféus—plantas em sua maioria inéditas em paisagismo, algumas até para a ciência—não vinham acompanhados de manual de instruções, era necessário descobrir o modo de mantê-las vivas e como se comportariam fora de seu habitat ao longo de um tempo razoável.")
38. Oscar Bressane, interviewed by author, September 24, 2014.
39. Dias, "O Sítio Santo Antônio da Bica" ("composições estéticas eram, enfim, ensaiadas").
40. Dias's comment on this description: "Non sequitur! What about 'from landscape designer to teacher'?"
41. Murray, "The Idea of Gardening," 48. Discussing Burle Marx's "tropical aesthetic," Murray describes how, during his visit to South Africa in the 1960s, gardeners in the tropical city of Durban styled their gardens using tropical plants from Brazil and biomorphic forms in his honor, but Burle Marx was more interested in the indigenous plants of South Africa, which he suggested they focus on.
42. Imbert, "Review: Roberto Burle Marx: La Permanence de l'instable," 247.
43. Quoted in Bill Marken, "Tropic of Jungles," *Landscape Architecture Magazine* 103, no. 3 (2013).
44. Parfit, "A Brazilian Master Who Finds the Art in Nature's Bounty."
45. Romão et al., "Brazilian Biodiversity for Ornamental Use and Conservation," 101.
46. There has been extensive discussion about changing notions of weeds, or spontaneous vegetation, in the context of irrevocable environmental change during the Anthropocene: Peter Del Tredici, *Wild Urban Plants of the Northeast: A Field Guide* (Ithaca: Cornell University Press, 2010); Emma Marris, *Rambunctious Garden: Saving Nature in a Post-Wild World* (New York: Bloomsbury, 2011); Fred Pearce, *The New Wild: Why Invasive Species Will Be Nature's Salvation* (London: Icon Books, 2015).
47. Ann Townsend, "The Ghost in the Garden," *North American Review* 282, no. 3/4 (1997), 63.
48. Carla Koop, "The Ecology of Home," *Discourse* 24, no. 2 (2002), 51.
49. Dias, "O Sítio Santo Antônio da Bica." ("Muito pelo contrário, é como se a coleção de plantas estivesse invadindo os jardins. Iniciava-se então, com copiosa diversidade e indeterminada duração, um, digamos assim, estágio probatório vegetal.")
50. Ibid. ("O jardim é a natureza ordenada pelo homem e para o homem.")
51. Francis Rambert, "In Praise of a Plant Amateur: Interview with Patrick Blanc," in Cavalcanti, El-Dahdah, and Rambert, *Roberto Burle Marx*, 287.
52. G. R. F. Ferrari, "The Meaninglessness of Gardens," *Journal of Aesthetics and Art Criticism* 68, no. 1 (2010), 35.
53. This is essentially what an arboretum aims to be.
54. It is from this kind of realization that the Laws of Thermodynamics arose.

55. Dias, "O Sítio Santo Antônio da Bica." ("As pessoas, de maneira geral, aturdidas com a beleza dos jardins que as envolvia, não estavam propensas a acreditar que aquilo tudo, aquelas verdadeiras sinfonias vegetais fossem apenas ensaio, rascunho, teste.")
56. Sima Eliovson, *The Gardens of Roberto Burle Marx* (London: Thames & Hudson, 1991), 96.
57. Dias, "O Sítio Santo Antônio da Bica" ("o trabalho desencadeado por RBM é, mais do que um produt ...").
58. <http://www.oxforddictionaries.com/definition/english/artefact?q=artifact>.
59. Bruno Latour and Steve Woolgar, *Laboratory Life: The Construction of Scientific Facts* (Princeton: Princeton University Press, 1986), 236.
60. Parfit, citing Costa, "A Brazilian Master Who Finds the Art in Nature's Bounty."
61. Ibid., citing Walmsley.
62. Daniel Buren and Thomas Repensek, "The Function of the Studio," *October* 10 (Autumn 1979), 53.
63. I use a similar phrase in my essay "'Landscape Symphonies': Gardening as a Source of Landscape Architectural Practice, Engaged with Change," paper presented at the PROGRESS conference of SAHANZ, University of Sydney, 2003.
64. Dias, "O Sítio Santo Antônio da Bica." ("Manter folcloricamente, perante estudiosos de paisagismo do mundo todo, os restos mortais de experiências que não deram certo é semelhante à atitude de pais que impingem como obras primas quaisquer rabiscos dos filhos.")
65. Dias, personal comment.
66. Dias, "O Sítio Santo Antônio da Bica" ("mesmo nas áreas mais elaboradas paisagisticamente, ele não considerava as composições vegetais como obra de arte finalizada, diferentemente dos demais jardins que projetou").
67. Ferrari, "The Meaninglessness of Gardens."
68. Dias, "O Sítio Santo Antônio da Bica." ("As experiências que tiveram, e têm, ocorrência ali também precisam ser mais bem compreendidas, pois diferem formalmente das praticadas em outras atividades, principalmente quanto ao fator tempo: são experiências de duração indeterminada, que podem levar décadas e, muitas vezes, depois de aparentemente fornecer certos resultados, apresenta outros, contrários aos primeiros.")
69. From Dias's email response to my draft of this chapter.
70. Gilles Deleuze, *Bergsonism* (New York: Zone Books, 1991).
71. This is the model used by most planting design texts, including: Brian Hackett, *Planting Design* (London: E & F N Spon, 1979); Ken Fieldhouse and Adrian Lisney, *Landscape Design*, vol. 1, *Soft Landscape* (Aldershot: Gower Publishing, 1990); Richard L. Austin, *Elements of Planting Design* (New York: John Wiley & Sons, 2002); Nick Robinson, *The Planting Design Handbook*, 2nd edn. (Aldershot:

Ashgate, 2004); R. E. Wörle and H. J. Wörle, *Designing with Plants* (Basel: Birkhäuser, 2008).

72. Aleca Le Blanc, "Palmeiras and Pilotis: Promoting Brazil with Modern Architecture," *Third Text* 26, no. 1 (2012), 106. Le Blanc claims that this pattern, also used at Copacabana, "is taken from the plaza in front of the Manaus Opera House, in the Brazilian Amazon. Usually rendered in black-and-white tile, it is said to mimic the soil in parts of the Amazon River."

73. Ferrari, "The Meaninglessness of Gardens," 35.

74. Dias, personal comment.

75. Parfit, citing Costa.

76. Imbert, "Review: Roberto Burle Marx: La Permanence de l'instable," 247.

77. Dias does not think that Burle Marx would have used the term ornamental, because all his plant selections were based on aesthetics.

78. All these definitions are from the *Oxford English Dictionary*.

79. H. Gitay and I. R. Noble, "What Are Functional Types and How Should We Seek Them?," in T. M. Smith, H. H. Shugart, and F. I. Woodward, eds., *Plant Functional Types: Their Relevance to Ecosystem Properties and Global Change* (Cambridge: Cambridge University Press, 1997), 4.

80. Quoted in ibid.

81. H. H. Shugart, "Plant and Ecosystem Functional Types," in Smith, Shugart, and Woodward, *Plant Functional Types*, 24.

82. Ibid., 23.

83. Cyrille Violle et al., "Let the Concept of Trait Be Functional!," *Oikos* 116, no. 5 (2007), 884.

84. Ibid., 890.

85. Deni Bown, *Aroids: Plants of the Arum Family*, 2nd edn. (Portland, OR: Timber Press, 2000), 23.

86. Ibid., 25.

87. Ibid., 156.

88. André Mantovani, "Leaf Morpho-Physiology and Distribution of Epiphytic Aroids along a Vertical Gradient in a Brazilian Rainforest," *Selbyana* 20, no. 2 (1999), 247.

89. Evan Weiher et al., "Challenging Theophrastus: A Common Core List of Plant Traits for Functional Ecology," *Journal of Vegetation Science* 10, no. 5 (1999), 612.

90. Mantovani, "Leaf Morpho-Physiology and Distribution of Epiphytic Aroids," 241.

91. From Dias's response to my draft.

92. Dugald C. Close and Christopher L. Beadle, "The Ecophysiology of Foliar Anthocyanin," *Botanical Review* 69, no. 2 (2003), 149.

93. Phyllis D. Coley and Thomas A. Kursar, "Anti-Herbivore Defenses of Young Tropical Leaves: Physiological Constraints and Ecological Trade-Offs," in Stephen

S. Mulkey, Robin L. Chazdon, and Alan P. Smith, eds., *Tropical Forest Plant Ecophysiology* (New York: Chapman and Hall, 1996), 311.

94. Parfit, "A Brazilian Master Who Finds the Art in Nature's Bounty."
95. Graham Harman, "Physical Nature and the Paradox of Qualities (2006)," in Harman, *Towards Speculative Realism: Essays and Lectures* (Winchester, UK: Zero Books, 2010), 124.
96. Ibid.
97. Michael Marder, *Plant-Thinking: A Philosophy of Vegetal Life* (New York: Columbia University Press, 2013).
98. Parfit, "A Brazilian Master Who Finds the Art in Nature's Bounty."

CHAPTER 6: MARGINALIA

1. G. F. Dutton, *Some Branch against the Sky: The Practice and Principles of Marginal Gardening* (Devon: David & Charles, 1997), 10.
2. Noël Kingsbury, "Contemporary Overview of Naturalistic Planting Design," in Nigel Dunnett and James Hitchmough, eds., *The Dynamic Landscape* (London: Spon Press, 2004), 79.
3. While McHarg's work had a scientific basis, the biographical and polemical texts that accompanied the mapping in *Design with Nature* (Ian L. McHarg, *Design with Nature* [New York: Natural History Press, 1969]) mirrored the kind of synthesis that Dutton spoke about.
4. I owe this reading of *sensibilité* to Martin Rein Cano, who discussed it with me in relation to students' work at ENSP Versailles during a workshop there in 2008, describing their drawings, in a characteristically German way, as "sensibilitization drawings."
5. Marc Claramunt and Catherine Mosbach, "Nature of a Landscape Project," *Pages Paysages*, no. 7 (1999), 56.
6. "A proposition is knowable a priori if it is knowable independently of experience, while a proposition knowable a posteriori is knowable on the basis of experience." Jason S. Baehr, "A Priori and a Posteriori," <http://www.iep.utm.edu/apriori/>.
7. In this sense his approach parallels that of Alfred North Whitehead, *Process and Reality* (1929; New York: Free Press, 1978).
8. Bernard Tschumi, *Architecture and Disjunction* (Cambridge, MA: MIT Press, 1996), 191.
9. The vehemence with which architects often deride landscape architects effectively constitutes bullying, which, nonetheless, landscape architects continue down the line to gardeners.
10. Brian Burchell, "Obituary: Professor Geoffrey J. F. Dutton (1924–2010)," *Biochemical Society*, August 2010, 52.

11. Geoffrey J. Dutton, ed., *Glucuronic Acid, Free and Combined: Chemistry, Biochemistry, Pharmacology, and Medicine* (New York: Academic Press, 1966).
12. Geoffrey J. Dutton, *Glucuronidation of Drugs and Other Compounds* (Boca Raton: CRC Press, 1980).
13. G. F. Dutton, *The Ridiculous Mountains: Tales of the Doctor and His Friends in the Scottish Highlands* (London: Diadem Books, 1984); G. F. Dutton, *Nothing So Simple as Climbing* (London: Diadem Books, 1993).
14. G. F. Dutton, *Swimming Free: On and Below the Surface of Lake, River, and Sea* (New York: St. Martin's Press, 1972).
15. G. F. Dutton, *The Bare Abundance: Selected Poems, 1975–2001* (Newcastle, UK: Bloodaxe, 2002); G. F. Dutton, *The Concrete Garden* (Newcastle, UK: Bloodaxe, 1991); G. F. Dutton, *Squaring the Waves: Poems* (Newcastle, UK: Bloodaxe, 1986).
16. G. F. Dutton, *Harvesting the Edge: Some Personal Explorations from a Marginal Garden* (London: Menard Press, 1995).
17. Burchell, "Obituary: Professor Geoffrey J. F. Dutton," 53.
18. Ibid.
19. Ibid.
20. "Man of All Parts at One with His World: Interview with Professor Geoffrey Dutton," 1999, <http://app.dundee.ac.uk/pressoffice/gcmagazine/gc99/final.htm>.
21. Kingsbury, "Contemporary Overview of Naturalistic Planting Design," 79.
22. Dutton, *Some Branch against the Sky*, 17.
23. Carl von Clausewitz, *On War* (1832; Princeton: Princeton University Press, 1976).
24. From email response from Kirsty Jones and family after draft review.
25. Ibid.
26. Ibid.
27. Ibid.
28. In the thick of poststructuralism, I wrote that site specificity was impossible because we project what we want to see onto sites (Julian Raxworthy, "Specificity: The Impossibility of Not Projecting," *Landscape Review* 3, no. 2 [1997]); however, this is not my position now, and site specificity is being well theorized in contemporary landscape architecture discourse, particularly in the discussion of site in Carol J. Burns and Andrea Kahn, eds., *Site Matters: Design Concepts, Histories and Strategies* (New York: Routledge, 2005).
29. Claramunt and Mosbach, "Nature of a Landscape Project," 55.
30. Christophe Girot, "Four Trace Concepts of Landscape Architecture," in James Corner, ed., *Recovering Landscape: Essays in Contemporary Landscape Architecture* (New York: Princeton Architectural Press, 1999), 60.
31. Ibid., 61.
32. Ibid.
33. Ibid., 62.

34. Ibid., 64.
35. Ibid., 65.
36. Ibid., 66.
37. Dutton, *Some Branch against the Sky*, 17.
38. Ibid., 18.
39. Bernard Tschumi famously referred to landscape architecture as "scribbling in the margins."
40. Dutton, *Some Branch against the Sky*, 13.
41. Ibid., 166.
42. Ibid., 14.
43. The context of the term in the development of the English landscape garden is discussed in John Dixon Hunt and Peter Willis, eds., *The Genius of Place: The English Landscape Garden 1620–1820* (London: Elek Books, 1975), but it was theorized for architecture in Christian Norberg-Schulz, *Genius Loci: Toward a Phenomenology of Architecture* (New York: Rizzoli, 1980). I mention *genius loci* in passing, since it is a term Dutton used that relates to a discourse of site specificity.
44. Dutton, *Some Branch against the Sky*, 14.
45. Ibid.
46. Ibid., 166.
47. Ibid., 14.
48. Ibid., 167.
49. Dutton, *Harvesting the Edge*, 1.
50. Ibid., 2.
51. Claramunt and Mosbach, "Nature of a Landscape Project," 58.
52. "Man of All Parts at One with His World: Interview with Professor Geoffrey Dutton."
53. Ibid.
54. David Ward, "Book Review: Enough of Green, by Anne Stevenson," *English* 27, no. 128–129 (1978), 258.
55. Alan Wall, "A Note on the Poetry of G. F. Dutton," *New Blackfriars* 60, no. 712 (1979), 372.
56. Anne Stevenson, "The Poetry of G. F. Dutton," *Ploughshares* 4, no. 3 (1978), 206.
57. Ibid.
58. "Review: Strange Minds in Muddy Waters," *Critical Survey* 14, no. 1 (2002), 120.
59. Ibid., 121.
60. Marian Macken, "The Book as Site: Alternative Modes of Representing and Documenting Architecture," University of Sydney, 2012, 18; emphasis added.
61. Ibid., 31.
62. Dutton, *Some Branch against the Sky*, 170.

63. Roel van Gerwen, "Force Fields in the Daily Practice of a Dutch Landscape Architect," in Julian Raxworthy and Jessica Blood, eds., *The Mesh Book: Infrastructure/Landscape* (Melbourne: RMIT Press, 2004).
64. Dutton, *Harvesting the Edge*, 22.
65. Ibid.
66. Ibid., 25.
67. Graham Harman, *Guerrilla Metaphysics: Phenomenology and the Carpentry of Things* (Chicago: Open Court, 2005).
68. Graham Harman, "Object-Oriented Philosophy (1999)," in Harman, *Towards Speculative Realism: Essays and Lectures* (Winchester, UK: Zero Books, 2010), 93–104.
69. Louis G. Le Roy, "Coconut Palms," in *Louis G. Le Roy: Nature Culture Fusion*, ed. Esther Boukema and Philippe Velez McIntyre (Rotterdam: NAi, 2002), 36.
70. Artist Robert Smithson famously described the resulting equilibrium state as a kind of "radical banality"—"a kind of architecture without values or qualities...if anything...a fact." Robert Smithson, "Entropy and the New Monuments," in *The Writings of Robert Smithson*, ed. Nancy Holt (New York: New York University Press, 1979), 9.
71. Erwin Schrödinger, *What Is Life? The Physical Aspect of the Living Cell, with Mind and Matter and Autobiographical Sketches* (Cambridge: Cambridge University Press, 1992), 73.
72. Luis Fernández-Galiano, *Fire and Memory: On Architecture and Energy*, trans. Gina Cariño (Cambridge, MA: MIT Press, 2000), 5.
73. Sanford Kwinter, "Landscapes of Change: Boccioni's 'Stati d'animo' as a General Theory of Models," *Assemblage*, no. 19 (1992).
74. Dilip Kondepudi and Ilya Prigogine, *Modern Thermodynamics: From Heat Engines to Dissipative Structures* (Chichester, UK: John Wiley & Sons, 1998), 87.
75. Dutton, *Harvesting the Edge*, 37. On a personal note, as the son of a sailor who used to eat fish and chips on the sea cliffs of Vaucluse in Sydney, in rare commune with my dad, I love the wind, whereas in Cape Town, my wife absolutely hates the southeaster which blows relentlessly and powerfully off Antarctica and over Table Mountain.
76. Ibid.
77. Ibid., 38.
78. Ibid.
79. Ibid.
80. Michael Marder, *Plant-Thinking: A Philosophy of Vegetal Life* (New York: Columbia University Press, 2013).
81. Dutton, *Harvesting the Edge*, 48.
82. Ibid.

83. Ibid.
84. Ibid., 49.
85. Ibid.
86. I have visited Parc Citroën twice: once in 1996, then on June 5, 2005. I visited Parc Henri Matisse on July 15, 2010. While both projects could have been case studies for this dissertation, I chose Marnas for the reasons I describe in this section: because it is both strongly formal in its intentions and strongly controlling in its use of gardening technique.
87. Gilles Clément, "The Garden in Movement," in *Planetary Gardens: The Landscape Architecture of Gilles Clément*, ed. Alessandro Rocca (Basel: Birkhäuser, 2007).
88. Mary in *JustAlchemy*, 6 April 2013, <http://justalchemy.com/2013/06/24/chop-wood-carry-water-lay-down-your-burden-then-pick-it-up-again/>.
89. Dutton, *Harvesting the Edge*, 49.
90. While Dutton said that "hogweed is preached against" because it can "provoke unpleasant reactions in susceptible persons who embrace it half-naked while sweating," "for reasonably normal people, it has been an entertaining and harmless monster."
91. G. F. Dutton, "The Year's Colour in a Marginal Garden" (self-published, 1998).
92. Dutton, *Harvesting the Edge*, 60.
93. Ibid.
94. Ibid., 66.
95. Ibid., 71.
96. Anne Stephen, ed., *Artists Think: The Late Work of Ian Burn* (Sydney: Power, 1996).
97. Dutton, "The Year's Colour in a Marginal Garden."
98. Dutton, *Harvesting the Edge*, 70.

CHAPTER 7: WAIT AND SEE

1. Thank you, Lisa Diedrich!
2. I interviewed Korte on July 21, 2015, in a park in Neuss, Damm in the Stiftung offices at the rocket station, and Fischedick in the Insel Hombroich garden on July 22, 2015.
3. Since I first heard it, this line from David Byrne has demonstrated the difference between physical speech as airwaves made by the body compared to meaning: "I open up my mouth, air comes rushing out" in *Lazy* by X-Press 2 featuring David Byrne, on Fat Boy Slim's mix CD *Dance Bitch* (2009).
4. Hannah Arendt, *The Human Condition* (Garden City, NY: Doubleday, 1958). I credit Kenneth Frampton with introducing me to Arendt, and thank him for our

brief correspondence about her, which influenced my lecture presented at the Inside Outside conference in 2005.

5. Kitty Kemr, "The Insel Hombroich Museum Collection, 'a Provisional Chronicle,'" in Kitty Kemr, Thomas King, and Brigitte Lohkamp, eds., *Stiftung Insel Hombroich: Museum und Raketenstation* (Neus: Stiftung Insel Hombroich, 2009), 247. Whether as a critique of the pavilions as architecture or because they were not designed by an architect, most architects tend to regard the buildings as "one-liners": superficial, lacking real depth.

6. Ibid., 248.

7. Jürgen Rüttgers, "The Insel Hombroich Foundation," in Kemr, King, and Lohkamp, *Stiftung Insel Hombroich*, 245.

8. Korte quotes Heerich. Bernhard Korte, "Topos," in Kemr, King, and Lohkamp, *Stiftung Insel Hombroich*, 254.

9. Rüttgers, "The Insel Hombroich Foundation," 245.

10. Ibid.

11. Ibid.

12. Kitty Kemr, "The Insel Hombroich Museum Collection," 247.

13. It is interesting to note that Valentine de Ganay emphasized this origin of the French Renaissance water garden when she discussed Courances: a serendipitous link between the projects.

14. Roberio Dias does not agree with me on this, arguing that the garden is only minimally ecological.

15. Korte, "Topos," 254.

16. Ibid. Reminiscent of Marder's notion of "plant-thinking."

17. G. R. F. Ferrari, "The Meaninglessness of Gardens," *Journal of Aesthetics and Art Criticism* 68, no. 1 (2010).

18. Walter Biemel, "The Happenings of Truth," in Kemr, King, and Lohkamp, *Stiftung Insel Hombroich*.

19. From my interview with Korte.

20. In the English garden, however, the restoration of which was underway when he started working at the Hombroich, he worked on the trees as a collection, since this was a part of the original garden's botanical character.

21. One cause of Korte's persistent anger about the project is how little he was paid compared to other artists, and how much of a businessman Müller was. Particularly upsetting for him was the day he had to tell the laborers that there was no more work for them, while just across the way the ticket office was collecting entry fees.

22. Much has been written recently on the relationship between landscape practice and walking: Rebecca Solnit, *Wanderlust: A History of Walking* (New York: Viking, 2000); Francesco Careri, *Walkscapes: Walking as an Aesthetic Practice* (Barcelona: Editorial Gustavo Gili, 2002); and Alice Foxley, *Distance and Engagement: Walking, Thinking and Making Landscape* (Baden, Switzerland: Lars Müller, 2010), for example.

23. Christophe Girot, "Four Trace Concepts of Landscape Architecture," in James Corner, ed., *Recovering Landscape: Essays in Contemporary Landscape Architecture* (New York: Princeton Architectural Press, 1999).

24. Erwin Heerich, "In Conversation," in Kemr, King, and Lohkamp, *Stiftung Insel Hombroich*.

25. Esther Boukema and Philippe Velez McIntyre, eds., *Louis G. Le Roy: Nature Culture Fusion* (Rotterdam: NAi, 2002).

26. Karl-Heinrich Müller, "Hombroich—an Open Experiment," in Kemr, King, and Lohkamp, *Stiftung Insel Hombroich*, 251.

27. Carl von Clausewitz, *On War* (1832; Princeton: Princeton University Press, 1976).

28. Henk Gerritsen, *Essay on Gardening* (Amsterdam: Architectura & Natura Press, 2008).

29. Ibid., 78.

30. Noël Kingsbury and Piet Oudolf, *Oudolf: Hummelo* (Amsterdam: Monacelli, 2015), 17.

31. Ibid., 56.

32. Ibid., 370.

33. Heerich, "In Conversation."

34. Gerritsen, *Essay on Gardening*, 13.

35. As I noted in chapter 5, the process of clearing forest for a house site and garden is called *limpiar* ("cleaning") in Spanish.

36. Müller, "Hombroich—an Open Experiment," 251.

37. Gerritsen, *Essay on Gardening*, 86.

38. Ibid., 85.

39. Ibid.

40. Ibid.

41. Ibid., 88.

42. Ibid.

43. Ibid., 90.

44. And too much interruption, as I realized with embarrassment while listening to the recording of our conversation in transit.

CHAPTER 8:
CONCLUSION: A MANIFESTO FOR THE VIRIDIC

1. Elizabeth K. Meyer, "Landscape Architecture as Modern *Other* and Post-Modern *Ground*," in Harriet Edquist and Vanessa Bird, eds., *The Culture of Landscape Architecture* (Melbourne: EDGE Publishing Committee, 1994).
2. Patrick Blanc, *Le bonheur d'être plante* (Paris: Maren Sell Éditeurs, 2005).
3. Luce Irigaray and Michael Marder, *Through Vegetal Being: Two Philosophical Perspectives* (New York: Columbia University Press, 2016).
4. Nicholas Nassim Taleb, *Antifragile: Things That Gain from Disorder* (London: Penguin, 2013).

INDEX

Acer spp., 312
adaptation
    of agricultural equipment to garden uses, 50
    of planting designs by gardening, 121
    of plants, 211, 212, 214, 257
aesthetics
    in Burle Marx, 171–173, 192–193, 197
    and Cicero's third nature, 25, 49
    and the Dutch Wave (Oudolf, Gerritsen, Leopold), 291, 303, 314
    Dutton's garden tastes, 259
    "everyday aesthetics" (Saito), 191–192
    Ferrari on gardening as aesthetic art, 17, 111, 208, 265, 290
    and Fischedick at Hombroich, 310, 314
    and Insel Hombroich, 289–290
    inseparable from plant performance, 191, 199, 202–203, 208, 211, 213, 289–290, 310, 330
    and Korte, 287–291, 294, 296, 298
    and management, 51, 54
    in planting design, 196
    plants used for, 25, 200
    qualities of growth and plants, 208–216
    relation to plant morphology, 211, 216
    relation to science, 172–173
    relation to site, 253, 289–290, 294, 314
    and the viridic, 208, 217, 327, 329–330
Agapanthus praecox, 287
allée
    at Courances, 43–45
    description of Honey Locust Allée, 74–76, 79–81
    history of Honey Locust Allée, 93–109
    spatial transformation over time, 48
Amazon, 192–193, 196, 323
analogue, plants as, for architecture, 75, 80–81, 83–86, 92, 94, 108–109
Andersson, Sven-Ingvar, 10, 117–119, 157, 164, 217, 248, 259
    biography, 121, 124
    on genetics and hawthorns, 163
    on Marnas, 117–119, 123, 128, 130, 135, 138, 139, 141–143, 163
anthocyanins, 216
apical dominance, 15
apical meristem, 15–16, 69, 137, 140
Araceae, 213
Arendt, Hannah, 275
aroids, 213
art
    Burle Marx as artist, 211, 217
    collection at Museum Insel Hombroich, 275, 277
    concepts in landscape architecture, 73, 116, 223
    garden as a work of, 1, 200–201, 203, 205
    gardening as an art (Ferrari), 17, 111, 208, 265, 290
    landscape architecture as an art, 19–20, 116
    medium specificity, 131–133, 136
    Müller's concept at Hombroich, 288–290
    and the veridic, 217
artifact, 14, 134, 199, 203, 223, 249, 269, 286

authorship
    concept in relation to gardens, 274, 286
    and Druimchardain, 243
    and Sítio, 184, 190
    valorization of designers, 269, 286
autumn, at Druimchardain, 266–269
auxin, 16
axis
    in the baroque garden, 84
    blurred axis at Courances, 37–48
    at Druimchardain, 233, 237
    at Vaux-le-Vicomte, 31
    at Versailles, 36
    visual axis at Marnas, 155

Betula spp., 259
Blanc, Patrick, 197
Bleam, Gregg, 11, 80–81
Brandt, G. N., 124
Bressane, Oscar, 192–193
Buczaki, Stefan, 17
building, and time or change, 67, 92, 251, 256, 286
Burle Marx, Roberto, 3, 11, 170–173, 179, 216
    and aroids, 213
    as artist, 191, 193, 201, 208–209, 211, 217
    on change, 202, 205, 208, 218
    as collector/plantsman, 192–193, 197
    on the garden, 190, 193, 197, 202, 208
    to "get" a plant, method of plant testing, 192–193, 197, 213
    on native plants, 190
    as scientist/researcher, 190–193, 196, 213
    on Sítio as laboratory, 190
    style of planting design, 173, 177, 191, 201–203, 205, 208–211, 214, 217
    to "use" a plant, method of plant testing, 192, 197, 213
Burn, Ian, 268
Buxus sempervirens, 155

Calocasia esculenta, 216
Cedrus spp., 264–265
change
    in autumn, 266
    Burle Marx on, 205, 208
    change of plant form without change of plan, 37, 155, 157, 159
    Damm on allowable landscape change, 300–305
    Dias and IPHAN on change at Sítio, 190
    and energy cost, according to Dutton, 248, 256–257
    of garden and gardener, 252–253, 265, 324
    plant growth as a model for, 3
    and the viridic, 286, 322, 324, 330–331, 332
Claramunt, Marc, 245, 251
Clausewitz, Carl von, 240, 299
Clément, Gilles, 261, 264
clipping, 58, 141, 161, 226
colonization, by plants, 145, 157
color
    autumn, 266
    Burle Marx and, 172, 211
    of foliage, 90, 208, 214, 216, 266
    history of the color green, 135
    of plants in planting design, 191, 202, 205, 209, 212
    and the viridic, 325
competition
    in forest at Courances, 51, 59, 65
    in Honey Locust Allée, 105
    at Marnas, 143
    in tropical rainforests, 214
    and weeds, 196, 319
Connolly, Peter, 8
Contre-allée, 44
Corajoud, Michel, 36
Costa, Lucio, 173, 179
    on Burle Marx, 201, 211
Courances, Château de, 30–70
    author's discovery of, 33
    English landscape garden, 46, 47
    forest at, 54, 56
    history of ownership, 41–46
    Hobhouse and Taylor on, 33
    hydrology of, 42–43
    relation of garden to park, 49–50, 51
    Scully on, 33
Crataegus monogyna (hawthorn), 124, 128, 135, 139, 140, 163–164
    Andersson on, 135, 163
    hedges at Marnas, 10, 117–119, 139

Damm, Burkhard, 295–306
    biography, 295
    concept of "frames" in terms of management, 300, 307
    concept of "the leash" in terms of allowable landscape change, 300–305
    on Gerritsen's *Essay on Gardening*, 303
    initial works at Hombroich, 298
    on Korte and work at Insel Hombroich, 296–298
    use of digital tools in management, 305
deconstruction, 4–5
design
    and aesthetics, 191
    and change in gardens, 124, 128, 137, 139, 145, 164
    dynamic, 3–5
    Eckbo and Kiley on landscape design, 11
    and form, 6, 9
    in gardening practice, 6–7, 19, 25, 245, 266, 269, 306
    generation processes, 169
    as judgment or decision, 6, 253, 299–300
    and landscape architecture, 4, 67, 73, 164, 223
    and representation, 269, 273
    and site, 222–223, 245–246, 286, 291
    subjectivity of, 222
    and the viridic, 109, 121, 274–275, 286, 321, 323–333
Dias, Roberio, 171, 177
    idea of the garden as a laboratory, 192–200
    time and work at Sítio, 182, 184, 190, 216
    working for Burle Marx, 191, 201, 209–211
DNA, 14, 163, 324
documentation
    in diaries by Dutton, 250, 270
    post-factum, 224, 251
Druimchardain, 221–270
    author's discovery of, 221
    description of, 226–240
    seasons in, according to Dutton, 254–268
Duchêne, Henri and Achille, 46
Dutton, G. F.
    biography, 224–226
    on marginal gardening, 245–248

Eckbo, Garrett, 11, 23, 73, 123
ecology
    Andersson's use of at Marnas, 124
    Burle Marx and, 191, 193, 208
    at Courances, 65–67
    at Druimchardain, 143, 258, 269
    Dutton on, 226, 247
    "enzyme ecology," 226
    Fischedick on, 310–311
    of the French garden, 70
    garden as, 130, 133, 199, 208, 252, 303
    Gerritsen and, 303, 314–315
    at Hombroich, 289, 300, 310–312
    Korte on, 289
    at Marnas, 143, 145
    at Miller Garden, 83, 104, 108
    and Oudolf, 291
    plant configuration as manipulation of, 133, 252
    of rainforest understory, 213–216
    relation to aesthetics, 211–213, 289–291
    relation to process discourse, 3, 8, 170–171, 323
    Spirn on, 116
    and thermodynamics, 256
    and the viridic, 325–327
economy
    of energy use in gardening, 247–248
    and forest at Courances, 59
    and gardening, 22, 24, 41, 44–46, 48, 68, 294, 300, 333
    of garden maintenance at Courances, 50–51
edge
    between garden and territory, 33–37, 51, 56, 59, 62, 65, 68
    between garden rooms at Marnas, 130, 145, 149, 157
    Harvesting the Edge, 223, 225, 245, 253, 254
    maintaining at Druimchardain, 261
    as margin, 247
    between meadow and forest at Hombroich, 311–312
    timed at Courances, 48–67
    trees creating, at Miller Garden, 78
Eliovson, Sima, 199

enquiry, Dutton and, 222–223, 249
entropy, 256–257
ephemerality
  ephemeral cues, 253
  "ephemerals of summer," 264
  of the garden over time, 203
  of the landscape, 273
  of landscape materials, 273
  of the living edge, 37, 68
  of phenomena, 223
  of watercourses at Hombroich, 289
Erft River, 275, 279, 281, 310
Excel spreadsheet, 305

Fagus spp., 155
Fern, 312
Ferrari, G. R. F., 16–17, 111, 132, 197, 203, 208, 265, 290
Fischedick, Klaus
  biography, 310
  on Gerritsen, 312
  on how to work with nature, 307, 311–312, 314
  on manpower, 310
  on the Niederrhein, 307
  on the rocket station and NATO, 310
  on waiting and seeing, 314
  on weeding, 314, 319
folly, sheds as, at Druimchardain, 240
forest
  at Courances, 48–67
  at Druimchardain, 261
  formation and succession, 314
  in the French garden/park, 31–34, 51, 54
  at Hombroich, 279, 300, 310–312
  Honey Locust Allée as, 105
  maintenance of edge, 33–37, 51, 56, 59, 62, 65, 68
  at the Sítio, 171, 182, 184
  tropical, 213–214, 216
form
  and change, 5–6, 12, 67
  definition, 14
  form-space dialectic, 10–12, 84, 85, 109, 211
  of the garden as provisional, 138
  and growth, 75–76

  in landscape architecture, 12
  as morphology, 211–212
  of plants and growth, 12, 67, 85, 93, 139, 163, 205
  of plants discussed by Dutton, 254, 261
  of plants shaped by gardening, 14, 135, 159, 260
  and process, 13–14, 68–69, 84, 257
  and the process discourse, 170
  as result of regulating natural forces, 321
  Rose on plants as, 84
  "sculptural," 146, 149
  as story of ownership, 38
  taxonomy of plant form, 83–93
  and the viridic, 68–69, 111, 324–325, 328, 329
formal
  compared to informal, 6, 68, 69
  French garden, 93
Frampton, Kenneth, 133–134
function
  and analogue, 80–81
  and Cicero's third nature, 25
  of hedges, 130, 138, 157
  in modernist landscape architecture, 76, 115, 171, 216
  plant physiology and plant functional type, 212–213

Ganay, Jean-Louis, 46, 50–51
Ganay, Valentine, 49, 50
garden
  artist's, 116
  as art studio, 200–208
  Burle Marx on, 190, 193, 197, 202, 208
  and change, 37–38, 67–68, 94, 111
  concept of authorship, 274, 286
  and ecology, 130, 133, 199, 208, 252, 303
  English landscape garden, 2, 20–21, 22, 25, 46, 47, 50, 69, 275, 284, 298, 300, 315
  French baroque garden, 34–37, 39, 41–42, 54, 69, 73–74, 76, 84, 93, 260, 300
  "French Renaissance water garden," xiv, 41–42
  and function, 25, 49
  and gardening as process, 1, 25

    Gerritsen on, 314–317
    as laboratory, 192–200
    and making, 115–116
    and meaning, 115
    and modernism, 80–81, 85
    Monet's, at Giverny, 319
    philosophy of, 1, 24–25, 115
    and privilege, 24
    as site for improvisation, 124, 138, 171, 294
    suburban, 24, 259
    and territory, 33–37, 51, 56, 59, 62, 65, 68
    as testing place, 24, 117, 119
    as third nature, 25
    time shared with gardener, 252–253, 265, 324

gardener
    as amateur, 1, 21, 24–25, 109
    author's experience as, 7, 274, 315, 321
    changing role due to technological change, 50
    Damm, as gardener at Hombroich, 295, 298
    differences from landscape architect, 307
    Fischedick, as gardener at Hombroich, 306–320
    as form maker, 19, 21, 223
    Gerritsen on, 314
    improvising, 124, 138, 171, 294
    Korte, as gardener at Hombroich, 288
    and landscape architect, 4–5, 19
    and plants, 17–18
    power relations with client or designer, 1, 296, 321
    sharing time with garden, 2, 23, 250, 252–253, 256, 265, 270, 324
    as tradesperson, 1, 22–23
    and the viridic, 326, 328, 331–333
    Wever, as gardener at Miller Garden, 94, 101, 104–105, 108

gardening
    as an art (Ferrari), 17, 111, 208, 265, 290
    and design, 6–7, 19, 25, 245, 266, 269, 306
    "Dutch Wave" school, 303, 317
    economics and, 22, 24, 41, 44–46, 48, 68, 294, 300, 333
    and energy use, 247–248
    and growth, 6, 19, 68–70, 224, 259, 269
    and landscape architecture, 4–6, 14
    learning while, 248, 268
    marginal, 245–248
    and plant form, 14, 135, 159, 260
    practices, 9, 19, 23, 65, 115, 117, 132, 171, 196, 259, 266, 274
    and seasons, 248, 254–268
    suburban, 24, 259
    and tactics, 322
    techniques, 36–37, 38, 68
    tools, 259, 261
    vernacular practices, 116–117
    as working-class trade, 22
genius loci, 247
Gerritsen, Henk, 303, 312–315, 317, 319, 321
Girot, Christophe, 245–246, 250
GIS, 305
Gleditsia tricanthos (honey locust), 74–75
Graubner, Gotthard, 277
Greenberg, Clement, 119, 131–132, 136
growth
    aesthetics of, 208–216
    biology of, 15–16, 69, 212–213, 247, 260
    and change of plan, 38, 48, 67–68
    definition, 9, 15
    form of plant growth, 12, 67, 75, 85, 93, 139, 163, 205
    and the French baroque garden, 34, 36
    and the garden, 23, 25–26
    and gardening or maintenance, 6, 19, 68–70, 224, 259, 269
    as a material, 5–6, 12
    as a medium for landscape architecture, 5–6
    and planting design, 128, 161, 171, 200, 205
    predictions and assumptions about, 76, 117–119, 124, 128, 130, 138, 164, 268, 294, 325
    qualities arising from, 4, 11, 15, 48, 75, 217, 260, 270
    and representation, 2, 5, 6, 7, 12
    uniting gardener and garden, 2, 23, 250, 265, 270
    and the viridic, 217, 270, 323–333
Guevrekian, Gabriel, 83

Harman, Graham, 217, 256, 257
Hedera helix, 146
hedge clippers, 136, 140–141, 161

hedgerow
  etymology, 140
  at Marnas, 140–145
hedges
  different effects over time, 130, 145, 149
  Dutton's use of, 258–260
  etymology of, 140
  hawthorn hedges at Marnas, 117–119, 124, 130
  hedge typology at Marnas, 139–163
  at Hombroich, 281
  making rooms/space, 10, 137–139, 143
  at Miller Garden, 76, 80, 86
  parterre de broderie, 36
  as plants, 18
  Rose on, 92–93
  as territorial edge, at Vaux-le-Vicomte, 33
  typologies at Courances, 56–62
Heerich, Erwin, 277–279, 295, 296, 307
Heliconia burle-marxii, 177
Helleborus spp., 312
Heracleum mantegazzianum (hogweed), 264
Hilderbrand, Gary, 80, 108–109

Imbert, Dorothée, 9
  on Burle Marx as artist, 191, 211
  on the Sítio, 190
improvisation, 124, 138, 171, 294
Indianapolis Museum of Art (IMA), 74, 104
Insel Hombroich
  description of, 279–286
  Graubner's curatorial agenda, 277–278
  history, 275, 277

Jekyll, Gertrude, 201
Jellicoe, Geoffrey, 2
Jewish Museum, Berlin, 296
Jungles, Raymond, 193

Kiley, Dan, 11–12, 31, 73–76, 171
  design of Miller Garden, 76, 80–83
  office correspondence about Miller Garden, 95–98
Korte, Bernhard
  and aesthetics, 287–291, 294, 296, 298
  biography, 287–288
  and cultural landscape of Niederrhein, 291
  on ecology, 289
  work on Insel Hombroich, 289–295
Krauss, Rosalind, 131, 133, 136–137
Krog, Steven, 73
Kwinter, Sanford, 13, 257

laboratory
  definition, 191, 192, 199–201
  Sítio as, 192–200
landscape
  compared to garden, 23
  hard, as real landscape design, 67
  maintenance, 25–26
  painting, 20–21
  public, 25
  and wilderness, 65
landscape architecture
  contemporary, 170, 222–223, 245–246, 275
  deconstructive reading of, 4–5
  definition, 3–4
  etymology, 20–21
  landscape architect and gardener, 4–5, 19, 23–26
  and maintenance or management, 25–26, 295–306, 321
  and modernism, 11, 24, 73, 75, 80, 84–85, 90, 92–93, 115, 116, 121, 169–170, 173, 211, 216
  office practice, 3, 6, 18, 76, 245, 294, 314
  postmodernism in, 8–9, 73, 115, 116–117, 169, 222
  professionalization of, 21
  and representation, 6, 93, 131–132
  role of plants in defining, 5, 84–85, 323
  and time, 4–5
  Tschumi on, 224
  and the viridic, 69, 131–135, 223, 324–333
landscape painting, 20–21, 290
landscape urbanism, 3, 8–9, 169, 222
Le Nôtre, André, 2, 31, 33
Leopold, Rob, 303
Le Roy, Louis G., 256
light
  and photosynthesis, 214, 258, 260

plant competition for, 105, 133, 141, 149, 298, 300, 312
and qualities of shadow, 12, 90, 161
Ligustrum sinense (privet), 149
Loudon, J. C., 20–22

maintenance, 5–7, 25–26, 38, 43, 58, 62, 68, 76, 93, 119, 121, 138–139, 205, 264, 275
  Andersson's schema of, 128
  Burle Marx on, 193
  as care, 58
  Damm on, at Hombroich, 305–306
  defining territory by, 67–69
  definition, 25
  equipment, 50–51, 261, 136, 140–141
  and form and space, 68, 138, 143
  Ganay on, 50–51, 58
  Gerritsen on, 314–315
  and growth, 68
  Kiley on, 108
  landscape, 23, 25–26
  mechanization of, 50–51, 58
  separation from design, 332
  techniques, 36–37, 38, 68
  as tool for shaping growth, 5
  and the viridic, 121, 326, 330, 332–333
Marder, Michael, 17, 19, 218, 323
margin
  landscape architecture as (Tschumi), 224
  marginal gardening method of Dutton, 245–248
  shape of Druimchardain, 229
Mariage, Thierry, 41–42, 54, 260
Marnas, garden at, 113–164
  Henyard, 117–119, 130, 141, 157, 179
  location, 124
  plant spacing at, 143
McHarg, Ian, 222
meadow
  at Marnas, 124, 143
  at Miller Garden, 74, 76, 78, 104, 105, 108
  Niederrhein meadow at Hombroich, 277, 279, 284, 289–291, 296, 298, 299, 300, 307, 310–312, 317
  pré Bernay at Courances, 42

Meyer, Elizabeth K., 9, 75, 81–83, 131, 323
  inspiration for the viridic, 131
  reading of Miller Garden, 81–83
microclimate, 14, 17, 69, 149, 161, 182, 299, 326
Miller Garden, 71–112
  analysis of problems by Wever, 104
  description of, 74
  first installation (1957), 95–100
  Kiley's design of, 76–80
  Office of Dan Kiley correspondence regarding, 95
  second installation (1986), 100–104
  third installation (2009), 104–109
modernism
  form-space dialectic, 10–12, 75, 84, 86, 109
  in landscape architecture, 11, 24, 73, 75, 80, 84–85, 90, 92–93, 115, 116, 121, 169–170, 173, 211, 216
  in painting, according to Greenberg, 131–132
morphogenesis, 3, 13, 15, 212
morphology, 15, 212
  of plants, 14, 15, 138–139, 212–214, 217, 329
Mosbach, Catherine, 245, 250
mowing
  at Courances, 51, 62, 65
  at Druimchardain, 226, 261, 264
  at Hombroich, 273, 300, 305, 307, 311–312, 319
Müller, Karl Heinrich, 275, 288, 294, 296, 315, 317
  landscape approach, 296, 298, 300, 305, 314, 319
  model of art and life, 288–290
Müller, Knippschild, Wehberg, 296
Museu de Arte Moderna do Rio de Janeiro (MAM), 205

Niederrhein (Lower Rhine), 277, 289, 291, 307
Niemeyer, Oscar, 170

Olmsted, Frederick Law, 3, 261, 311
Oudolf, Piet, 209, 291, 303

painting
  and Burle Marx, 173, 201, 208–209, 211
  Burn on, 268
  cubism, 84
  Greenberg on, 131–132
  landscape, 20–21, 290
palisade
  at Courances, 43–44, 50–51, 56–59
  regular, 58–59
  thickened, 56–58
parametric design, 3, 169–170
Parc de la Villette, 169
parterre, definition, 36
parti, definition, 34
parti-parterre model, 34–40, 48, 67–68
Pechère, René, 58
perennial garden, at Hombroich, 315, 319
phenomenology, 12, 256
Philodendron spp., 177, 213–216
Philodendron burle-marxii, 177
photosynthesis, 149, 214, 216, 258, 260
phototropism, 149
physiology
  Dutton on, 249
  of plants, 212–214, 260, 327
  and the viridic, 327
plan
  Andersson's plan of Marnas, 124, 128, 130, 139, 155
  Burle Marx's, 202, 211
  changes over time due to growth, at Courances, 10, 12, 48, 67
  Dutton's imaginary plan of Druimchardain, 260–261
  for landscape architects, 273, 307, 321
  Miller Garden, 76
  and *parti* diagram, 34
  planting plan, 128, 138, 332
  unchanged despite growth, at Marnas, 119, 145, 149, 155, 157, 164
  and the viridic, 326, 330
plant functional types, 212–213
planting design
  category of "form," 6, 11, 109
  category of "texture," 87, 90, 191, 202, 209
  conventional model and its critique, 87, 171–172, 191, 200, 205
  "Dutch Wave" approach, 303
  and ecology, 196
  and growth managed by gardening, 128, 161, 171, 200, 205
  Jekyll and, 201
  Kiley as a planting designer, 74
  of Marnas, 124, 130
  Miller Garden as an icon of, 75, 111
  and modernism, 74, 83–84
  and nature, 302–303
  and planting plan, 128
  plant morphological and physiological basis for categories, 211–214
  and Burle Marx, 170, 172, 177, 205, 208–211, 217
  relation to gardening, 121
  Rose as researcher into "form" category, 84–93
  and the viridic, 208, 325–326, 329
  Walling and, 201
plants
  adaptation to stress, 69
  and humans sharing life, 2, 23, 250, 252–253, 256, 265, 270, 324
  as living "beings," 16–18, 324
  physiology and morphology, 9, 15–16
  role in defining landscape architecture in relation to change, 5
plant thinking, Marder's idea of, 17
poetry, 221
  for Dutton, 222–224, 248–249, 251, 268
pollard, at Hombroich, 274, 281, 284, 291, 300, 305, 307, 317
postmodernism
  in landscape architecture, 8–9, 73, 115, 116–117, 169, 222
  and Vaux-le-Vicomte, 8–9, 73, 116
practices, gardening, 9, 19, 23, 65, 115, 117, 132, 171, 196, 259, 266, 274
process discourse, 3–4, 13, 169–172, 226, 323, 329
pruning, 9, 16, 18, 115, 132
  Dutton on, 259–260
  of honey locusts at Miller Garden, 98, 105

at Insel Hombroich, 298, 305–306, 307, 312, 317
of Marnas by Andersson, 117, 119, 124, 138, 143, 146, 149, 157
mechanization of at Courances, 51, 59
of plane trees at Courances, 46–47
and plant physiology and morphology, 15–16, 69, 136, 139, 161
"pruned space," 137–163
tools, 136, 140–141, 161, 243

qualities
aesthetic, 191, 197, 287, 289–290
arising from growth, 4, 48, 75, 211, 217, 260, 270
in conventional planting design, 205, 209
definition, 18, 191
enhanced by maintenance, 50
of light, 257
from plant functional types, 212–213
of plants, 11, 83, 90, 92, 172–173, 191–192, 197, 202, 209, 212
plants', adding to design, 68, 171
of site, 245
and the viridic, 325–332

representation
in architecture and landscape architecture, 5, 93, 131–132
for Burle Marx, 202, 211
and design judgment, 299–300
and plant growth or change, 2, 4, 6, 12, 86, 269
of plants in design, 86
poems, for Dutton, 222–224, 248–249, 251, 268
"post-factum," 251
vs. practice, 119, 132, 137, 222, 253, 273, 275, 291, 324, 330–331
and site, 245
staticness compared to growth, 2, 5, 6, 12
Repton, Humphry, 2, 20–21, 23
response
of plants to environmental condition, 214–216, 259, 327–328
of plants to pruning, 69, 138–139, 164

room
author's description of Courances, 33
author's description of Miller Garden, 76
at Marnas, 117, 124–125, 130, 138, 143, 145–146, 149, 155, 157, 159, 161
root in concepts of space (*Raum*), 10
Rosa spp., 264
Rose, James, 11
theorizing planting design, 75, 84–90
Ryoan-ji, 111

Saito, Yuriko, 191–192
Salix spp. (willow), 307
science
and aesthetics at Sítio, 199–200
and Burle Marx, 170, 172, 193
and Dutton, 223, 224–226, 249, 259
and McHarg, 222
and modernist painting, 131
and poetry, 250
for Rose, 84–85
for Spirn, 116
and the viridic, 217
seasons, 15, 49, 90, 145, 253
in Druimchardain, 254–269
in Dutton's writing, 221
and gardening, 248
in planting design, 205
secateurs, 50, 51, 137, 140–141, 149, 259
Semper, Gottfried, 121, 133–136
serendipity, 128
Shulgin, Alexander, 80–81
site-specific discourse, 222, 245–246
Sítio Roberto Burle Marx
as botanical collection, 177
history, 173, 184, 190–191
plants named after, 177
tour of, 177–184
Sørensen, C. Th., 121–122
space, dialectic with form, 10–12, 84, 85, 109, 211
specific leaf area, 213
Spirn, Anne Whiston, 116
on Andersson and Marnas, 117–119, 128, 143–145

spring, in Druimchardain, 257–260
Steele, Fletcher, 69, 84
Stevenson, Anne, 250, 254
strimming, 261
studio
   garden as, 200–208
   as testing space, 172, 191, 201
suburban gardens, 24, 259
succession, 314–315, 328
summer, in Druimchardain, 260–266

tactics, 115–116, 240, 299–300
   de Certeau on, 115
   at Druimchardain, 240
   gardening using, 322
   at Hombroich, 299–300, 307
   vs. strategy, in Clausewitz, 240, 299
Taxodium distichum (swamp cypress), 284
taxonomy
   Dutton's taxonomy of plant forms, 254, 261
   Rose's taxonomy of plants, 11, 83, 86–93, 109, 131
   Semper's, 134
tectonic
   in architecture, 133–135
   Semper's model as the basis of, 121, 133
   the viridic as an equivalent of, 5, 121, 135, 217, 331
territory
   Corajoud's definition of, 36
   at Courances, 42, 48–49
   defined by maintenance, 67
   parti-parterre model, 34–40, 48
   territoriality of Vaux-le-Vicomte, 32–33
thermodynamics, 248, 253, 256–258, 327
   and the viridic, 327
time
   Burle Marx on, 208
   role in landscape architecture, 4–5
   shared by gardener and garden, 2, 23, 117, 250, 252–253, 256, 265–266, 268, 270, 324
   and the viridic, 321–332
tools, 50–51, 136, 140–141, 261
   Dutton's, at Druimchardain, 259, 261
   mechanization at Courances, 50–51, 58
   secateurs, 50, 51, 137, 140–141, 149, 259

topiary, 24, 44, 117, 317
transparency, 11, 86–87, 90, 92, 157
traumatic reiteration, 69
Treib, Marc, 9, 83–84, 140
Tschumi, Bernard, 169, 224

Ungers, Oswald Mathias, 296

Vaux, Calvert, 3
vernacular gardening practices, 116–117
viridic
   and aesthetics, 208, 217, 327, 329–330
   and change, 286, 322, 324, 330–331, 332
   compared to tectonics, 5, 121, 135, 217, 331
   definition, 5
   and design, 109, 121, 274–275, 286, 321, 323–333
   and ecology, 325–327
   and the gardener, 326, 328, 331–333
   and growth, 217, 270, 323–333
   and landscape architecture, 69, 131–135, 223, 324–333
   and maintenance or gardening, 121, 326, 330, 332–333
   and physiology, 327
   and plan, 326, 330
   and planting design, 208, 325–326, 329
   and qualities, 325–332
   and science, 217
   theoretical or historiographic basis, 131–136
   and thermodynamics, 327
   and time, 321–332
vita activa (Arendt), 275

walking
   as a garden practice for Dutton, 223
   for Korte as a practice at Hombroich, 294–295
Walling, Edna, 201, 247
weed, 43, 116, 196, 253
   definition, 193, 319
weeding, 193, 196, 205, 312–315, 319
weedscape, 65
Wever, Benjamin, 94, 101, 104–105, 108
winter, in Druimchardain, 254–257